Weimer

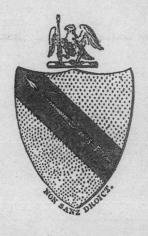

NON SANZ DROICT.

William Shakespeare

The Tragedy of
KING LEAR

Edited by Russell Fraser

The Signet Classic Shakespeare
GENERAL EDITOR: SYLVAN BARNET

C

A SIGNET CLASSIC from
NEW AMERICAN LIBRARY
TIMES MIRROR
New York and Scarborough, Ontario
The New English Library Limited, London

This book is for Allan Macdonald
Requiescat a labore
Doloroso et amore

C

SIGNET CLASSIC TRADEMARK REG. U.S. PAT. OFF. AND FOREIGN COUNTRIES
REGISTERED TRADEMARK—MARCA REGISTRADA
HECHO EN CHICAGO, U.S.A.

SIGNET, SIGNET CLASSICS, MENTOR, PLUME AND MERIDIAN BOOKS
are published *in the United States* by
The New American Library, Inc.,
1301 Avenue of the Americas, New York, New York 10019,
in Canada by The New American Library of Canada Limited,
81 Mack Avenue, Scarborough, 704, Ontario,
in the United Kingdom by The New English Library Limited,
Barnard's Inn, Holborn, London, E.C. 1, England

First Printing, May, 1963

13 14 15 16 17 18 19 20 21

PRINTED IN THE UNITED STATES OF AMERICA

Contents

Shakespeare: Prefatory Remarks

Between the record of his baptism in Stratford on 26 April 1564 and the record of his burial in Stratford on 25 April 1616, some forty documents name Shakespeare, and many others name his parents, his children, and his grandchildren. More facts are known about William Shakespeare than about any other playwright of the period except Ben Jonson. The facts should, however, be distinguished from the legends. The latter, inevitably more engaging and better known, tell us that the Stratford boy killed a calf in high style, poached deer and rabbits, and was forced to flee to London, where he held horses outside a playhouse. These traditions are only traditions; they may be true, but no evidence supports them, and it is well to stick to the facts.

Mary Arden, the dramatist's mother, was the daughter of a substantial landowner; about 1557 she married John Shakespeare, who was a glove-maker and trader in various farm commodities. In 1557 John Shakespeare was a member of the Council (the governing body of Stratford), in 1558 a constable of the borough, in 1561 one of the two town chamberlains, in 1565 an alderman (entitling him to the appellation "Mr."), in 1568 high bailiff—the town's highest political office, equivalent to mayor. After 1577, for an unknown reason he drops out of local politics. The birthday of William Shakespeare, the eldest son of this locally prominent man, is unrecorded; but the Stratford parish register records that the infant was baptized on 26 April 1564. (It is quite possible that he was born on 23 April, but this date has probably been assigned by tradition because it is the date on which, fifty-two years later, he died.) The attendance records of the Stratford grammar school of the period are not extant, but it is reasonable to assume that the son of a local official attended the school and received substantial training in Latin. The masters of the school from Shakespeare's seventh to fifteenth years held Oxford degrees; the Elizabethan curriculum excluded mathematics and the natural sciences but taught a good deal of Latin rhetoric, logic, and literature. On 27 November 1582 a marriage license was issued to Shakespeare and Anne Hathaway, eight years his senior. The couple had a child in May, 1583. Perhaps the marriage was necessary, but perhaps the couple had earlier engaged in a formal "troth-plight," which would render their children legitimate even if no further ceremony were performed. In 1585 Anne Hathaway bore Shakespeare twins.

That Shakespeare was born is excellent; that he married and had children is pleasant; but that we know nothing about his departure from Stratford to London, or about the beginning of his theatrical career, is lamentable and must be admitted. We would gladly sacrifice details about his children's baptism for details about his earliest days on the stage. Perhaps the poaching episode is true (but it is first reported almost a century after Shakespeare's death), or perhaps he first left Stratford to be a schoolteacher, as another tradition holds; perhaps he was moved by

Such wind as scatters young men through the world,
To seek their fortunes further than at home
Where small experience grows.

In 1592, thanks to the cantankerousness of Robert Greene, a rival playwright and a pamphleteer, we have our first reference, a snarling one, to Shakespeare as an actor and playwright. Greene warns those of his own educated friends who wrote for the theater against an actor who has presumed to turn playwright:

> There is an upstart crow, beautified with our feathers, that with his *tiger's heart wrapped in a player's hide* supposes he is as well able to bombast out a blank verse as the best of you, and being an absolute Johannes-factotum is in his own conceit the only Shake-scene in a country.

The reference to the player, as well as the allusion to Aesop's crow (who strutted in borrowed plumage, as an actor struts in fine words not his own), makes it clear that by this date Shakespeare had both acted and written. That Shakespeare is meant is indicated not only by "Shake-scene" but by the parody of a line from one of Shakespeare's plays, *3 Henry VI*: "O, tiger's heart wrapped in a woman's hide." If Shakespeare in 1592 was prominent enough to be attacked by an envious dramatist, he probably had served an apprenticeship in the theater for at least a few years.

In any case, by 1592 Shakespeare had acted and written, and there are a number of subsequent references to him as an actor: documents indicate that in 1598 he is a "principal comedian," in 1603 a "principal tragedian," in 1608 he is one of the "men players." The profession of actor was not for a gentleman, and it occasionally drew the scorn of university men who resented writing speeches for persons less educated than themselves, but it was respectable enough: players, if prosperous, were in effect members of the bourgeoisie, and there is nothing to suggest that Stratford considered William Shakespeare lesse than a solid citizen. When, in 1596, the Shakespeares were granted a coat of arms, the grant was made to Shakespeare's father, but probably William Shakespeare (who the next year bought the second-largest house in town) had arranged the matter on his own behalf. In subsequent transactions he is occasionally styled a gentleman.

Although in 1593 and 1594 Shakespeare published

two narrative poems dedicated to the Earl of Southampton, *Venus and Adonis* and *The Rape of Lucrece,* and may well have written most or all of his sonnets in the middle nineties, Shakespeare's literary activity seems to have been almost entirely devoted to the theater. (It may be significant that the two narrative poems were written in years when the plague closed the theaters for several months.) In 1594 he was a charter member of a theatrical company called the Chamberlain's Men (which in 1603 changed its name to the King's Men); until he retired to Stratford (about 1611, apparently), he was with this remarkably stable company. From 1599 the company acted primarily at the Globe Theatre, in which Shakespeare held a one-tenth interest. Other Elizabethan dramatists are known to have acted, but no other is known also to have been entitled to a share in the profits of the playhouse.

Shakespeare's first eight published plays did not have his name on them, but this is not remarkable; the most popular play of the sixteenth century, Thomas Kyd's *The Spanish Tragedy,* went through many editions without naming Kyd, and Kyd's authorship is known only because a book on the profession of acting happens to quote (and attribute to Kyd) some lines on the interest of Roman emperors in the drama. What is remarkable is that after 1598 Shakespeare's name commonly appears on printed plays—some of which are not his. Another indication of his popularity comes from Francis Meres, author of *Palladis Tamia: Wit's Treasury* (1598): in this anthology of snippets accompanied by an essay on literature, many playwrights are mentioned, but Shakespeare's name occurs more often than any other, and Shakespeare is the only playwright whose plays are listed.

From his acting, playwriting, and share in a theater, Shakespeare seems to have made considerable money. He put it to work, making substantial investments in Stratford real estate. When he made his will (less than a month before he died), he sought to leave his property intact to his descendants. Of small bequests to relatives and to friends (including three actors, Richard Burbage,

John Heminges, and Henry Condell), that to his wife of the second-best bed has provoked the most comment; perhaps it was the bed the couple had slept in, the best being reserved for visitors. In any case, had Shakespeare not excepted it, the bed would have gone (with the rest of his household possessions) to his daughter and her husband. On 25 April 1616 he was buried within the chancel of the church at Stratford. An unattractive monument to his memory, placed on a wall near the grave, says he died on 23 April. Over the grave itself are the lines, perhaps by Shakespeare, that (more than his literary fame) have kept his bones undisturbed in the crowded burial ground where old bones were often dislodged to make way for new:

> Good friend, for Jesus' sake forbear
> To dig the dust enclosèd here.
> Blessed be the man that spares these stones
> And cursed be he that moves my bones.

Thirty-seven plays, as well as some nondramatic poems, are held to constitute the Shakespeare canon. The dates of composition of most of the works are highly uncertain, but there is often evidence of a *terminus a quo* (starting point) and/or a *terminus ad quem* (terminal point) that provides a framework for intelligent guessing. For example, *Richard II* cannot be earlier than 1595, the publication date of some material to which it is indebted; *The Merchant of Venice* cannot be later than 1598, the year Francis Meres mentioned it. Sometimes arguments for a date hang on an alleged topical allusion, such as the lines about the unseasonable weather in *A Midsummer Night's Dream*, II.i.81–117, but such an allusion (if indeed it is an allusion) can be variously interpreted, and in any case there is always the possibility that a topical allusion was inserted during a revision, years after the composition of a play. Dates are often attributed on the basis of style, and although conjectures about style usually rest on other conjectures, sooner or later one must rely on one's literary sense. There is no real proof, for example, that *Othello* is not as early as *Romeo and Juliet,* but one feels *Othello* is later, and because the first record of its performance is 1604, one is glad enough to set its composition at that date and not push it back into Shakespeare's early years. The following chronology, then, is as much indebted to informed guesswork and sensitivity as it is to fact. The dates, necessarily imprecise, indicate something like a scholarly consensus.

PLAYS

1588–93	*The Comedy of Errors*
1588–94	*Love's Labor's Lost*
1590–91	*2 Henry VI*
1590–91	*3 Henry VI*
1591–92	*1 Henry VI*
1592–93	*Richard III*
1592–94	*Titus Andronicus*
1593–94	*The Taming of the Shrew*
1593–95	*The Two Gentlemen of Verona*
1594–96	*Romeo and Juliet*
1595	*Richard II*
1594–96	*A Midsummer Night's Dream*
1596–97	*King John*
1596–97	*The Merchant of Venice*
1597	*1 Henry IV*
1597–98	*2 Henry IV*
1598–99	*Henry V*
1598–1600	*Much Ado About Nothing*
1599	*Julius Caesar*
1599–1600	*As You Like It*
1599–1600	*Twelfth Night*
1600–01	*Hamlet*
1597–1601	*The Merry Wives of Windsor*
1601–02	*Troilus and Cressida*
1602–04	*All's Well That Ends Well*
1603–04	*Othello*
1603–06	*King Lear*

Shakespeare's Theater

In Shakespeare's infancy, Elizabethan actors performed wherever they could—in great halls, at court, in the courtyards of inns. The innyards must have made rather unsatisfactory theaters: on some days they were unavailable because carters bringing goods to London used them as depots; when available, they had to be rented from the innkeeper; perhaps most important, London inns were subject to the Common Council of London, which was not well disposed toward theatricals. In 1574 the Common Council required that plays and playing places in London be licensed. It asserted that

sundry great disorders and inconveniences have been found to ensue to this city by the inordinate haunting of great multitudes of people, specially youth, to plays, interludes, and shows, namely occasion of frays and quarrels, evil practices of incontinency in great inns having chambers and secret places adjoining to their open stages and galleries, and ordered that innkeepers who wished licenses to hold performances put up a bond and make contributions to the poor.

The requirement that plays and innyard theaters be licensed, along with the other drawbacks of playing at inns, probably drove James Burbage (a carpenter-turned-actor) to rent in 1576 a plot of land northeast of the city walls and to build here—on property outside the jurisdiction of the city—England's first permanent construction designed for plays. He called it simply the Theatre. About all that is known of its construction is that it was wood. It soon had imitators, the most famous being the Globe (1599), built across the Thames (again outside the city's jurisdiction), out of timbers of the Theatre, which had been dismantled when Burbage's lease ran out.

There are three important sources of information about the structure of Elizabethan playhouses—drawings, a contract, and stage directions in plays. Of drawings, only the so-called De Witt drawing (c. 1596) of the Swan—really a friend's copy of De Witt's drawing—is of much significance. It shows a building of three tiers, with a stage jutting from a wall into the yard or center of the building. The tiers are roofed, and part of the stage is covered by a roof that projects from the rear and is supported at its front on two posts, but the groundlings, who paid a penny to stand in front of the stage, were exposed to the sky. (Performances in such a playhouse were held only in the daytime; artificial illumination was not used.) At the rear of the stage are two doors; above the stage is a gallery. The second major source of information, the contract for the Fortune, specifies that although the Globe is to be the model, the Fortune is to be square, eighty feet outside and fifty-five inside. The stage is to be forty-three feet broad, and is to extend into the middle of the yard (i.e., it is twenty-seven and a half feet deep). For patrons willing to pay more than the general admission charged of the groundlings, there were to be three galleries provided with seats. From the third chief source, stage directions, one learns that entrance to the stage was by doors, presumably spaced widely apart at the rear ("Enter one citizen at one door, and another at the other"), and that in addition to the platform stage there was occasionally some sort of curtained booth or alcove allowing for "discovery" scenes, and some sort of playing space "aloft" or "above" to represent (for example) the top of a city's walls or a room above the street. Doubtless each theater had its own peculiarities, but perhaps we can talk about a "typical" Elizabethan theater if we realize that no theater need exactly have fit the description, just as no father is the typical father with 3.7 children. This hypothetical theater is wooden, round or polygonal (in *Henry V* Shakespeare calls it a "wooden *O*"), capable of holding some eight hundred spectators standing in the yard around the projecting elevated stage and some fifteen hundred additional spectators seated in the three roofed galleries. The stage, protected by a "shadow" or "heavens" or roof, is entered by two doors; behind the doors is the "tiring house" (attiring house, i.e., dressing room), and above the doors is some sort of gallery that may sometimes hold spectators but that can be used (for example) as the bedroom from which Romeo—according to a stage direction in one text—"goeth down." Some evidence suggests that a throne can be lowered on to the platform stage, perhaps from the "shadow"; certainly characters can descend from the stage through a trap or traps into the cellar or "hell." Sometimes this space beneath the platform accommodates a sound-effects man or musician (in *Antony and Cleopatra* "music of the hautboys is under the stage") or an actor (in *Hamlet* the "Ghost cries under the stage"). Most characters simply walk on and off, but because there is no curtain in front of the platform, corpses will have to be carried off (Hamlet must lug Polonius' guts into the neighbor room) or will have to fall at the rear, where the curtain on the alcove or booth can be drawn to conceal them.

Such may have been the so-called "public theater." Another kind of theater, called the "private theater" because its much greater admission charge limited its audience to the wealthy or the prodigal, must be briefly mentioned. The private theater was basically a large room, entirely roofed, and therefore artificially illluminated, with a stage at one end. In 1576 one such theater was established in Blackfriars, a Dominican priory in London that had been suppressed in 1538 and confiscated by the Crown and thus was not under the city's jurisdiction. All the actors in the Blackfriars theater were boys about eight to thirteen years old (in the public theaters similar boys played female parts; a boy Lady Macbeth played to a man Macbeth). This private theater had a precarious existence, and ceased operations in 1584. In 1596 James Burbage, who had already made theatrical history by building the Theatre, began to construct a second Blackfriars theater. He died in 1597, and for several years this second Blackfriars theater was used by a troupe of boys, but in 1608 two of Burbage's sons and five other actors (including Shakespeare) became joint operators of the theater, using it in the winter when the open-air Globe was unsuitable. Perhaps such a smaller theater, roofed, artificially illuminated, and with a tradition of a courtly audience, exerted an influence on Shakespeare's late plays.

Performances in the private theaters may well have had intermissions during which music was played, but in the public theaters the action was probably uninterrupted, flowing from scene to scene almost without a break. Actors would enter, speak, exit, and others would immediately enter and establish (if necessary) the new locale by a few properties and by words and gestures. Here are some samples of Shakespeare's scene painting:

> This is Illyria, lady.

> Well, this is the Forest of Arden.

> This castle hath a pleasant seat; the air
> Nimbly and sweetly recommends itself
> Unto our gentle senses.

On the other hand, it is a mistake to conceive of the Elizabethan stage as bare. Although Shakespeare's Chorus in *Henry V* calls the stage an "unworthy scaffold" and urges the spectators to "eke out our performance with your mind," there was considerable spectacle. The last act of *Macbeth*, for example, has five stage directions calling for "drum and colors," and another sort of appeal to the eye is indicated by the stage direction "Enter Macduff, with Macbeth's head." Some scenery and properties may have been substantial; doubtless a throne was used, and in one play of the period we encounter this direction: "Hector takes up a great piece of rock and casts at Ajax, who tears up a young tree by the roots and assails Hector." The matter is of some importance, and will be glanced at again in the next section.

The Texts of Shakespeare

Though eighteen of his plays were published during his lifetime, Shakespeare seems never to have supervised their publication. There is nothing unusual here; when a playwright sold a play to a theatrical company he surrendered his ownership of it. Normally a company would not publish the play, because to publish it meant to allow competitors to acquire the piece. Some plays, however, did get published: apparently treacherous actors sometimes pieced together a play for a publisher, sometimes a company in need of money sold a play, and sometimes a company allowed a play to be published that no longer drew audiences. That Shakespeare did not concern himself with publication, then, is scarcely remarkable; of his contemporaries only Ben Jonson carefully supervised the publication of his own plays. In 1623, seven years after Shakespeare's death, John Heminges and Henry Condell (two senior members of Shakespeare's company, who had performed with him for about twenty years) collected his plays—published and unpublished —into a large volume, commonly called the First Folio.

(A folio is a volume consisting of sheets that have been folded once, each sheet thus making two leaves, or four pages. The eighteen plays published during Shakespeare's lifetime had been issued one play per volume in small books called quartos. Each sheet in a quarto has been folded twice, making four leaves, or eight pages.) The First Folio contains thirty-six plays; a thirty-seventh, *Pericles,* though not in the Folio, is regarded as canonical. Heminges and Condell suggest in an address "To the great variety of readers" that the republished plays are presented in better form than in the quartos: "Before you were abused with diverse stolen and surreptitious copies, maimed and deformed by the frauds and stealths of injurious impostors that exposed them; even those, are now offered to your view cured and perfect of their limbs, and all the rest absolute in their numbers, as he [i.e., Shakespeare] conceived them."

Whoever was assigned to prepare the texts for publication in the First Folio seems to have taken his job seriously and yet not to have performed it with uniform care. The sources of the texts seem to have been, in general, good unpublished copies or the best published copies. The first play in the collection, *The Tempest,* is divided into acts and scenes, has unusually full stage directions and descriptions of spectacle, and concludes with a list of the characters, but the editor was not able (or willing) to present all of the succeeding texts so fully dressed. Later texts occasionally show signs of carelessness: in one scene of *Much Ado About Nothing* the names of actors, instead of characters, appear as speech prefixes, as they had in the quarto, which the Folio reprints; proofreading throughout the Folio is spotty and apparently was done without reference to the printer's copy; the pagination of *Hamlet* jumps from 156 to 257.

A modern editor of Shakespeare must first select his copy; no problem if the play exists only in the Folio, but a considerable problem if the relationship between a quarto and the Folio—or an early quarto and a later one—is unclear. When an editor has chosen what seems to him to be the most authoritative text or texts for his copy, he has not done with making decisions. First of all, he must reckon with Elizabethan spelling. If he is not producing a facsimile, he probably modernizes it, but ought he to preserve the old form of words that apparently were pronounced quite unlike their modern forms—"lanthorn," "alablaster"? If he preserves these forms, is he really preserving Shakespeare's forms or perhaps those of a compositor in the printing house? What is one to do when one finds "lanthorn" and "lantern" in adjacent lines? (The editors of this series in general, but not invariably, assume that words should be spelled in their modern form.) Elizabethan punctuation, too, presents problems. For example, in the First Folio, the only text for the play, Macbeth rejects his wife's idea that he can wash the blood from his hand:

> no: this my Hand will rather
> The multitudinous Seas incarnardine,
> Making the Greene one, Red.

Obviously an editor will remove the superfluous capitals, and he will probably alter the spelling to "incarnadine," but will he leave the comma before "red," letting Macbeth speak of the sea as "the green one," or will he (like most modern editors) remove the comma and thus have Macbeth say that his hand will make the ocean *uniformly* red?

An editor will sometimes have to change more than spelling or punctuation. Macbeth says to his wife:

> I dare do all that may become a man,
> Who dares no more, is none.

For two centuries editors have agreed that the second line is unsatisfactory, and have emended "no" to "do": "Who dares do more is none." But when in the same play Ross says that fearful persons

> floate vpon a wilde and violent Sea
> Each way, and moue,

need "move" be emended to "none," as it often is, on the hunch that the compositor misread the manuscript? The editors of the Signet Classic Shakespeare have restrained themselves from making abundant emendations. In their minds they hear Dr. Johnson on the dangers of emending: "I have adopted the Roman sentiment, that it is more honorable to save a citizen than to kill an enemy." Some departures (in addition to spelling, punctuation, and lineation) from the copy text have of course been made, but the original readings are listed in a note following the play, so that the reader can evaluate them for himself.

The editors of the Signet Classic Shakespeare, following tradition, have added line numbers and in many cases act and scene divisions as well as indications of locale at the beginning of scenes. The Folio divided most of the plays into acts and some into scenes. Early eighteenth-century editors increased the divisions. These divisions, which provide a convenient way of referring to passages in the plays, have been retained, but when not in the text chosen as the basis for the Signet Classic text they are enclosed in square brackets [ ] to indicate that they are editorial additions. Similarly, although no play of Shakespeare's published during his lifetime was equipped with indications of locale at the heads of scene divisions, locales have here been added in square brackets for the convenience of the reader, who lacks the information afforded to spectators by costumes, properties, and gestures. The spectator can tell at a glance he is in the throne room, but without an editorial indication the reader may be puzzled for a while. It should be mentioned, incidentally, that there are a few authentic stage directions—perhaps Shakespeare's, perhaps a prompter's—that suggest locales: for example, "Enter Brutus in his orchard," and "They go up into the Senate house." It is hoped that the bracketed additions provide the reader with the sort of help provided in these two authentic directions, but it is equally hoped that the reader will remember that the stage was not loaded with scenery.

No editor during the course of his work can fail to recollect some words Heminges and Condell prefixed to the Folio:

> It had been a thing, we confess, worthy to have been wished, that the author himself had lived to have set forth and overseen his own writings. But since it hath been ordained otherwise, and he by death departed from that right, we pray you do not envy his friends the office of their care and pain to have collected and published them.

Nor can an editor, after he has done his best, forget Heminges and Condell's final words: "And so we leave you to other of his friends, whom if you need can be your guides. If you need them not, you can lead yourselves, and others. And such readers we wish him."

SYLVAN BARNET
Tufts University

Introduction

In structure *Lear* differs significantly from the other tragedies of Shakespeare. It is like them in this. It dramatizes the fall of a hero who, assailed by the rebel passion, gives it sovereign sway and masterdom, and is in consequence destroyed. That is the case of Brutus, Othello, and Macbeth. But the resemblance is more ostensible than real. Ostensibly the play is one long denouement. In fact the declining action, which is the dogging of the hero to death, is complemented by a rising action, which is the hero's regeneration. Yeats's metaphor of the gyres is apposite. As the one wanes to nothing, the other, which lives within it, emerges. This emergent, or renascent, action is a condition of the hero's loss of the world. The play fools us. Its primary story is not the descent of the King into Hell, but the ascent of the King as he climbs the Mountain of Purgatory and is fulfilled. The suspense the play develops is a function of the ascending action, which is not material but spiritual. Battles and thrones are nugatory. What does it profit a man if he gain the whole world and suffer the loss of his soul?

The rising and falling curves, the hero tasting his folly, the hero triumphing over it, intersect in the center of the play, in the fourth scene of Act III. It is on the heath that Lear reaches his nadir. His characteristic utterance is the imperative mood: the wonted reversal follows: he is made less than the slave and sumpter to a detested groom. These are the injuries that he himself has procured. So far the parallel is precise to the action of the other tragedies.

But now the crucial difference. It is also on the heath that Lear is made pregnant to pity. That is another and an unexpected kind of reversal. "In boy, go first." These words, addressed to the Fool, who stands shivering in the rain before a hovel that is the refuge of a madman, constitute the real, as opposed to the apparent, hinge of the play. They do not signal the decay but the metamorphosis of the King: Lear in a red shirt. The great apostrophe to the poor follows at once. From this point, the action turns upward.

The structure of the subplot duplicates and so of course clarifies and confirms that of the central story. As the King is limed, and by his own folly, so are Gloucester and Edgar: "A credulous father, and a brother noble." The one is, initially, an unthinking sensualist. The other, the younger, is initially a kind of clown: "and pat he comes like the catastrophe of the old comedy." But the degradation of Gloucester is not ratified. He also undergoes a miraculous transformation. The critical point or pivot at which this transformation is announced is located, like Lear's, in the mathematical center of the play (III, iii), which is also, with a fit symmetry, the metaphysical center. The placatory man, who would have all well between the contending parties, is emboldened suddenly to choose. "If I die for it, as no less is threatened me, the King my old master must be relieved." In that decision is his death, but also his salvation.

The retrieving of Edgar is more spectacular, if not so abruptly achieved. Edgar is conceded the chance to grow and prosper. He seizes his chance; he makes himself over. "Bear free and patient thoughts." The dupe of the opening scenes is the philosopher who dominates in the close of the play.

This is not to pretend that the close is thereby made happy. "All's cheerless, dark, and deadly." Kent's somber valediction is approved. If the kindness of the one daughter hints at the redemption of Nature, it does not deprecate entirely the general curse which twain have brought her to. The implication is uneasy in Edgar's assertion (as of one who is saying "what we ought to say") that man must obey the weight of the time. His flawed heart, on the evidence of the play, is too weak to support it. His nature cannot carry the affliction or the fear.

> What ribs of oak, when mountains melt on them,
> Can hold the mortise?

Man endures until he expires, dying the pain of death every hour, in a night that pities neither wise man nor fool. What is more unsettling, to be wise is not to be provident. "Man may his fate foresee, but not prevent." And thus Webster's conclusion, in *The White Devil*: " 'Tis better to be fortunate than wise." Man is the natural fool of fortune. That is the title he is born with. It is the stars, and not our own endeavors, that govern. After all we are their tennis balls, struck and bandied which way please them. We do not get our deserts. The optimism is foolishness, to which we are prone.

> I would not take this from report. It is,
> And my heart breaks at it.

The wry conjunctions contrived by the playwright—who knows out of what bitterness or whimsy—attest to its fatuity. Edgar, in a sanguine mood, is sure that the worst returns to laughter. He is confronted at once with the bleeding visage of his father.

> The worst is not
> So long as we can say "This is the worst."

But Shakespeare is not done with him yet. "If ever I return to you again, I'll bring you comfort." That is Edgar's promise to Gloucester before the battle. It is a rash promise, and poor comfort attends on it. A hiatus ensues, filled up with alarums and excursions. Then Edgar reenters and speaks again: "Away, old man. . . . King Lear hath lost."

The optimism of Albany, as it is more eupeptic, is more sternly reproved.

> All friends shall taste
> The wages of their virtue, and all foes
> The cup of their deservings.

In that cheerful saying his philosophy is embodied. But the pentameter line wants its conclusion. Albany, rather cruelly, is made to supply it: "O, see, see!" It is the last agony of Lear to which his attention is directed.

Albany, as he presents the hopeful man who insists, a little too suavely, that God's in His Heaven, is Shakespeare's particular butt. It is he who cries, of Cordelia: "The gods defend her!" The stage direction follows, enforcing the most monstrous conjunction in the play: "Enter Lear with Cordelia in his arms." The gods do not defend us. Perhaps they are unable to do so. "The gods reward your kindness," says Kent to Gloucester. That is the reading of the Folio, and surely it is the right reading. But the reading of the Quarto provokes speculation: "The gods deserve your kindness." It is as if the gods are weak, and require that man collaborate with them in wielding the world (Shakespeare imitating Will James). Lear, as his ardor for the right grows upon him, shakes the superflux to the wretched. His intent is, as he says, to show the heavens more just. It is at least tenable to interpret: his intent is to justify their feckless ways as he can.

Maybe the heavens are worse than insufficient. What is said of the King,

> If Fortune brag of two she loved and hated,
> One of them we behold,

suggests not merely a lack of capacity in the ordering of things, but a malevolent purpose, as if the gods had marked us down for their sport. On this reading, Lear's reference to himself and Cordelia as "God's spies" will mean, as Warburton suggested long ago, "spies placed over God Almighty, to watch his motions." Maybe there is need of surveillance, if the human sacrifices on which the gods themselves throw incense are offered up for their delectation; if the brand of fire that parts the pre-destined victims is handed down, and with an antique malice, from Heaven. *Tantaene animis coelestibus irae!* The chill that invades us as, huddled with the others against the roaring wind and rain, we await the advent of unaccommodated man: "What art thou that dost grumble there i' th' straw?" is occasioned by the wild surmise, so much more fearful because it is involuntary, that the fiend is really walking up and down in the earth, and with the sufferance and even the connivance of Heaven. In the pitiless conclusion of *King Lear,*

> Thou'lt come no more,
> Never, never, never, never, never,

the dominion of the Prince of Darkness seems confirmed, and his presence a substantial presence as, with his terrible vans, he enshadows and overwhelms the just and the unjust alike.

That is, I daresay, only an apparition, the disnatured child of night thoughts, and as such may be dispelled. But it needs more than to rub one's eyes, or to mutter a pious ejaculation. To such a degree is this true that even critics so tough-minded as Dr. Johnson have averted their eyes rather than acquiesce in the final horror with which the dramatist confronts them. It is too literal, too realistic for "dramatick exhibition." And yet it is remarkable that this play, in which Shakespeare's unremitting fidelity to fact is almost an occasion for scandal, manifests in its beginning a studied and a deliberate indifference to fact. If subsequent scenes are so realistic as hardly to be endured, the opening scenes have not to do with realism but with ritual and romance. Their abiding characteristic is a niggling formality. They do not wear the aspect of life so much as the aspect of art. Kent, lapsing into rude rhyme as he takes his departure, catches and communicates that aspect. His language is gnomic, admonitory, and simple—not naïvely but consciously simple: "artificial." He is not, for the moment, a real (an eccentric) man who displaces air like Hamlet or

Parolles. He is, and by design, a flat character, highly conventionalized, who figures in a mumming or mystery. He would speak a prophecy before he goes.

The language of the other protagonists is of a piece with his. It does not evoke—not yet—the savage business of dragons of the prime (for all that the dragon is portentous in the comminatory speeches of the King), so much as the ceremonious (the otherworldly!) business of proceedings at law and finance. Legal and fiscal metaphors reverberate. Gloucester, treating of his sons, asserts that the elder is no more dear than the younger, in his account. Lear, enacting his intention to abdicate the throne, renounces interest of territory, or possession. In lieu of Kent's insistence that he reserve his state, he stipulates his troop of knights as reservation, explicitly a legalism, in which the action of retaining a privilege is denoted. He would extend his largest bounty where nature challenges merit, or makes title to it. Regan, whose tenders of affection aim at that title, finds that Goneril has anticipated her very deed of love. The King, in whose lexicon love is a commodity, urges his youngest daughter to discover what portion her protestations can draw. But Cordelia loves only according to her bond. Failing to please, her price is fallen. Goneril pleases, in that she is taken as permitting to her father twice the retinue permitted by Regan. Her devotion may therefore be measured. She is precisely twice her sister's love.

Lear is not easily persuaded of his error, that devotion—in his psychology, a ponderable thing—is to be assessed and ought to be requited in ponderable ways. The inadmissible equation is there still, in the crass appeal to Regan when his agony is upon him:

> Thy half o' th' kingdom hast thou not forgot,
> Wherein I thee endowed.

He is appropriately answered, since that respects of fortune are his love:

> Good sir, to the purpose.

This patina of the unreal and the ritualistic, overlaying the initial action of the play, is not peculiar to the love test. The characters themselves move in an air of unreality. There is about them a felt sense of disjunction, as between what they are and what they seem to be. Lear is not a king but the show of a king. It is an insubstantial pageant over which he presides, recalling, in its unreality, the specious parade with which an earlier tragedy of Shakespeare's commences, that of Richard II, the mockery king of snows. Kent's acumen is verified when, with a lack of respect that is intended to shock and thereby to quicken perception, he sees and salutes his master, not as a monarch but as an old man.

But if Lear is a simulacrum, so are the wicked daughters. Their essential vacuity, echoing to the touch, announces itself as it issues in their fulsome avowals of love. Kent points to it obliquely in his praise of Cordelia:

> Nor are those empty-hearted whose low sounds
> Reverb no hollowness.

Gloucester discerns it, magnified to cosmic proportions, in the disordered state of the macrocosm, riven by machinations, by the hollowness that is hypocrisy. All that glisters is taken for gold. The pretension of the hypocrite, who professes herself

> an enemy to all other joys
> Which the most precious square of sense professes,

weighs more than the practice of the candid and guileless retainer, who professes himself to be no less than he seems. The vizard is everything, and hence what is lifelike and vital is eclipsed. The characters are cut in alabaster. The same metaphor describes the fool and the knave and the paragon of virtue, divesting each of human personality. Gloucester, who seems a good old man, is brazed by self-indulgence, become like hard metal. Regan, in whom nature appears tender-hefted, is hardened to insensibility, made of that self metal as her sister. Cordelia is, conversely, a little-seeming substance. But Cordelia is rendered also in nonhuman terms: her love, a precious metal, is more ponderous than her tongue.

Stylization of language and gesture is notable in such a play as *The Tempest,* and for excellent and obvious reasons. Shakespeare's resort to it in *King Lear* seems, however, gratuitous, and even antipathetic to the spirit of the play. *Lear* is not masquelike nor, certainly, romantic, in the harrowing story it tells. But observe that *The Tempest* begins, not formally, but realistically, with the faithful depicting of a ship driving on the rocks, a wild and literal scene in which the blasphemy and execration of real and affrighted persons bass the throbbing of the storm. And then the scene shifts abruptly. The auditor or reader, whose belief is purchased at the outset by a terrific glimpse of the real world, is brought safe to shore: is induced to enter, and willingly, the world of enchantment and romance. The fact of the transition, and the implausibility attendant on it, elude him. The tempest is still dinning in his ears.

In *King Lear* the dramatic problem is exactly reversed. It is to ensure that those whose disenchantment the playwright is already preparing, who are to be compelled to look on the Gorgon-features, will not evince incredulity or petrifaction. The problem is resolved by emphasizing at the outset the elements of unreality and romance. The impelling action of *Lear* is made to resemble a fairy tale, which is, I suppose, its ultimate provenance. The auditor or reader is cozened. Before he is aware, he has become a participant in the fierce and excessively painful dispute between damnation and impassioned clay.

But there is more than craft to Shakespeare's design in thus introducing his drama. He makes his characters unreal initially because he means them, at least in part, to be symbolic. The stylized quality of the beginning, as of a charade, its legalistic and ceremonious nature, the exalting in it of appearance as against reality, all work to the fulfilling of that primary intention. And though

Lear is essentially representational drama, though realism very quickly takes precedence over ritual, the element of the symbolic is never dissipated altogether but figures in important ways until the end. Just as in *Twelfth Night,* whose burden is mistaken identity and the hocus-pocus of identical twins, realism intrudes persistently to temper and give substance to romance—

> In nature there's no blemish but the mind;
> None can be called deformed but the unkind.
> Virtue is beauty, but the beauteous evil
> Are empty trunks o'erflourished by the devil

—so in *King Lear,* an anti-romantic play in that its burden is a relentless anatomizing of evil, the symbolic declines to yield entirely to the representational. It persists, not to give substance to the real, which is substantial enough—

> Out, vile jelly!
> Where is thy luster now?

—but to order the real and make it meaningful, to avoid a confounding of it with the merely sensational. Not to grasp this ordering function is, necessarily, to run counter, to smell a fault where no fault is. Thus the embarrassment of critics so estimable as Goethe (for whom the action of the play was a tissue of the improbable and absurd), and Coleridge (who saw the first scene as dispensable), and A. C. Bradley (who detected and enumerated in the whole, more and grosser inconsistencies than in any other of the great tragedies).

Misconstruction of the role and character of Cordelia typifies this failure to come to terms with the symbolic. Cordelia is, of old, a deeply disquieting figure. Why does she love, and yet remain silent? The question has engendered a little galaxy of answers. It is a question not to be asked. The first principle of good dramatic manners is to concede to the dramatist his given, so long as he is able to exploit it. Here, the given is the heroine's fatal reserve. It is the lever or prise that starts the play on its progress. As such, it may not be queried, any more thàn the procedure that governs in chess or in the writing of an Italian sonnet.

But "reserve" is after all the wrong word. It suggests the wrong frame of reference. It leads to the rationalization of conduct, on realistic grounds. To make the horrid point, this judgment of a contemporary critic may be cited, that Cordelia loved her father "less than she loved her own way and hated her sisters." That is a fair sample of the appeal to realism. It is at all costs to be avoided. Cordelia does not betray, what Coleridge thought to perceive, "some little faulty admixture of pride and sullenness." No faintest stain of guilt or responsibility attaches to her. She is not imperious, like the King, not headstrong, not intractable. The appeal to heredity is a variation of the appeal to realism, and is, in this context, equally and altogether inapposite. Shakespeare's characters, unlike Eugene O'Neill's, have no antecedents. It is of no use to say that Cordelia is her father's daughter. The reason she will not speak is because she cannot speak; and she cannot because the heart of a fool is in his mouth but the mouth of the wise is in his heart.

This is to say that the muteness of Cordelia (like the fantastic credulity of Gloucester) is not so much a reflection of character as it is the embodiment of an idea. Less real than symbolic, her affinity is more to a creature of fairy tale like Cinderella than to a heroine of the realistic drama like Blanche DuBois. In delineating her behavior the playwright may be, psychologically, so penetrating and exact as really to catch the manners living as they rise: that is partly a gratuity. More important is his intention, not to portray a veritable woman, but to dramatize the proposition that plainness is more than eloquence, that beauty is to be purchased by the weight, that meager lead, which rather threatens than promises aught, buys more than silver and gold. The agitation of those who worry the details of the love test in an attempt to make it credible, which means to make it conformable to the canons of the realistic theater, is founded on their misapprehension of symbolic action.

When Cordelia is depicted as the last and least, it is not her slightness of stature that the dramatist is glancing at—or not that, decisively. He is preparing an ironic and a pregnant echo, to amplify Kent's assertion, a little later:

> Thy youngest daughter does not love thee least.

But more than that, he is invoking the promise of Scripture, unspoken in the play, and yet close to the theme, which is the heart (but not the moral!) of the play: The first shall be last and the last shall be first. When Cordelia herself exclaims, as she prepares to engage the British powers,

> O dear father,
> It is thy business that I go about,

it is not altogether the realistic business of an imminent battle to which she is adverting. (Certainly that business does not much preoccupy Shakespeare.) And therefore we are not to wonder why the King of France was, so inopportunely, called back to his kingdom, nor whether Shakespeare's allegiance or circumspection dictated the victory of the English. We want to catch in what is said an anterior saying, the sentence of the Evangelist, so much more than a literary reminiscence, and estimate accordingly the symbolic role the speaker plays: "Knew ye not that I must go about my father's business." It may be that Cordelia is that quintessence of womanhood celebrated reverentially (and with an appropriate taciturnity as to particulars) by critics like A. W. Schlegel: "Of Cordelia's heavenly beauty of soul, I do not dare to speak." But it is not after all the literal woman to whom Shakespeare is holding up the mirror. Compare Beatrice in *Much Ado,* or Rosalind in *As You Like It.*

It is a nice but an indispensable point to adjudicate, just when the dramatist intends that the canons of ordi-

nary realism are to be set aside or, better, transcended.
Pretty clearly he wishes to transcend them when, in
Act II, Kent is made to sleep in the stocks, and Edgar,
unmindful of him, to step forward and tell of his purposed transformation. Bradley is bemused: "One cannot
help asking . . . whether Edgar is mad that he should return from his hollow tree . . . to his father's castle in
order to soliloquize." But Shakespeare, in juxtaposing
the two characters, is not concerned with motivation
or, certainly, with locale. No doubt the Bedlam is understood to remain on the heath. But precisely where he
is, is not a question that ought to detain us. Neither are
we to ask why he fails to perceive that someone else is
up there with him on stage, in full view of the audience,
and so, presumably, of himself; nor how Kent, for all
his travails, can sleep undisturbed through twenty lines
of blank verse. In the bringing together of the two good
men, each of whom has been driven to the lowest
and most dejected point of fortune, a dramatic emblem
is achieved, a speaking picture, whose purport is not
realistic but symbolic. What Shakespeare is after is this
dark collocation, or sequence:

A good man's fortune may grow out at heels.

Edgar I nothing am.

In the same way the symbolic overtops the conven-
tionally real when, in the final act, Edgar issues his
challenge to Edmund. One is not to belabor the improbability of Edmund's failure to recognize his brother,
though, in point of fact, the failure is itself symbolic:
the villain is indeed cozened and beguiled, and not for
reasons of dramatic exigency but by virtue of his own
willful behavior. But what is central to the scene is the
intimation one hears, in the blast of the trumpet that announces the combat, of that final trump that vindicates
the right and summons the perpetrator of wrong to the
Judgment. When—another illustration—Edgar, opposing
Oswald, assumes the character of a rustic, the clown-

ish dialect he speaks is, realistically, absurd: what is its occasion? Symbolically, however, it is deeply congruous. The power of truth is attested to, however ludicrous its aspect, and the frailty which is falsehood exposed, in this meeting of the ragged fellow, whose West Country accent gives him out to be a bumpkin, but who intrinsically merits and possesses all honors, and the gilded courtier, whose extrinsic show and sophistication betoken all honors and are as paste and cover to none.

> The Prince of Darkness is a gentleman.

In Edgar's vanquishing of Oswald, which is the triumph of the lowly and the unprepossessing over the world of robes and furred gowns, Lear's great social speeches are enacted and answered.

A similar intention, to effect on stage a symbolic tableau, dictates the grouping of the protagonists at the end of the play. All are there in the resolution, occupying, I think, the same positions they assumed at first, and not least the wicked sisters, whose dead bodies are brought on, no doubt to exemplify this judgment of the heavens, but more, to direct the attention of the audience back and back, over all the dreadful ground that has been traced, to the opening scene. In their beginning is their ending. Perhaps the great wheel of the play, now come full circle, is impelled in its progress by something more than mechanical law.

What this other law may be is the central question Shakespeare poses and endeavors to answer. Lear, as is fitting, is made to enunciate it: "Who is it that can tell me who I am?" But the question is not peculiar to Lear but is implicit in the utterance and conduct of all those who inhabit the darkness with him. Kent as Caius is interrogated by the King:

> What art thou?
> A man, sir.

But what is it, to be a man? What is man to profess?

To what law are his services bound? Gloucester interrogates Edgar: "Now, good sir, what are you?" and is answered:

> A most poor man, made tame to fortune's blows,
> Who, by the art of known and feeling sorrows,
> Am pregnant to good pity.

Cornwall, whose disposition will not be rubbed or stopped, does not manifest that pity. It is ascendant, though tardily, in Gloucester, who, if he dies for it, must relieve his master. Why is that? And why had Kent rather break his own heart than the King's? How does one construe that fitness to which Albany appeals, in declining to let his hands obey his blood; or that pleasure, a more intriguing word, which inclines the Old Man to succor the blinded Gloucester, "Come on't what will"? What point inheres in Albany's characterization of Oswald, as Oswald reports it:

> he called me sot,
> And told me I had turned the wrong side out;

and in what manner does it comment on the Captain's decision to collaborate in the killing of the King and Cordelia:

> If it be man's work, I'll do it.

There ought here to ensue a brief though perceptible silence, in token of the irony and expectation with which these laconic words are charged. The dramatist is bidding us essay a definition of the nature of man's work and, concomitantly, of the nature of man. Edmund, with his customary *sang-froid,* addresses himself to the task:

> men
> Are as the time is.

Kent speaks to it, describing Oswald:

> A tailor made thee.

So in whimsical ways does the Fool, begging pardon of Goneril:

> Cry you mercy, I took you for a joint stool;

and also the King, whose confusion is at once real and assumed:

> Your name, fair gentlewoman?

and, in sterner ways, the Servant, drawing his sword against Cornwall:

> Nay, then, come on, and take the chance of anger.

To divine the way in which these lines reticulate is to resolve at least a corner of the mystery which is the play.

RUSSELL FRASER
Princeton University

The Tragedy of
KING LEAR

[DRAMATIS PERSONAE

Lear, King of Britain
King of France
Duke of Burgundy
Duke of Cornwall, husband to Regan
Duke of Albany, husband to Goneril
Earl of Kent
Earl of Gloucester
Edgar, son to Gloucester
Edmund, bastard son to Gloucester
Curan, a courtier
Oswald, steward to Goneril
Old Man, tenant to Gloucester
Doctor
Lear's Fool
A Captain, subordinate to Edmund
Gentlemen, attending on Cordelia
A Herald
Servants to Cornwall
Goneril 〉
Regan 〉 daughters to Lear
Cordelia 〉
Knights attending on Lear, Officers,
    Messengers, Soldiers, Attendants

Scene: Britain]

The Tragedy of King Lear

ACT I

Scene I.   [*King Lear's palace.*]

Enter Kent, Gloucester, and Edmund.

Kent. I thought the King had more affected°¹ the Duke
of Albany° than Cornwall.

Gloucester. It did always seem so to us; but now, in
the division of the kingdom, it appears not which
of the dukes he values most, for equalities are so   5
weighed that curiosity in neither can make choice
of either's moiety.°

Kent. Is not this your son, my lord?

Gloucester. His breeding,° sir, hath been at my
charge. I have so often blushed to acknowledge   10
him that now I am brazed° to't.

Kent. I cannot conceive° you.

Gloucester. Sir, this young fellow's mother could;
whereupon she grew round-wombed, and had indeed, sir, a son for her cradle ere she had a hus-   15
band for her bed. Do you smell a fault?

---

¹ The degree sign (°) indicates a footnote, which is keyed to the text by
line number. Text references are printed in *italic* type; the annotation
follows in roman type.
I.i. 1 *affected* loved   2 *Albany* Albanacte, whose domain extended "from
the river Humber to the point of Caithness" (Holinshed)   5-7 *equalities . . . moiety* i.e., shares are so balanced against one another that
careful examination by neither can make him wish the other's portion
9 *breeding* upbringing   11 *brazed* made brazen, hardened   12 *conceive*
understand (pun follows)

Kent. I cannot wish the fault undone, the issue° of it
being so proper.°

20 *Gloucester.* But I have a son, sir, by order of law,
some year elder than this, who yet is no dearer
in my account:° though this knave° came something saucily° to the world before he was sent
for, yet was his mother fair, there was good sport
at his making, and the whoreson° must be acknowl-
25 edged. Do you know this noble gentleman, Edmund?

Edmund. No, my lord.

Gloucester. My Lord of Kent. Remember him here-
after as my honorable friend.

30 *Edmund.* My services to your lordship.

Kent. I must love you, and sue° to know you better.

Edmund. Sir, I shall study deserving.

Gloucester. He hath been out° nine years, and away
he shall again. The King is coming.

*Sound a sennet.° Enter one bearing a coronet,°
then King Lear, then the Dukes of Cornwall and
Albany, next Goneril, Regan, Cordelia, and Attendants.*

35 *Lear.* Attend the lords of France and Burgundy,
Gloucester.

Gloucester. I shall, my lord.   *Exit [with Edmund].*

Lear. Meantime we shall express our darker purpose.°
Give me the map there. Know that we have divided
40 In three our kingdom; and 'tis our fast° intent
To shake all cares and business from our age,
Conferring them on younger strengths, while we

17 *issue* result (child)   18 *proper* handsome   21 *account* estimation
21 *knave* fellow (without disapproval)   22 *saucily* (1) insolently (2)
lasciviously   24 *whoreson* fellow (lit., son of a whore)   31 *sue* entreat
33 *out* away, abroad   34 s.d. *sennet* set of notes played on a trumpet,
signalizing the entrance or departure of a procession   34 s.d. *coronet*
small crown, intended for Cordelia   38 *darker purpose* hidden intention   40 *fast* fixed

Unburthened crawl toward death. Our son of
   Cornwall,
And you our no less loving son of Albany,
We have this hour a constant will to publish°   45
Our daughters' several° dowers, that future strife
May be prevented° now. The Princes, France and
   Burgundy,
Great rivals in our youngest daughter's love,
Long in our court have made their amorous sojourn,
And here are to be answered. Tell me, my daughters   50
(Since now we will divest us both of rule,
Interest° of territory, cares of state),
Which of you shall we say doth love us most,
That we our largest bounty may extend
Where nature doth with merit challenge.° Goneril,   55
Our eldest-born, speak first.

Goneril. Sir, I love you more than word can wield°
   the matter;
Dearer than eyesight, space° and liberty;
Beyond what can be valued, rich or rare;
No less than life, with grace, health, beauty, honor;   60
As much as child e'er loved, or father found;
A love that makes breath° poor, and speech
   unable:
Beyond all manner of so much° I love you.

Cordelia. [*Aside*] What shall Cordelia speak? Love,
   and be silent.

Lear. Of all these bounds, even from this line to this,   65
With shadowy forests, and with champains riched,°
With plenteous rivers, and wide-skirted meads,°
We make thee lady. To thine and Albany's issues°
Be this perpetual.° What says our second daughter,

---

45 *constant will to publish* fixed intention to proclaim   **46** *several* separate   **47** *prevented* forestalled   **52** *Interest* legal right   **55** *nature . . . challenge* i.e., natural affection contends with desert for (or lays claim to) bounty   **57** *wield* handle   **58** *space* scope   **62** *breath* language   **62** *unable* impotent   **63** *Beyond . . . much* beyond all these comparisons   **66** *champains riched* enriched plains   **67** *wide-skirted meads* extensive grasslands   **68** *issues* descendants   **69** *perpetual* in perpetuity

70   Our dearest Regan, wife of Cornwall? Speak.

Regan. I am made of that self mettle° as my sister,
And prize me at her worth.° In my true heart
I find she names my very deed of love;°
Only she comes too short, that° I profess
75   Myself an enemy to all other joys
Which the most precious square of sense
    professes,°
And find I am alone felicitate°
In your dear Highness' love.

Cordelia.   [*Aside*] Then poor Cordelia!
And yet not so, since I am sure my love's
80   More ponderous° than my tongue.

Lear. To thee and thine hereditary ever
Remain this ample third of our fair kingdom,
No less in space, validity,° and pleasure
Than that conferred on Goneril. Now, our joy,
85   Although our last and least;° to whose young love
The vines of France and milk° of Burgundy
Strive to be interest;° what can you say to draw
A third more opulent than your sisters? Speak.

Cordelia. Nothing, my lord.

90   *Lear.* Nothing?

Cordelia. Nothing.

Lear. Nothing will come of nothing. Speak again.

Cordelia. Unhappy that I am, I cannot heave
My heart into my mouth. I love your Majesty
95   According to my bond,° no more nor less.

Lear. How, how, Cordelia? Mend your speech a little,
Lest you may mar your fortunes.

---

71 *self mettle* same material or temperament   72 *prize . . . worth* value
me the same (imperative)   73 *my . . . love* what my love really is (a
legalism)   74 *that* in that   76 *Which . . . professes* which the choicest
estimate of sense avows   77 *felicitate* made happy   80 *ponderous* weighty
83 *validity* value   85 *least* youngest, smallest   86 *milk* i.e., pastures
87 *interest* closely connected, as interested parties   95 *bond* i.e., filial
obligation

Cordelia.   Good my lord,
    You have begot me, bred me, loved me. I
    Return those duties back as are right fit,°
    Obey you, love you, and most honor you.   *100*
    Why have my sisters husbands, if they say
    They love you all? Haply,° when I shall wed,
    That lord whose hand must take my plight° shall
        carry
    Half my love with him, half my care and duty.
    Sure I shall never marry like my sisters,   *105*
    To love my father all.

Lear. But goes thy heart with this?

Cordelia.   Ay, my good lord.

Lear. So young, and so untender?

Cordelia. So young, my lord, and true.

Lear. Let it be so, thy truth then be thy dower!   *110*
    For, by the sacred radiance of the sun,
    The mysteries of Hecate° and the night,
    By all the operation of the orbs°
    From whom we do exist and cease to be,
    Here I disclaim all my paternal care,   *115*
    Propinquity and property of blood,°
    And as a stranger to my heart and me
    Hold thee from this for ever. The barbarous
        Scythian,°
    Or he that makes his generation messes°
    To gorge his appetite, shall to my bosom   *120*
    Be as well neighbored, pitied, and relieved,
    As thou my sometime° daughter.

Kent.   Good my liege——

Lear. Peace, Kent!

---

⁹⁹ *Return . . . fit* i.e., am correspondingly dutiful ¹⁰² *Haply* perhaps
¹⁰³ *plight* troth plight ¹¹² *mysteries of Hecate* secret rites of Hecate
(goddess of the infernal world, and of witchcraft) ¹¹³ *operation of
the orbs* astrological influence ¹¹⁶ *Propinquity and property of blood*
relationship and common blood ¹¹⁸ *Scythian* (type of the savage)
¹¹⁹ *makes his generation messes* eats his own offspring ¹²² *sometime*
former

Come not between the Dragon° and his wrath.
125   I loved her most, and thought to set my rest°
      On her kind nursery.° Hence and avoid my sight!
      So be my grave my peace, as here I give
      Her father's heart from her! Call France. Who stirs?
      Call Burgundy. Cornwall and Albany,
130   With my two daughters' dowers digest° the third;
      Let pride, which she calls plainness, marry her.°
      I do invest you jointly with my power,
      Pre-eminence, and all the large effects
      That troop with majesty.° Ourself,° by monthly
          course,
135   With reservation° of an hundred knights,
      By you to be sustained, shall our abode
      Make with you by due turn. Only we shall retain
      The name, and all th' addition° to a king. The sway,
      Revènue, execution of the rest,
140   Belovèd sons, be yours; which to confirm,
      This coronet° part between you.

Kent.   Royal Lear,
      Whom I have ever honored as my king,
      Loved as my father, as my master followed,
      As my great patron thought on in my prayers——

Lear. The bow is bent and drawn; make from the
145   shaft.°

Kent. Let it fall° rather, though the fork° invade
      The region of my heart. Be Kent unmannerly
      When Lear is mad. What wouldst thou do, old
          man?
      Think'st thou that duty shall have dread to speak

---

124 *Dragon* (1) heraldic device of Britain (2) emblem of ferocity
125 *set my rest* (1) stake my all (a term from the card game of primero)
(2) find my rest   126 *nursery* care, nursing   130 *digest* absorb
131 *Let . . . her* i.e., let her pride be her dowry and gain her a husband   133-34 *effects/That troop with majesty* accompaniments that go with
kingship   134 *Ourself* (the royal "we")   135 *reservation* the action of
reserving a privilege (a legalism)   138 *addition* titles and honors   141 *coronet* (the crown which was to have been Cordelia's)   145 *make from
the shaft* avoid the arrow   146 *fall* strike   146 *fork* forked head of the
arrow

When power to flattery bows? To plainness honor's
   bound   150
When majesty falls to folly. Reserve thy state,°
And in thy best consideration° check
This hideous rashness. Answer my life my
   judgment,°
Thy youngest daughter does not love thee least,
Nor are those empty-hearted whose low sounds   155
Reverb° no hollowness.°

Lear.   Kent, on thy life, no more!

Kent. My life I never held but as a pawn°
   To wage° against thine enemies; nor fear to lose it,
   Thy safety being motive.°

Lear.   Out of my sight!

Kent. See better, Lear, and let me still° remain   160
   The true blank° of thine eye.

Lear. Now by Apollo——

Kent.   Now by Apollo, King,
   Thou swear'st thy gods in vain.

Lear.   O vassal! Miscreant!°
                    [*Laying his hand on his sword.*]

Albany, Cornwall. Dear sir, forbear!

Kent. Kill thy physician, and the fee bestow   165
   Upon the foul disease. Revoke thy gift,
   Or, whilst I can vent clamor° from my throat,
   I'll tell thee thou dost evil.

Lear.   Hear me, recreant!°
   On thine allegiance,° hear me!
   That thou hast sought to make us break our vows,   170

---

151 *Reserve thy state* retain your kingly authority   152 *best consideration* most careful reflection   153 *Answer . . . judgment* I will stake my
life on my opinion   156 *Reverb* reverberate   156 *hollowness* (1) empti-
ness (2) insincerity   157 *pawn* stake in a wager   158 *wage* (1) wager
(2) carry on war   159 *motive* moving cause   160 *still* always   161 *blank*
the white spot in the center of the target (at which Lear should aim)
163 *vassal! Miscreant!* base wretch! Misbeliever!   167 *vent clamor* utter
a cry   168 *recreant* traitor   169 *On thine allegiance* (to forswear, which
is to commit high treason)

Which we durst never yet, and with strained° pride
To come betwixt our sentence° and our power,
Which nor our nature nor our place can bear,
Our potency made good,° take thy reward.
175 Five days we do allot thee for provision°
To shield thee from diseases° of the world,
And on the sixth to turn thy hated back
Upon our kingdom. If, on the tenth day following,
Thy banished trunk° be found in our dominions,
180 The moment is thy death. Away! By Jupiter,
This shall not be revoked.

    Kent. Fare thee well, King. Sith° thus thou wilt appear,
    Freedom lives hence, and banishment is here.
    [*To Cordelia*] The gods to their dear shelter take
        thee, maid,
185 That justly think'st, and hast most rightly said.
    [*To Regan and Goneril*] And your large speeches
        may your deeds approve,°
    That good effects° may spring from words of love.
    Thus Kent, O Princes, bids you all adieu;
    He'll shape his old course° in a country new.   *Exit.*

    Flourish.° Enter Gloucester, with France and
        Burgundy; Attendants.

190 *Gloucester.* Here's France and Burgundy, my noble
    lord.

    Lear. My Lord of Burgundy,
    We first address toward you, who with this king
    Hath rivaled for our daughter. What in the least
    Will you require in present° dower with her,
    Or cease your quest of love?

195 *Burgundy.*   Most royal Majesty,
    I crave no more than hath your Highness offered,

---

171 *strained* forced (and so excessive)   172 *sentence* judgment, decree
174 *Our potency made good* my royal authority being now asserted
175 *for provision* for making preparation   176 *diseases* troubles
179 *trunk* body   182 *Sith* since   186*approve* prove true   187 *effects* results
189 *shape . . . course* pursue his customary way   189 s.d. *Flourish* trumpet
fanfare   194 *present* immediate

Nor will you tender° less.

Lear.   Right noble Burgundy,
When she was dear° to us, we did hold her so;
But now her price is fallen. Sir, there she stands.
If aught within that little seeming substance,°   200
Or all of it, with our displeasure pieced,°
And nothing more, may fitly like° your Grace,
She's there, and she is yours.

Burgundy.   I know no answer.

Lear. Will you, with those infirmities she owes,°
Unfriended, new adopted to our hate,   205
Dow'red with our curse, and strangered° with our
    oath,
Take her, or leave her?

Burgundy.   Pardon me, royal sir.
Election makes not up° on such conditions.

Lear. Then leave her, sir; for, by the pow'r that made
    me,
I tell you all her wealth. [*To France*.] For you,
    great King,   210
I would not from your love make such a stray
To° match you where I hate; therefore beseech°
    you
T' avert your liking a more worthier way°
Than on a wretch whom nature is ashamed
Almost t' acknowledge hers.

France.   This is most strange,   215
That she whom even but now was your best object,°
The argument° of your praise, balm of your age,
The best, the dearest, should in this trice of time
Commit a thing so monstrous to dismantle°

---

197 *tender* offer   198 *dear* (1) beloved   (2) valued at a high price
200 *little seeming substance* person who is (1) inconsiderable (2) out-
spoken   201 *pieced* added to it   202 *fitly like* please by its fitness
204 *owes* possesses   206 *strangered* made a stranger   208 *Election makes
not up* no one can choose   211-12 *make such a stray/To* stray so far as to
212 *beseech* I beseech   213 *avert . . . way* turn your affections from her
and bestow them on a better person   216 *best object* i.e., the one you
loved most   217 *argument* subject   219 *dismantle* strip off

220   So many folds of favor. Sure her offense
     Must be of such unnatural degree
     That monsters it,° or your fore-vouched° affection
     Fall into taint;° which to believe of her
     Must be a faith that reason without miracle
     Should never plant in me.°

225 *Cordelia.*   I yet beseech your Majesty,
     If for° I want that glib and oily art
     To speak and purpose not,° since what I well intend
     I'll do't before I speak, that you make known
     It is no vicious blot, murder, or foulness,
230   No unchaste action or dishonored step,
     That hath deprived me of your grace and favor;
     But even for want of that for which I am richer,
     A still-soliciting° eye, and such a tongue
     That I am glad I have not, though not to have it
     Hath lost° me in your liking.

235 *Lear.*   Better thou
     Hadst not been born than not t' have pleased me
       better.

France. Is it but this? A tardiness in nature°
     Which often leaves the history unspoke°
     That it intends to do. My Lord of Burgundy,
240   What say you° to the lady? Love's not love
     When it is mingled with regards° that stands
     Aloof from th' entire point.° Will you have her?
     She is herself a dowry.

Burgundy.   Royal King,
     Give but that portion which yourself proposed,
245   And here I take Cordelia by the hand,
     Duchess of Burgundy.

---

222 *That monsters it* as makes it monstrous, unnatural 222 *fore-vouched* previously sworn 223 *Fall into taint* must be taken as having been unjustified all along i.e., Cordelia was unworthy of your love from the first 224-25 *reason . . . me* my reason would have to be supported by a miracle to make me believe 226 *for* because 227 *purpose not* not mean to do what I promise 233 *still-soliciting* always begging 235 *lost* ruined 237 *tardiness in nature* natural reticence 238 *leaves the history unspoke* does not announce the action 240 *What say you* i.e., will you have 241 *regards* considerations (the dowry) 241-42 *stands . . . point* have nothing to do with the essential question (love)

Lear. Nothing. I have sworn. I am firm.

Burgundy. I am sorry then you have so lost a father
That you must lose a husband.

Cordelia.   Peace be with Burgundy.
Since that respects of fortune° are his love,   250
I shall not be his wife.

France. Fairest Cordelia, that art most rich being
    poor,
Most choice forsaken, and most loved despised,
Thee and thy virtues here I seize upon.
Be it lawful I take up what's cast away.   255
Gods, gods! 'Tis strange that from their cold'st
    neglect
My love should kindle to inflamed respect.°
Thy dow'rless daughter, King, thrown to my
    chance,°
Is Queen of us, of ours, and our fair France.
Not all the dukes of wat'rish° Burgundy   260
Can buy this unprized precious° maid of me.
Bid them farewell, Cordelia, though unkind.
Thou losest here, a better where° to find.

Lear. Thou hast her, France; let her be thine, for we
Have no such daughter, nor shall ever see   265
That face of hers again. Therefore be gone,
Without our grace, our love, our benison.°
Come, noble Burgundy.

    *Flourish. Exeunt [Lear, Burgundy, Cornwall,
        Albany, Gloucester, and Attendants].*

France. Bid farewell to your sisters.

Cordelia. The jewels of our father,° with washed°
    eyes   270
Cordelia leaves you. I know you what you are,

---

250 *respects of fortune* mercenary considerations   257 *inflamed respect*
more ardent affection   258 *chance* lot   260 *wat'rish* (1) with many
rivers (2) weak, diluted   261 *unprized precious* unappreciated by others, and yet precious   263 *here . . . where* in this place, in another
place   267 *benison* blessing   270 *The jewels of our father* you creatures
prized by our father   270 *washed* (1) weeping (2) clear-sighted

And, like a sister,° am most loath to call
Your faults as they are named.° Love well our
    father.
To your professèd° bosoms I commit him.
275 But yet, alas, stood I within his grace,
I would prefer° him to a better place.
So farewell to you both.

Regan. Prescribe not us our duty.

Goneril.   Let your study
Be to content your lord, who hath received you
280 At Fortune's alms.° You have obedience scanted,°
And well are worth the want that you have wanted.°

Cordelia. Time shall unfold what plighted° cunning
    hides,
Who covers faults, at last shame them derides.°
Well may you prosper.

France.   Come, my fair Cordelia.
                    Exit France and Cordelia.

285 *Goneril.* Sister, it is not little I have to say of what
    most nearly appertains to us both. I think our
    father will hence tonight.

Regan. That's most certain, and with you; next month
    with us.

290 *Goneril.* You see how full of changes his age is. The
    observation we have made of it hath not been lit-
    tle. He always loved our sister most, and with
    what poor judgment he hath now cast her off ap-
    pears too grossly.°

295 *Regan.* 'Tis the infirmity of his age; yet he hath ever
    but slenderly known himself.

---

272 *like a sister* because I am a sister i.e., loyal, affectionate 273 *as
they are named* i.e., by their right and ugly names 274 *professèd*
pretending to love 276 *prefer* recommend 280 *At Fortune's alms* as
a charitable bequest from Fortune (and so, by extension, as one beg-
gared or cast down by Fortune) 280 *scanted* stinted 281 *worth . . .
wanted* deserve to be denied, even as you have denied 282 *plighted*
pleated, enfolded 283 *Who . . . derides* those who hide their evil are
finally exposed and shamed ("He that hideth his sins, shall not prosper") 294 *grossly* obviously

Goneril. The best and soundest of his time° hath
 been but rash; then must we look from his age to
 receive not alone the imperfections of long-in-
 grafted° condition,° but therewithal° the unruly *300*
 waywardness that infirm and choleric years bring
 with them.

Regan. Such unconstant starts° are we like to have
 from him as this of Kent's banishment.

Goneril. There is further compliment° of leave-taking *305*
 between France and him. Pray you, let's hit° together; if our father carry authority with such disposition as he bears,° this last surrender° of his
 will but offend° us.

Regan. We shall further think of it.   *310*

Goneril. We must do something, and i' th' heat.°

            Exeunt.

Scene II. [*The Earl of Gloucester's castle.*]

Enter Edmund [*with a letter*].

Edmund. Thou, Nature,° art my goddess; to thy law
 My services are bound. Wherefore should I
 Stand in the plague of custom,° and permit
 The curiosity° of nations to deprive me,
 For that° I am some twelve or fourteen
  moonshines °   *5*

---

297 *of his time* period of his life up to now 299-300 *long-ingrafted* im-
planted for a long time 300 *condition* disposition 300 *therewithal*
with them 303 *unconstant starts* impulsive whims 305 *compliment*
formal courtesy 306 *hit* agree 307-8 *carry . . . bears* continues, and
in such frame of mind, to wield the sovereign power 308 *last surren-
der* recent abdication 309 *offend* vex 311 *i' th' heat* while the iron is
hot I.ii. 1 *Nature* (Edmund's conception of Nature accords with our
description of a bastard as a natural child) 3 *Stand . . . custom*
respect hateful convention 4 *curiosity* nice distinctions 5 *For that*
because 5 *moonshines* months

Lag of° a brother? Why bastard? Wherefore base?
When my dimensions are as well compact,°
My mind as generous,° and my shape as true,
As honest° madam's issue? Why brand they us
10   With base? With baseness? Bastardy? Base? Base?
Who, in the lusty stealth of nature, take
More composition° and fierce° quality
Than doth, within a dull, stale, tired bed,
Go to th' creating a whole tribe of fops°
15   Got° 'tween asleep and wake? Well then,
Legitimate Edgar, I must have your land.
Our father's love is to the bastard Edmund
As to th' legitimate. Fine word, "legitimate."
Well, my legitimate, if this letter speed,°
20   And my invention° thrive, Edmund the base
Shall top th' legitimate. I grow, I prosper.
Now, gods, stand up for bastards.

Enter Gloucester.

Gloucester. Kent banished thus? and France in choler
    parted?
And the King gone tonight? prescribed° his pow'r?
25   Confined to exhibition?° All this done
Upon the gad?° Edmund, how now? What news?

Edmund. So please your lordship, none.

Gloucester. Why so earnestly seek you to put up°
    that letter?

30   *Edmund.* I know no news, my lord.

Gloucester. What paper were you reading?

Edmund. Nothing, my lord.

Gloucester. No? What needed then that terrible dis-
    patch° of it into your pocket? The quality of noth-

---

6 *Lag of* short of being (in age)   7 *compact* framed   8 *generous* gal-
lant   9 *honest* chaste   12 *composition* completeness   12 *fierce* energetic
14 *fops* fools   15 *Got* begot   19 *speed* prosper   20 *invention* plan
24 *prescribed* limited   25 *exhibition* an allowance or pension   26 *Upon
the gad* on the spur of the moment (as if pricked by a gad or goad)
28 *put up* put away, conceal   33-34 *terrible dispatch* hasty putting away

ing hath not such need to hide itself. Let's see.   35
Come, if it be nothing, I shall not need spectacles.

Edmund. I beseech you, sir, pardon me. It is a letter
from my brother that I have not all o'er-read; and
for so much as I have perused, I find it not fit
for your o'erlooking.°   40

Gloucester. Give me the letter, sir.

Edmund. I shall offend, either to detain or give .it.
The contents, as in part I understand them, are
to blame.°

Gloucester. Let's see, let's see.   45

Edmund. I hope, for my brother's justification, he
wrote this but as an essay or taste° of my virtue.

Gloucester. (*Reads*) "This policy and reverence° of
age makes the world bitter to the best of our
times;° keeps our fortunes from us till our oldness   50
cannot relish° them. I begin to find an idle and
fond° bondage in the oppression of aged tyranny,
who sways, not as it hath power, but as it is suffered.° Come to me, that of this I may speak more.
If our father would sleep till I waked him, you   55
should enjoy half his revenue° for ever, and live
the beloved of your brother,   EDGAR."
Hum! Conspiracy? "Sleep till I waked him, you
should enjoy half his revenue." My son Edgar! Had
he a hand to write this? A heart and brain to   60
breed it in? When came you to this? Who brought
it?

Edmund. It was not brought me, my lord; there's the
cunning of it. I found it thrown in at the casement of my closet.°   65

---

40 *o'erlooking* inspection   44 *to blame* blameworthy   47 *essay or taste*
test   48 *policy and reverence* policy of reverencing (hendiadys)
49-50 *best of our times* best years of our lives (i.e., our youth)   51 *relish*
enjoy   51-52 *idle and fond* foolish   53-54 *who . . . suffered* which rules,
not from its own strength, but from our allowance   56 *revenue* income
64-65 *casement of my closet* window of my room

Gloucester. You know the character° to be your
  brother's?

Edmund. If the matter were good, my lord, I durst
  swear it were his; but in respect of that,° I would
70 fain° think it were not.

Gloucester. It is his.

Edmund. It is his hand, my lord; but I hope his
  heart is not in the contents.

Gloucester. Has he never before sounded° you in this
75 business?

Edmund. Never, my lord. But I have heard him
  oft maintain it to be fit that, sons at perfect° age,
  and fathers declined, the father should be as ward
  to the son, and the son manage his revenue.

80 *Gloucester.* O villain, villain! His very opinion in the
  letter. Abhorred villain, unnatural, detested,° brutish villain; worse than brutish! Go, sirrah,° seek
  him. I'll apprehend him. Abominable villain! Where
  is he?

85 *Edmund.* I do not well know, my lord. If it shall
  please you to suspend your indignation against my
  brother till you can derive from him better testi-
  mony of his intent, you should run a certain
  course;° where, if you violently proceed against
90 him, mistaking his purpose, it would make a great
  gap° in your own honor, and shake in pieces the
  heart of his obedience. I dare pawn down° my life
  for him that he hath writ this to feel° my affection to your honor, and to no other pretense of
95 danger.°

Gloucester. Think you so?

66 *character* handwriting   69 *in respect of that* in view of what it is
70 *fain* prefer to   74 *sounded* sounded you out   77 *perfect* mature
81 *detested* detestable   82 *sirrah* sir (familiar form of address)   88-89 *run
a certain course* i.e., proceed safely, know where you are going   91 *gap*
breach   92 *pawn down* stake   93 *feel* test   94-95 *pretense of danger*
dangerous purpose

Edmund. If your honor judge it meet,° I will place
you where you shall hear us confer of this, and
by an auricular assurance° have your satisfaction,
and that without any further delay than this very   *100*
evening.

Gloucester. He cannot be such a monster.

Edmund. Nor is not, sure.

Gloucester. To his father, that so tenderly and entirely loves him. Heaven and earth! Edmund, seek   *105*
him out; wind me into him,° I pray you; frame°
the business after your own wisdom. I would unstate myself to be in a due resolution.°

Edmund. I will seek him, sir, presently;° convey° the
business as I shall find means, and acquaint you   *110*
withal.°

Gloucester. These late° eclipses in the sun and moon
portend no good to us. Though the wisdom of Na-
ture° can reason° it thus and thus, yet Nature
finds itself scourged by the sequent effects.° Love   *115*
cools, friendship falls off,° brothers divide. In
cities, mutinies;° in countries, discord; in palaces,
treason; and the bond cracked 'twixt son and
father. This villain of mine comes under the prediction,° there's son against father; the King falls   *120*
from bias of nature,° there's father against child.
We have seen the best of our time.° Machinations,
hollowness,° treachery, and all ruinous disorders
follow us disquietly° to our graves. Find out this

97 *meet* fit   99 *auricular assurance* proof heard with your own ears
106 *wind me into him* insinuate yourself into his confidence for me
106 *frame* manage   107–08 *unstate . . . resolution* forfeit my earldom
to know the truth   109 *presently* at once   109 *convey* manage   111 *withal*
with it   112 *late* recent   113–14 *wisdom of Nature* scientific learning   114 *reason* explain   114–15 *yet . . . effects* nonetheless our world
is punished with subsequent disasters   116 *falls off* revolts   117 *mutinies*
riots   119–20 *This . . . prediction* i.e., my son's villainous behavior is
included in these portents, and bears them out   121 *bias of nature*
natural inclination (the metaphor is from the game of bowls)   122 *best
of our time* our best days   123 *hollowness* insincerity   124 *disquietly*
unquietly

125   villain, Edmund; it shall lose thee nothing.° Do it
       carefully. And the noble and true-hearted Kent
       banished; his offense, honesty. 'Tis strange.

                                                    Exit.

   Edmund. This is the excellent foppery° of the world,
       that when we are sick in fortune, often the surfeits
130   of our own behavior,° we make guilty of our dis-
       asters the sun, the moon, and stars; as if we were
       villains on° necessity; fools by heavenly compul-
       sion; knaves, thieves, and treachers by spherical
       predominance;° drunkards, liars, and adulterers by
135   an enforced obedience of planetary influence;° and
       all that we are evil in, by a divine thrusting on.°
       An admirable evasion of whoremaster° man, to
       lay his goatish° disposition on the charge of a
       star. My father compounded° with my mother
140   under the Dragon's Tail,° and my nativity° was
       under Ursa Major,° so that it follows I am rough
       and lecherous. Fut!° I should have been that° I
       am, had the maidenliest star in the firmament twin-
       kled on my bastardizing. Edgar——

                           Enter Edgar.

145   and pat he comes, like the catastrophe° of the old
       comedy. My cue is villainous melancholy, with a
       sigh like Tom o' Bedlam.°—O, these eclipses do
       portend these divisions. Fa, sol, la, mi.°

   Edgar. How now, brother Edmund; what serious con-
150   templation are you in?

---

125 *it . . . nothing* you will not lose by it   128 *foppery* folly
129-30 *often . . . behavior* often caused by our own excesses   132 *on* of
133-34 *treachers . . . predominance* traitors because of the ascen-
dancy of a particular star at our birth   134-35 *by . . . influence* because
we had to submit to the influence of our star   136 *divine thrusting on*
supernatural compulsion   137 *whoremaster* lecherous   138 *goatish* las-
civious   139 *compounded* (1) made terms (2) formed (a child)
140 *Dragon's Tail* the constellation Draco   140 *nativity* birthday
141 *Ursa Major* the Great Bear   142 *Fut!* 's foot (an impatient oath)
142 *that* what   145 *catastrophe* conclusion   146-47 *My . . . Bedlam* I must
be doleful, like a lunatic beggar out of Bethlehem (Bedlam) Hospital, the
London madhouse   148 *Fa, sol, la, mi* (Edmund's humming of the
musical notes is perhaps prompted by his use of the word "division,"
which describes a musical variation)

Edmund. I am thinking, brother, of a prediction I read this other day, what should follow these eclipses.

Edgar. Do you busy yourself with that?

Edmund. I promise you, the effects he writes of suc- 155
ceed° unhappily: as of unnaturalness° between the child and the parent, death, dearth, dissolutions of ancient amities,° divisions in state, menaces and maledictions against King and nobles, needless diffidences,° banishment of friends, dissipation of co- 160
horts,° nuptial breaches, and I know not what.

Edgar. How long have you been a sectary astronomical?°

Edmund. Come, come, when saw you my father last?

Edgar. Why, the night gone by. 165

Edmund. Spake you with him?

Edgar. Ay, two hours together.

Edmund. Parted you in good terms? Found you no displeasure in him by word nor countenance?°

Edgar. None at all. 170

Edmund. Bethink yourself wherein you may have offended him; and at my entreaty forbear his pres-
ence° until some little time hath qualified° the heat of his displeasure, which at this instant so rageth in him that with the mischief of your person it 175
would scarcely allay.°

Edgar. Some villain hath done me wrong.

Edmund. That's my fear, brother I pray you have a continent forbearance° till the speed of his rage goes slower; and, as I say, retire with me to my 180

155-56 *succeed* follow **157** *unnaturalness* unkindness **158** *amities* friend-
ships **159-60** *diffidences* distrusts **160-61** *dissipation of cohorts* falling
away of supporters **162-63** *sectary astronomical* believer in astrology
169 *countenance* expression **172-73** *forbear his presence* keep away from
him **173** *qualified* lessened **175-76** *with . . . allay* even an injury to you
would not appease his anger **178-79** *have a continent forbearance* be restrained and keep yourself withdrawn

lodging, from whence I will fitly° bring you to hear
my lord speak. Pray ye, go; there's my key. If
you do stir abroad, go armed.

Edgar. Armed, brother?

185   *Edmund.* Brother, I advise you to the best. Go armed.
I am no honest man if there be any good meaning
toward you. I have told you what I have seen and
heard; but faintly, nothing like the image and hor-
ror° of it. Pray you, away.

190   *Edgar.* Shall I hear from you anon?°

Edmund. I do serve you in this business.

Exit Edgar.

A credulous father, and a brother noble,
Whose nature is so far from doing harms
That he suspects none; on whose foolish honesty
195   My practices° ride easy. I see the business.
Let me, if not by birth, have lands by wit.
All with me's meet° that I can fashion fit.°   *Exit.*

Scene III.   [*The Duke of Albany's palace.*]

Enter Goneril, and [Oswald, her] Steward.

Goneril. Did my father strike my gentleman for chid-
ing of his Fool?°

Oswald. Ay, madam.

Goneril. By day and night he wrongs me. Every hour
5   He flashes into one gross crime° or other

---

181 *fitly* at a fit time   188-89 *image and horror* true horrible picture
190 *anon* in a little while   195 *practices* plots   197 *meet* proper   197 *fashion fit* shape to my purpose   I.iii. 2 *Fool* court jester   5 *crime* offense

That sets us all at odds. I'll not endure it.
His knights grow riotous,° and himself upbraids us
On every trifle. When he returns from hunting,
I will not speak with him. Say I am sick.
If you come slack of former services,°   10
You shall do well; the fault of it I'll answer.°

                                    [*Horns within.*]

Oswald. He's coming, madam; I hear him.

Goneril. Put on what weary negligence you please,
You and your fellows. I'd have it come to question.°
If he distaste° it, let him to my sister,   15
Whose mind and mine I know in that are one,
Not to be overruled. Idle° old man,
That still would manage those authorities
That he hath given away. Now, by my life,
Old fools are babes again, and must be used   20
With checks as flatteries, when they are seen
    abused.°
Remember what I have said.

Oswald.   Well, madam.

Goneril. And let his knights have colder looks among
    you.
What grows of it, no matter; advise your fellows so.
I would breed from hence occasions, and I shall,   25
That I may speak.° I'll write straight° to my sister
To hold my course. Go, prepare for dinner.

                                    Exeunt.

---

7 *riotous* dissolute **10** *come . . . services* are less serviceable to him
than formerly **11** *answer* answer for **14** *come to question* be discussed
openly **15** *distaste* dislike **17** *Idle* foolish **21** *With . . . abused*
with restraints as well as soothing words when they are misguided
25-26 *breed . . . speak* find in this opportunities for speaking out
26 *straight* at once

Scene IV.   [*A hall in the same.*]

Enter Kent [disguised].

Kent. If but as well I other accents borrow
    That can my speech defuse,° my good intent
    May carry through itself to that full issue°
    For which I razed my likeness.° Now, banished
        Kent,
    If thou canst serve where thou dost stand
        condemned,
5   So may it come,° thy master whom thou lov'st
    Shall find thee full of labors.

        *Horns within.° Enter Lear, [Knights] and
                Attendants.*

Lear. Let me not stay° a jot for dinner; go, get it
    ready. [*Exit an Attendant.*] How now, what art
10 thou?

Kent. A man, sir.

Lear. What dost thou profess?° What wouldst thou
    with us?

Kent. I do profess° to be no less than I seem, to
15 serve him truly that will put me in trust, to love
    him that is honest, to converse with him that is
    wise and says little, to fear judgment,° to fight
    when I cannot choose, and to eat no fish.°

I.iv. 2 *defuse* disguise   3 *full issue* perfect result   4 *razed my likeness*
shaved off, disguised my natural appearance   6 *So may it come* so may
it fall out   7 s.d. *within* offstage   8 *stay* wait   12 *What dost thou profess* what do you do   14 *profess* claim   17 *judgment* (by a heavenly or
earthly judge)   18 *eat no fish* i.e., (1) I am no Catholic, but a loyal
Protestant (2) I am no weakling (3) I use no prostitutes

Lear. What art thou?

Kent. A very honest-hearted fellow, and as poor as   20
the King.

Lear. If thou be'st as poor for a subject as he's for a
king, thou art poor enough. What wouldst thou?

Kent. Service.

Lear. Who wouldst thou serve?   25

Kent. You.

Lear. Dost thou know me, fellow?

Kent. No, sir, but you have that in your countenance°
which I would fain° call master.

Lear. What's that?   30

Kent. Authority.

Lear. What services canst thou do?

Kent. I can keep honest counsel,° ride, run, mar a
curious tale in telling it,° and deliver a plain message bluntly. That which ordinary men are fit for, I   35
am qualified in, and the best of me is diligence.

Lear. How old art thou?

Kent. Not so young, sir, to love a woman for singing, nor so old to dote on her for anything. I have
years on my back forty-eight.   40

Lear. Follow me; thou shalt serve me. If I like thee
no worse after dinner, I will not part from thee
yet. Dinner, ho, dinner! Where's my knave?° my
Fool? Go you and call my Fool hither.

                         [Exit an Attendant.]

               Enter Oswald.

You, you, sirrah, where's my daughter?   43

Oswald. So please you——   *Exit.*

---

²⁸ *countenance* bearing ²⁹ *fain* like to ³³ *honest counsel* honorable
secrets ³³⁻³⁴ *mar . . . it* i.e., I cannot speak like an affected courtier
("curious" = "elaborate," as against "plain") ⁴³ *knave* boy

Lear. What says the fellow there? Call the clotpoll°
    back. [*Exit a Knight*.] Where's my Fool? Ho, I
    think the world's asleep.

                 [*Re-enter Knight*.]

50   How now? Where's that mongrel?

Knight. He says, my lord, your daughter is not well.

Lear. Why came not the slave back to me when I
    called him?

Knight. Sir, he answered me in the roundest° manner,
55   he would not.

Lear. He would not?

Knight. My lord, I know not what the matter is;
    but to my judgment your Highness is not enter-
    tained° with that ceremonious affection as you
60   were wont. There's a great abatement of kindness
    appears as well in the general dependants° as in the
    Duke himself also and your daughter.

Lear. Ha? Say'st thou so?

Knight. I beseech you pardon me, my lord, if I be
65   mistaken; for my duty cannot be silent when I
    think your Highness wronged.

Lear. Thou but rememb'rest° me of mine own con-
    ception.° I have perceived a most faint neglect°
    of late, which I have rather blamed as mine own
70   jealous curiosity° than as a very pretense° and
    purpose of unkindness. I will look further into't.
    But where's my Fool? I have not seen him this two
    days.

Knight. Since my young lady's going into France, sir,
75   the Fool hath much pined away.

Lear. No more of that; I have noted it well. Go you

---

47 *clotpoll* clodpoll, blockhead   54 *roundest* rudest   58-59 *entertained*
treated 61 *dependants* servants 67 *rememb'rest* remindest 67-68 *conception* idea 68 *faint neglect* i.e., "weary negligence" (I.iii.13)
69-70 *mine own jealous curiosity* suspicious concern for my own dignity
70 *very pretense* actual intention

and tell my daughter I would speak with her. Go
you, call hither my Fool.   [*Exit an Attendant.*]

           Enter Oswald.

O, you, sir, you! Come you hither, sir. Who am I,
sir?   80

Oswald. My lady's father.

Lear. "My lady's father"? My lord's knave, you
whoreson dog, you slave, you cur!

Oswald. I am none of these, my lord; I beseech your
pardon.   85

Lear. Do you bandy° looks with me, you rascal?
                              [*Striking him.*]

Oswald. I'll not be strucken,° my lord.

Kent. Nor tripped neither, you base football° player.
                     [*Tripping up his heels.*]

Lear. I thank thee, fellow. Thou serv'st me, and I'll
love thee.   90

Kent. Come, sir, arise, away. I'll teach you differences.° Away, away. If you will measure your lubber's° length again, tarry; but away. Go to!° Have
you wisdom?° So.°   [*Pushes Oswald out.*]

Lear. Now, my friendly knave, I thank thee. There's 95
earnest° of thy service.   [*Giving Kent money.*]

            Enter Fool.

Fool. Let me hire him too. Here's my coxcomb.°
                  [*Offering Kent his cap.*]

Lear. How now, my pretty knave? How dost thou?

Fool. Sirrah, you were best° take my coxcomb.

Kent. Why, Fool?   100

---

86 *bandy* exchange insolently (metaphor from tennis) 87 *strucken*
struck 88 *football* (a low game played by idle boys to the scandal of
sensible men) 91-92 *differences* (of rank) 92-93 *lubber's* lout's 93 *Go
to* (expression of derisive incredulity) 93-94 *Have you wisdom* i.e., do
you know what's good for you 94 *So* good 96 *earnest* money for services rendered 97 *coxcomb* professional fool's cap, shaped like a coxcomb 99 *you were best* you had better

Fool. Why? For taking one's part that's out of favor.
Nay, an° thou canst not smile as the wind sits,°
thou'lt catch cold shortly. There, take my coxcomb.
Why, this fellow has banished° two on's daughters,
105 and did the third a blessing against his will. If thou
follow him, thou must needs wear my coxcomb.
—How now, Nuncle?° Would I had two coxcombs
and two daughters.

Lear. Why, my boy?

110 *Fool.* If I gave them all my living,° I'd keep my coxcombs myself. There's mine; beg another of thy
daughters.

Lear. Take heed, sirrah—the whip.

Fool. Truth's a dog must to kennel; he must be
115 whipped out, when Lady the Brach° may stand by
th' fire and stink.

Lear. A pestilent gall° to me.

Fool. Sirrah, I'll teach thee a speech.

Lear. Do.

120 *Fool.* Mark it, Nuncle.
    Have more than thou showest,
    Speak less than thou knowest,
    Lend less than thou owest,°
    Ride more than thou goest,°
125   Learn more than thou trowest,°
    Set less than thou throwest;°
    Leave thy drink and thy whore,
    And keep in-a-door,
    And thou shalt have more
130   Than two tens to a score.°

Kent. This is nothing, Fool.

---

102 *an* if   102 *smile . . . sits* ingratiate yourself with those in power
104 *banished* alienated (by making them independent)   107 *Nuncle*
(contraction of "mine uncle")   110 *living* property   115 *Brach* bitch
117 *gall* sore   123 *owest* ownest   124 *goest* walkest   125 *trowest* knowest
126 *Set . . . throwest* bet less than you play for (get odds from your
opponent)   129-30 *have . . . score* i.e., come away with more than you
had (two tens, or twenty shillings, make a score, or one pound)

Fool. Then 'tis like the breath of an unfeed° lawyer
—you gave me nothing for't. Can you make no use
of nothing, Nuncle?

Lear. Why, no, boy. Nothing can be made out of 135
nothing.

Fool. [*To Kent*] Prithee tell him, so much the
rent of his land comes to; he will not believe a
Fool.

Lear. A bitter° Fool. 140

Fool. Dost thou know the difference, my boy, between
a bitter Fool and a sweet one?

Lear. No, lad; teach me.

Fool.

> That lord that counseled thee
>   To give away thy land,
> Come place him here by me,
>   Do thou for him stand.
> The sweet and bitter fool
>   Will presently appear;
> The one in motley° here, 150
>   The other found out° there.°

Lear. Dost thou call me fool, boy?

Fool. All thy other titles thou hast given away; that
thou wast born with.

Kent. This is not altogether fool, my lord. 155

Fool. No, faith; lords and great men will not let me.°
If I had a monopoly° out, they would have part
on't. And ladies too, they will not let me have all
the fool to myself; they'll be snatching. Nuncle,
give me an egg, and I'll give thee two crowns. 160

---

132 *unfeed* unpaid for   140 *bitter* satirical   150 *motley* the drab costume
of the professional jester   151 *found out* revealed   151 *there* (the Fool
points at Lear, as a fool in the grain)   156 *let me* (have all the folly to
myself)   157 *monopoly* (James I gave great scandal by granting to his
"snatching" courtiers royal patents to deal exclusively in some commodity)

Lear. What two crowns shall they be?

Fool. Why, after I have cut the egg i' th' middle
and eat up the meat, the two crowns of the egg.
When thou clovest thy crown i' th' middle and
165 gav'st away both parts, thou bor'st thine ass on
thy back o'er the dirt.° Thou hadst little wit in thy
bald crown when thou gav'st thy golden one away.
If I speak like myself° in this, let him be whipped°
that first finds it so.
170 [*Singing*] Fools had ne'er less grace in a year,
        For wise men are grown foppish,
And know not how their wits to wear,
        Their manners are so apish.°

Lear. When were you wont to be so full of songs,
175 sirrah?

Fool. I have used° it, Nuncle, e'er since thou mad'st
thy daughters thy mothers; for when thou gav'st
them the rod, and put'st down thine own breeches,
[*Singing*] Then they for sudden joy did weep,
180   And I for sorrow sung,
That such a king should play bo-peep°
        And go the fools among.
Prithee, Nuncle, keep a schoolmaster that can teach
thy Fool to lie. I would fain learn to lie.

185 *Lear.* And° you lie, sirrah, we'll have you whipped.

Fool. I marvel what kin thou and thy daughters are.
They'll have me whipped for speaking true; thou'lt
have me whipped for lying; and sometimes I am
whipped for holding my peace. I had rather be any
190 kind o' thing than a Fool, and yet I would not be

165-66 *bor'st . . . dirt* (like the foolish and unnatural countryman in
Aesop's fable) 168 *like myself* like a Fool 168 *let him be whipped* i.e.,
let the man be whipped for a Fool who thinks my true saying to be
foolish 170-73 *Fools . . . apish* i.e., fools were never in less favor than
now, and the reason is that wise men, turning foolish, and not knowing
how to use their intelligence, imitate the professional fools and so make
them unnecessary 176 *used* practiced 181 *play bo-peep* (1) act like a
child (2) blind himself 185 *And* if

thee, Nuncle: thou hast pared thy wit o' both sides
and left nothing i' th' middle. Here comes one o'
the parings.

Enter Goneril.

Lear. How now, daughter? What makes that frontlet°
on? Methinks you are too much of late i' th'   195
frown.

Fool. Thou wast a pretty fellow when thou hadst no
need to care for her frowning. Now thou art an O
without a figure.° I am better than thou art now: I
am a Fool, thou art nothing. [*To Goneril.*] Yes,   200
forsooth, I will hold my tongue. So your face bids
me, though you say nothing. Mum, mum,
> He that keeps nor crust nor crum,°
> Weary of all, shall want° some.

[*Pointing to Lear*] That's a shealed peascod.°   205

Goneril. Not only, sir, this your all-licensed° Fool,
But other° of your insolent retinue
Do hourly carp and quarrel, breaking forth
In rank° and not-to-be-endurèd riots. Sir,
I had thought by making this well known unto you   210
To have found a safe° redress, but now grow
    fearful,
By what yourself too late° have spoke and done,
That you protect this course, and put it on
By your allowance;° which if you should, the fault
Would not 'scape censure, nor the redresses sleep,° 215
Which, in the tender of° a wholesome weal,°
Might in their working do you that offense,
Which else were shame, that then necessity
Will call discreet proceeding.°

---

194 *frontlet* frown (lit., ornamental band) 199 *figure* digit, to give
value to the cipher (Lear is a nought) 203 *crum* soft bread inside
the loaf 204 *want* lack 205 *shealed peascod* empty pea pod 206 *all-
licensed* privileged to take any liberties 207 *other* others 209 *rank*
gross 211 *safe* sure 212 *too late* lately 213-14 *put . . . allowance*
promote it by your approval 214 *allowance* approval 215 *redresses
sleep* correction fail to follow 216 *tender of* desire for 216 *weal* state
217-19 *Might . . . proceeding* as I apply it, the correction might humiliate you; but the need to take action cancels what would otherwise be
unfilial conduct in me

220 *Fool.* For you know, Nuncle,
           The hedge-sparrow fed the cuckoo° so long
           That it had it head bit off by it° young.
      So out went the candle, and we were left darkling.°

Lear. Are you our daughter?

225 *Goneril.* Come, sir,
           I would you would make use of your good wisdom
           Whereof I know you are fraught° and put away
           These dispositions° which of late transport you
           From what you rightly are.

230 *Fool.* May not an ass know when the cart draws the
      horse? Whoop, Jug,° I love thee!

Lear. Does any here know me? This is not Lear.
      Does Lear walk thus? Speak thus? Where are his
      eyes?
      Either his notion° weakens, or his discernings°
235   Are lethargied°—Ha! Waking? 'Tis not so.
      Who is it that can tell me who I am?

Fool. Lear's shadow.

Lear. I would learn that; for, by the marks of sover-
      eignty,° knowledge, and reason, I should be false°
240   persuaded I had daughters.

Fool. Which° they will make an obedient father.

Lear. Your name, fair gentlewoman?

Goneril. This admiration,° sir, is much o' th' savor°
      Of other your° new pranks. I do beseech you
245   To understand my purposes aright.
      As you are old and reverend, should be wise.
      Here do you keep a hundred knights and squires,

---

221 *cuckoo* (who lays its eggs in the nests of other birds)   222 *it* its
223 *darkling* in the dark   227 *fraught* endowed   228 *dispositions* moods
231 *Jug* Joan (? a quotation from a popular song)   234 *notion* understanding   234 *discernings* faculties   235 *lethargied* paralyzed   238-39 *marks
of sovereignty* i.e., tokens that Lear is king, and hence father to his
daughters   239 *false* falsely   241 *Which* whom (Lear)   243 *admiration*
(affected)   wonderment   243 *is much o' th' savor* smacks much
244 *other your* others of your

Men so disordered, so deboshed,° and bold,
That this our court, infected with their manners,
Shows° like a riotous inn. Epicurism° and lust   250
Makes it more like a tavern or a brothel
Than a graced° palace. The shame itself doth speak
For instant remedy. Be then desired°
By her, that else will take the thing she begs,
A little to disquantity your train,°   255
And the remainders° that shall still depend,°
To be such men as may besort° your age,
Which know themselves, and you.

Lear.   Darkness and devils!
Saddle my horses; call my train together.
Degenerate° bastard, I'll not trouble thee: 260
Yet have I left a daughter.

Goneril. You strike my people, and your disordered
    rabble
Make servants of their betters.

Enter Albany.

Lear. Woe, that too late repents. O, sir, are you
    come?
Is it your will? Speak, sir. Prepare my horses.   265
Ingratitude! thou marble-hearted fiend,
More hideous when thou show'st thee in a child
Than the sea-monster.

Albany.   Pray, sir, be patient

Lear. Detested kite,° thou liest.
My train are men of choice and rarest parts,°   270
That all particulars of duty know,
And, in the most exact regard,° support
The worships° of their name. O most small fault,

---

248 *deboshed* debauched   **250** *Shows* appears   **250** *Epicurism* riotous living   **252** *graced* dignified   **253** *desired* requested   **255** *disquantity your train* reduce the number of your dependents   **256** *remainders* those who remain   **256** *depend* attend on you   **257** *besort* befit   **260** *Degenerate* unnatural   **269** *kite* scavenging bird of prey   **270** *parts* accomplishments   **272** *exact regard* strict attention to detail   **273** *worships* honor

How ugly didst thou in Cordelia show!
Which, like an engine,° wrenched my frame of
275   nature
From the fixed place;° drew from my heart all love,
And added to the gall.° O Lear, Lear, Lear!
Beat at this gate that let thy folly in [*Striking
        his head.*]
And thy dear judgment out. Go, go, my people.

280 *Albany.* My lord, I am guiltless, as I am ignorant
Of what hath moved you.

Lear.   It may be so, my lord.
Hear, Nature, hear; dear Goddess, hear:
Suspend thy purpose if thou didst intend
To make this creature fruitful.
285 Into her womb convey sterility,
Dry up in her the organs of increase,°
And from her derogate° body never spring
A babe to honor her. If she must teem,°
Create her child of spleen,° that it may live
290 And be a thwart disnatured° torment to her.
Let it stamp wrinkles in her brow of youth,
With cadent° tears fret° channels in her cheeks,
Turn all her mother's pains and benefits°
To laughter and contempt, that she may feel
295 How sharper than a serpent's tooth it is
To have a thankless child. Away, away!   *Exit.*

Albany. Now, gods that we adore, whereof comes
        this?

Goneril. Never afflict yourself to know the cause,
But let his disposition° have that scope
300 As° dotage gives it.

                Enter Lear.

Lear. What, fifty of my followers at a clap?°

---

275 *engine* destructive contrivance   274-76 *wrenched . . . place* i.e.,
disordered my natural self   277 *gall* bitterness   286 *increase* childbear-
ing   287 *derogate* degraded   288 *teem* conceive   289 *spleen* ill humor
290 *thwart disnatured* perverse unnatural   292 *cadent* falling   292 *fret*
wear   293 *benefits* the mother's beneficent care of her child   299 *disposition* mood   300 *As* that   301 *at a clap* at one stroke

Within a fortnight?

Albany. What's the matter, sir?

Lear. I'll tell thee. [*To Goneril*] Life and death,
   I am ashamed
   That thou hast power to shake my manhood°
      thus!
   That these hot tears, which break from me
      perforce,° 305
   Should make thee worth them. Blasts and fogs
      upon thee!
   Th' untented woundings° of a father's curse
   Pierce every sense about thee! Old fond° eyes,
   Beweep° this cause again, I'll pluck ye out
   And cast you, with the waters that you loose,° 310
   To temper° clay. Yea, is it come to this?
   Ha! Let it be so. I have another daughter,
   Who I am sure is kind and comfortable.°
   When she shall hear this of thee, with her nails
   She'll flay thy wolvish visage. Thou shalt find 315
   That I'll resume the shape° which thou dost think
   I have cast off for ever.
                Exit [*Lear with Kent and Attendants*].

Goneril. Do you mark that?

Albany. I cannot be so partial, Goneril,
   To the great love I bear you°——

Goneril. Pray you, content. What, Oswald, ho! 320
   [*To the Fool*] You, sir, more knave than fool,
      after your master!

Fool. Nuncle Lear, Nuncle Lear, tarry. Take the Fool°
   with thee.

---

304 *shake my manhood* i.e., with tears 305 *perforce* involuntarily,
against my will 307 *untented woundings* wounds too deep to be
probed with a tent (a roll of lint) 308 *fond* foolish 309 *Beweep* if you
weep over 310 *loose* (1) let loose (2) lose, as of no avail 311 *temper*
mix with and soften 313 *comfortable* ready to comfort 316 *shape* i.e.,
kingly role 318-19 *I cannot . . . you* i.e., even though my love inclines
me to you, I must protest 322 *Fool* (1) the Fool himself (2) the
epithet or character of "fool"

A fox, when one has caught her,
825 And such a daughter,
Should sure to the slaughter,
If my cap would buy a halter.°
So the Fool follows after.°   *Exit.*

Goneril. This man hath had good counsel. A hundred
knights!
830 'Tis politic° and safe to let him keep
At point° a hundred knights: yes, that on every
dream,
Each buzz,° each fancy, each complaint, dislike,
He may enguard° his dotage with their pow'rs
And hold our lives in mercy.° Oswald, I say!

Albany. Well, you may fear too far.

835 *Goneril.*   Safer than trust too far.
Let me still take away the harms I fear,
Not fear still to be taken.° I know his heart.
What he hath uttered I have writ my sister.
If she sustain him and his hundred knights,
When I have showed th' unfitness——

Enter Oswald.

840   How now, Oswald?
What, have you writ that letter to my sister?

Oswald. Ay, madam.

Goneril. Take you some company,° and away to
horse.
Inform her full of my particular° fear,
845 And thereto add such reasons of your own
As may compact° it more. Get you gone,
And hasten your return. [*Exit Oswald.*] No, no,
my lord,
This milky gentleness and course° of yours,
Though I condemn not,° yet under pardon,

327-28 *halter, after* pronounced "hauter," "auter" 330 *politic* good
policy 331 *At point* armed 332 *buzz* rumor 333 *enguard* protect
334 *in mercy* at his mercy 337 *Not . . . taken* rather than remain fearful of being overtaken by them 343 *company* escort 344 *particular*
own 346 *compact* strengthen 348 *milky . . . course* mild and gentle
way (hendiadys) 349 *condemn not* condemn it not

 You are much more attasked° for want of wisdom 350
 Than praised for harmful mildness.°

Albany. How far your eyes may pierce I cannot tell;
 Striving to better, oft we mar what's well.

Goneril. Nay then——

Albany. Well, well, th' event.°   *Exeunt.* 355

Scene V. [*Court before the same.*]

Enter Lear, Kent, and Fool.

Lear. Go you before to Gloucester with these letters.
 Acquaint my daughter no further with anything
 you know than comes from her demand out of
 the letter.° If your diligence be not speedy, I shall
 be there afore you.   5

Kent. I will not sleep, my lord, till I have delivered
 your letter.   *Exit.*

Fool. If a man's brains were in's heels, were't° not
 in danger of kibes?°

Lear. Ay, boy.   10

Fool. Then I prithee be merry. Thy wit shall not go
 slipshod.°

Lear. Ha, ha, ha.

Fool. Shalt° see thy other daughter will use thee
 kindly;° for though she's as like this as a crab's° 15
 like an apple, yet I can tell what I can tell.

350 *attasked* taken to task, blamed 351 *harmful mildness* dangerous indulgence 355 *th' event* i.e., we'll see what happens I.v. 3-4 *than . . . letter* than her reading of the letter brings her to ask 8 *were't* i.e., the brains 9 *kibes* chilblains 11-12 *Thy . . . slipshod* your brains shall not go in slippers (because you have no brains to be protected from chilblains) 14 *Shalt* thou shalt 15 *kindly* (1) affectionately (2) after her kind or nature 15 *crab* crab apple

Lear. Why, what canst thou tell, my boy?

Fool. She will taste as like this as a crab does to a crab. Thou canst tell why one's nose stands i' th' middle on's° face?

Lear. No.

Fool. Why, to keep one's eyes of° either side's nose, that what a man cannot smell out, he may spy into.

Lear. I did her wrong.

Fool. Canst tell how an oyster makes his shell?

Lear. No.

Fool. Nor I neither; but I can tell why a snail has a house.

Lear. Why?

Fool. Why, to put 's head in; not to give it away to his daughters, and leave his horns° without a case.

Lear. I will forget my nature.° So kind a father! Be my horses ready?

Fool. Thy asses are gone about 'em. The reason why the seven stars° are no moe° than seven is a pretty° reason.

Lear. Because they are not eight.

Fool. Yes indeed. Thou wouldst make a good Fool.

Lear. To take't again perforce!° Monster ingratitude!

Fool. If thou wert my Fool, Nuncle, I'd have thee beaten for being old before thy time.

Lear. How's that?

Fool. Thou shouldst not have been old till thou hadst been wise.

---

20 *on's* of his **22** *of* on **32** *horns* (1) snail's horns (2) cuckold's horns **33** *nature* paternal instincts **36** *seven stars* the Pleiades **36** *moe* more **36** *pretty* apt **40** *To . . . perforce* (1) of Goneril, who has forcibly taken away Lear's privileges; or (2) of Lear, who meditates a forcible resumption of authority

Lear. O, let me not be mad, not mad, sweet heaven!
    Keep me in temper;° I would not be mad!

[*Enter Gentleman.*]

How now, are the horses ready?

Gentleman. Ready, my lord.

Lear. Come, boy.   50

Fool. She that's a maid now, and laughs at my
        departure,
    Shall not be a maid long, unless things be cut
        shorter.°   *Exeunt.*

---

⁴⁷ *in temper* sane ⁵¹⁻⁵² *She . . . shorter* the maid who laughs, missing
the tragic implications of this quarrel, will not have sense enough to
preserve her virginity ("things" = penises)

ACT II

Scene I. [*The Earl of Gloucester's castle.*]

Enter Edmund and Curan, severally.°

Edmund. Save° thee, Curan.

Curan. And you, sir. I have been with your father, and given him notice that the Duke of Cornwall and Regan his duchess will be here with him this night.

Edmund. How comes that?

Curan. Nay, I know not. You have heard of the news abroad? I mean the whispered ones, for they are yet but ear-kissing arguments.°

Edmund. Not I. Pray you, what are they?

Curan. Have you heard of no likely° wars toward,° 'twixt the Dukes of Cornwall and Albany?

Edmund. Not a word.

Curan. You may do, then, in time. Fare you well, sir.   *Exit.*

Edmund. The Duke be here tonight? The better!° best!

II.i. ¹ s.d. *severally* separately (from different entrances on stage) ¹ *Save* God save ⁹ *ear-kissing arguments* subjects whispered in the ear ¹¹ *likely* probable ¹¹ *toward* impending ¹⁶ *The better* so much the better

This weaves itself perforce° into my business.
My father hath set guard to take my brother,
And I have one thing of a queasy question°
Which I must act. Briefness° and Fortune, work!   20
Brother, a word; descend. Brother, I say!

Enter Edgar.

My father watches. O sir, fly this place.
Intelligence° is given where you are hid.
You have now the good advantage of the night.
Have you not spoken 'gainst the Duke of Cornwall?   25
He's coming hither, now i' th' night, i' th' haste,°
And Regan with him. Have you nothing said
Upon his party° 'gainst the Duke of Albany?
Advise yourself.°

Edgar.   I am sure on't,° not a word.

Edmund. I hear my father coming. Pardon me: 30
In cunning° I must draw my sword upon you.
Draw, seem to defend yourself; now quit you° well.
Yield! Come before my father! Light ho, here!
Fly, brother. Torches, torches! —So farewell.

Exit Edgar.

Some blood drawn on me would beget opinion°   35

[*Wounds his arm*]

Of my more fierce endeavor. I have seen drunkards
Do more than this in sport. Father, father!
Stop, stop! No help?

Enter Gloucester, and Servants with torches.

Gloucester. Now, Edmund, where's the villain?

Edmund. Here stood he in the dark, his sharp sword
    out,   40
Mumbling of wicked charms, conjuring the moon
To stand auspicious mistress.

Gloucester.   But where is he?

---

17 *perforce* necessarily   19 *of a queasy question* that requires delicate
handling (to be "queasy" is to be on the point of vomiting)   20 *Brief-
ness* speed   23 *Intelligence* information   26 *i' th' haste* in great haste
28 *Upon his party* censuring his enmity   29 *Advise yourself* reflect
29 *on't* of it   31 *In cunning* as a pretense   32 *quit you* acquit yourself
35 *beget opinion* create the impression

Edmund. Look, sir, I bleed.

Gloucester.   Where is the villain, Edmund?

Edmund. Fled this way, sir, when by no means he
  could——

Gloucester. Pursue him, ho! Go after.

                                        [*Exeunt some Servants.*]

45   By no means what?

Edmund. Persuade me to the murder of your lordship;
  But that I told him the revenging gods
  'Gainst parricides did all the thunder bend;°
  Spoke with how manifold and strong a bond
50   The child was bound to th' father. Sir, in fine,°
  Seeing how loathly opposite° I stood
  To his unnatural purpose, in fell° motion°
  With his preparèd sword he charges home
  My unprovided° body, latched° mine arm;
55   But when he saw my best alarumed° spirits
  Bold in the quarrel's right,° roused to th'
    encounter,
  Or whether gasted° by the noise I made,
  Full suddenly he fled.

Gloucester.   Let him fly far.
  Not in this land shall he remain uncaught;
60   And found—dispatch.° The noble Duke my master,
  My worthy arch° and patron, comes tonight.
  By his authority I will proclaim it,
  That he which finds him shall deserve our thanks,
  Bringing the murderous coward to the stake.
65   He that conceals him, death.°

Edmund. When I dissuaded him from his intent,
  And found him pight° to do it, with curst° speech
  I threatened to discover° him. He replied,

---

48 *bend* aim   50 *in fine* finally   51 *loathly opposite* bitterly opposed
52 *fell* deadly   52 *motion* thrust (a term from fencing)   54 *unprovided*
unprotected   54 *latched* wounded (lanced)   55 *best alarumed* wholly
aroused   56 *Bold . . . right* confident in the rightness of my cause
57 *gasted* struck aghast   60 *dispatch* i.e., he will be killed   61 *arch* chief
65 *death* (the same elliptical form that characterizes "dispatch," 1.60)
67 *pight* determined   67 *curst* angry   68 *discover* expose

"Thou unpossessing° bastard, dost thou think,
If I would stand against thee, would the reposal°   70
Of any trust, virtue, or worth in thee
Make thy words faithed?° No. What I should
    deny—
As this I would, ay, though thou didst produce
My very character°—I'd turn it all
To thy suggestion,° plot, and damnèd practice.°   75
And thou must make a dullard of the world,°
If they not thought° the profits of my death
Were very pregnant° and potential spirits°
To make thee seek it."

Gloucester.   O strange and fastened° villain!
Would he deny his letter, said he? I never got° him.   80

                                    Tucket° within.

Hark, the Duke's trumpets. I know not why he
    comes.
All ports° I'll bar; the villain shall not 'scape;
The Duke must grant me that. Besides, his picture
I will send far and near, that all the kingdom
May have due note of him; and of my land,   85
Loyal and natural° boy, I'll work the means
To make thee capable.°

        Enter Cornwall, Regan, and Attendants.

Cornwall. How now, my noble friend! Since I came
    hither,
Which I can call but now, I have heard strange
    news.

Regan. If it be true, all vengeance comes too short   90
Which can pursue th' offender. How dost, my lord?

Gloucester. O madam, my old heart is cracked, it's
    cracked.

---

69 *unpossessing* beggarly (landless) 70 *reposal* placing 72 *faithed* believed 74 *character* handwriting 75 *suggestion* instigation 75 *practice* device 76 *make . . . world* think everyone stupid 77 *not thought* did not think 78 *pregnant* teeming with incitement 78 *potential spirits* powerful evil spirits 79 *fastened* hardened 80 *got* begot 80 s.d. *Tucket* (Cornwall's special trumpet call) 82 *ports* exits, of whatever sort 86 *natural* (1) kind (filial) (2) illegitimate 87 *capable* able to inherit

Regan. What, did my father's godson seek your life?
    He whom my father named, your Edgar?

95 *Gloucester.* O lady, lady, shame would have it hid.

Regan. Was he not companion with the riotous knights
    That tended upon my father?

Gloucester. I know not, madam. 'Tis too bad, too bad.

Edmund. Yes, madam, he was of that consort.°

100 *Regan.* No marvel then, though he were ill affected.°
    'Tis they have put° him on the old man's death,
    To have th' expense and waste° of his revenues.
    I have this present evening from my sister
    Been well informed of them, and with such cautions
105   That, if they come to sojourn at my house,
    I'll not be there.

Cornwall.   Nor I, assure thee, Regan.
    Edmund, I hear that you have shown your father
    A childlike° office.

Edmund. It was my duty, sir.

110 *Gloucester.* He did bewray his practice,° and received
    This hurt you see, striving to apprehend him.

Cornwall. Is he pursued?

Gloucester.   Ay, my good lord.

Cornwall. If he be taken, he shall never more
    Be feared of doing° harm. Make your own purpose,
115   How in my strength you please.° For you, Edmund,
    Whose virtue and obedience° doth this instant
    So much commend itself, you shall be ours.
    Natures of such deep trust we shall much need;
    You we first seize on.

Edmund.   I shall serve you, sir,
    Truly, however else.

120 *Gloucester.*   For him I thank your Grace.

---

99 *consort* company 100 *ill affected* disposed to evil 101 *put* set
102 *expense and waste* squandering 108 *childlike* filial 110 *bewray his
practice* disclose his plot 114 *of doing* because he might do
114-15 *Make . . . please* use my power freely, in carrying out your plans
for his capture 116 *virtue and obedience* virtuous obedience

Cornwall. You know not why we came to visit you?

Regan. Thus out of season, threading dark-eyed night.
    Occasions, noble Gloucester, of some prize,°
    Wherein we must have use of your advice.
    Our father he hath writ, so hath our sister,   *125*
    Of differences,° which° I best thought it fit
    To answer from° our home. The several
       messengers
    From hence attend dispatch.° Our good old friend,
    Lay comforts to your bosom,° and bestow
    Your needful° counsel to our businesses,   *130*
    Which craves the instant use.°

Gloucester.   I serve you, madam.
    Your Graces are right welcome.

                              Exeunt. Flourish.

Scene II.   [*Before Gloucester's castle.*]

Enter Kent and Oswald, severally.

Oswald. Good dawning° to thee, friend. Art of this
    house?°

Kent. Ay.

Oswald. Where may we set our horses?

Kent. I' th' mire.   *5*

Oswald. Prithee, if thou lov'st me, tell me.

Kent. I love thee not.

---

122 *prize* importance 125 *differences* quarrels 125 *which* (referring not
to "differences," but to the letter Lear has written) 126 *from* away
from 127 *attend dispatch* are waiting to be sent off 128 *Lay . . .
bosom* console yourself (about Edgar's supposed treason) 129 *needful*
needed 131 *craves the instant use* demands immediate transaction
II.ii. 1 *dawning* (dawn is impending, but not yet arrived) 1-2 *Art of
this house* i.e., do you live here

Oswald. Why then, I care not for thee.

Kent. If I had thee in Lipsbury Pinfold,° I would make
10   thee care for me.

Oswald. Why dost thou use me thus? I know thee not.

Kent. Fellow, I know thee.

Oswald. What dost thou know me for?

Kent. A knave, a rascal, an eater of broken meats;°
15   a base, proud, shallow, beggarly, three-suited,°
    hundred-pound,° filthy worsted-stocking° knave;
    a lily-livered, action-taking,° whoreson, glass-gaz-
    ing,° superserviceable,° finical° rogue; one-trunk-
    inheriting° slave; one that wouldst be a bawd in
20   way of good service,° and art nothing but the com-
    position° of a knave, beggar, coward, pander, and
    the son and heir of a mongrel bitch; one whom I
    will beat into clamorous whining if thou deniest the
    least syllable of thy addition.°

25 *Oswald.* Why, what a monstrous fellow art thou, thus
    to rail on one that is neither known of thee nor
    knows thee!

Kent. What a brazen-faced varlet art thou to deny
    thou knowest me! Is it two days since I
30   tripped up thy heels and beat thee before the
    King? [*Drawing his sword*] Draw, you rogue,
    for though it be night, yet the moon shines. I'll
    make a sop o' th' moonshine° of you. You whore-
    son cullionly barbermonger,° draw!

9 *Lipsbury Pinfold* a pound or pen in which strayed animals are enclosed ("Lipsbury" may denote a particular place, or may be slang for
"between my teeth")   14 *broken meats* scraps of food   15 *three-suited*
(the wardrobe permitted to a servant or "knave")   16 *hundred-pound*
(the extent of Oswald's wealth, and thus a sneer at his aspiring to
gentility)   16 *worsted-stocking* (worn by servants)   17 *action-taking*
one who refuses a fight and goes to law instead   17-18 *glass-gazing*
conceited   18 *superserviceable* sycophantic, serving without principle.
18 *finical* overfastidious   18-19 *one-trunk-inheriting* possessing only a
trunkful of goods   19-20 *bawd . . . service* pimp, to please his master
20-21 *composition* compound   24 *addition* titles   33 *sop o' th' moonshine*
i.e., Oswald will admit the moonlight, and so sop it up, through the
open wounds Kent is preparing to give him   34 *cullionly barbermonger*
base patron of hairdressers (effeminate man)

Oswald. Away, I have nothing to do with thee.   35

Kent. Draw, you rascal. You come with letters
against the King, and take Vanity the puppet's° part
against the royalty of her father. Draw, you rogue,
or I'll so carbonado° your shanks. Draw, you rascal. Come your ways!°   40

Oswald. Help, ho! Murder! Help!

Kent. Strike, you slave! Stand, rogue! Stand, you neat°
slave! Strike! [*Beating him*]

Oswald. Help, ho! Murder, murder!

*Enter Edmund, with his rapier drawn, Cornwall,
Regan, Gloucester, Servants.*

Edmund. How now? What's the matter? Part!   45

Kent. With you,° goodman boy,° if you please! Come,
I'll flesh° ye, come on, young master.

Gloucester. Weapons? Arms? What's the matter here?

Cornwall. Keep peace, upon your lives.
He dies that strikes again. What is the matter?   50

Regan. The messengers from our sister and the King.

Cornwall. What is your difference?° Speak.

Oswald. I am scarce in breath, my lord.

Kent. No marvel, you have so bestirred° your valor.
You cowardly rascal, nature disclaims in thee.° A   55
tailor made thee.°

Cornwall. Thou art a strange fellow. A tailor make a
man?

Kent. A tailor, sir. A stonecutter or a painter could

---

37 *Vanity the puppet's* Goneril, here identified with one of the personified characters in the morality plays, which were sometimes put
on as puppet shows   39 *carbonado* cut across, like a piece of meat
before cooking   40 *Come your ways* get along   42 *neat* (1) foppish
(2) unmixed, as in "neat wine"   46 *With you* i.e., the quarrel is with
you   46 *goodman boy* young man (peasants are "goodmen"; "boy" is
a term of contempt)   47 *flesh* introduce to blood (term from hunting)
52 *difference* quarrel   54 *bestirred* exercised   55 *nature disclaims in thee*
nature renounces any part in you   55-56 *A tailor made thee* (from the
proverb "The tailor makes the man")

60 　　　not have made him so ill, though they had been
　　　　　but two years o' th' trade.

　　　Cornwall. Speak yet, how grew your quarrel?

　　　Oswald. This ancient ruffian, sir, whose life I have
　　　　　spared at suit of° his gray beard——

65 　*Kent.* Thou whoreson zed,° thou unnecessary letter!
　　　　　My lord, if you will give me leave, I will tread this
　　　　　unbolted° villain into mortar and daub the wall of
　　　　　a jakes° with him. Spare my gray beard, you wag-
　　　　　tail!°

70 　*Cornwall.* Peace, sirrah!
　　　　　You beastly° knave, know you no reverence?

　　　Kent. Yes, sir, but anger hath a privilege.

　　　Cornwall. Why art thou angry?

　　　Kent. That such a slave as this should wear a sword,
　　　　　Who wears no honesty. Such smiling rogues as
75 　　　　　these,
　　　　　Like rats, oft bite the holy cords° atwain
　　　　　Which are too intrince° t' unloose; smooth°
　　　　　　every passion
　　　　　That in the natures of their lords rebel,
　　　　　Being oil to fire, snow to the colder moods;
80 　　　　Renege,° affirm, and turn their halcyon beaks°
　　　　　With every gale and vary° of their masters,
　　　　　Knowing naught, like dogs, but following.
　　　　　A plague upon your epileptic° visage!
　　　　　Smile you° my speeches, as I were a fool?

64 *at suit of* out of pity for　65 *zed* the letter Z, generally omitted in
contemporary dictionaries　67 *unbolted* unsifted, i.e., altogether a villain　68 *jakes* privy　68-69 *wagtail* a bird that bobs its tail up and down,
and thus suggests obsequiousness　71 *beastly* irrational　76 *holy cords*
sacred bonds of affection (as between husbands and wives, parents and children)　77 *intrince* entangled, intricate　77 *smooth* appease
80 *Renege* deny　80 *halcyon beaks* (the halcyon or kingfisher serves
here as a type of the opportunist because, when hung up by the tail or
neck, it was supposed to turn with the wind, like a weathervane)
81 *gale and vary* varying gale (hendiadys)　83 *epileptic* distorted by
grinning　84 *Smile you* do you smile at

Goose, if I had you upon Sarum Plain,°   85
  I'd drive ye cackling home to Camelot.°

Cornwall. What, art thou mad, old fellow?

Gloucester. How fell you out? Say that.

Kent. No contraries° hold more antipathy
  Than I and such a knave.   90

Cornwall. Why dost thou call him knave? What is his
  fault?

Kent. His countenance likes° me not.

Cornwall. No more perchance does mine, nor his, nor
  hers.

Kent. Sir, 'tis my occupation to be plain:
  I have seen better faces in my time   95
  Than stands on any shoulder that I see
  Before me at this instant.

Cornwall.   This is some fellow
  Who, having been praised for bluntness, doth
    affect
  A saucy roughness, and constrains the garb
  Quite from his nature.° He cannot flatter, he;   100
  An honest mind and plain, he must speak truth.
  And° they will take it, so; if not, he's plain.
  These kind of knaves I know, which in this
    plainness
  Harbor more craft and more corrupter ends
  Than twenty silly-ducking observants°   105
  That stretch their duties nicely.°

Kent. Sir, in good faith, in sincere verity,
  Under th' allowance° of your great aspect,°
  Whose influence,° like the wreath of radiant fire

---

85 *Sarum Plain* Salisbury Plain   86 *Camelot* the residence of King
Arthur (presumably a particular point, now lost, is intended here)
89 *contraries* opposites   92 *likes* pleases   99-100 *constrains . . . nature*
forces the manner of candid speech to be a cloak, not for candor but
for craft   102 *And* if   105 *silly-ducking observants* ridiculously obsequious attendants   106 *nicely* punctiliously   108 *allowance* approval
108 *aspect* (1) appearance (2) position of the heavenly bodies   109 *influence* astrological power

On flick'ring Phoebus' front°——

110   *Cornwall.*   What mean'st by this?

Kent. To go out of my dialect,° which you discommend
    so much. I know, sir, I am no flatterer. He° that
    beguiled you in a plain accent was a plain knave,
    which, for my part, I will not be, though I should
115 win your displeasure to entreat me to't.°

Cornwall. What was th' offense you gave him?

Oswald. I never gave him any.
    It pleased the King his master very late°
    To strike at me, upon his misconstruction;°
120 When he, compact,° and flattering his displeasure,
    Tripped me behind; being down, insulted, railed,
    And put upon him such a deal of man°
    That worthied him,° got praises of the King
    For him attempting who was self-subdued;°
125 And, in the fleshment° of this dread exploit,
    Drew on me here again.

Kent.   None of these rogues and cowards
    But Ajax is their fool.°

Cornwall.   Fetch forth the stocks!
    You stubborn° ancient knave, you reverent°
        braggart,
    We'll teach you.

    Kent.   Sir, I am too old to learn.

110 *Phoebus' front* forehead of the sun   111 *dialect* customary manner
of speaking   112 *He* i.e., the sort of candid-crafty man Cornwall has
been describing   114-15 *though . . . to't* even if I were to succeed in
bringing your graceless person ("displeasure" personified, and in lieu
of the expected form, "your grace") to beg me to be a plain knave
118 *very late* recently   119 *misconstruction* misunderstanding   120 *compact* in league with the king   122 *put . . . man* pretended such manly
behavior   123 *worthied him* made him seem heroic   124 *For . . . self-
subdued* for attacking a man (Oswald) who offered no resistance
125 *fleshment* the bloodthirstiness excited by his first success or "flesh-
ing"   126-27 *None . . . fool* i.e., cowardly rogues like Oswald always
impose on fools like Cornwall (who is likened to Ajax: [1] the brag-
gart Greek warrior [2] a jakes or privy)   128 *stubborn* rude   128 *rev-
erent* old

Call not your stocks for me, I serve the King,   *130*
On whose employment I was sent to you.
You shall do small respect, show too bold malice
Against the grace and person° of my master,
Stocking his messenger.

Cornwall. Fetch forth the stocks. As I have life and
    honor,   *135*
There shall he sit till noon.

Regan. Till noon? Till night, my lord, and all night
    too.

Kent. Why, madam, if I were your father's dog,
You should not use me so.

Regan.   Sir, being his knave, I will.

Cornwall. This is a fellow of the selfsame color°   *140*
Our sister speaks of. Come, bring away° the stocks.
                           Stocks brought out.

Gloucester. Let me beseech your Grace not to do so.
His fault is much, and the good King his master
Will check° him for't. Your purposed° low
    correction
Is such as basest and contemnèd'st° wretches   *145*
For pilf'rings and most common trespasses
Are punished with.
The King his master needs must take it ill
That he, so slightly valued in° his messenger,
Should have him thus restrained.

Cornwall.   I'll answer° that.   *150*

Regan. My sister may receive it much more worse,
To have her gentleman abused, assaulted,
For following her affairs. Put in his legs.
               [Kent is put in the stocks.]
Come, my good lord, away!
           [Exeunt all but Gloucester and Kent.]

---

133 *grace and person* i.e., Lear as sovereign and in his personal character   **140** *color* kind   **141** *away* out   **144** *check* correct   **144** *purposed* intended   **145** *contemnèd'st* most despised   **149** *slightly valued in* little honored in the person of   **150** *answer* answer for

Gloucester. I am sorry for thee, friend. 'Tis the Duke's
155   pleasure,
    Whose disposition° all the world well knows
    Will not be rubbed° nor stopped. I'll entreat for
    thee.

Kent. Pray do not, sir. I have watched° and traveled
    hard.
    Some time I shall sleep out, the rest I'll whistle.
160   A good man's fortune may grow out at heels.°
    Give° you good morrow.

Gloucester. The Duke's to blame in this. 'Twill be
    ill taken.°   *Exit.*

Kent. Good King, that must approve° the common
    saw,°
    Thou out of Heaven's benediction com'st
165   To the warm sun.°
    Approach, thou beacon to this under globe,°
    That by thy comfortable° beams I may
    Peruse this letter. Nothing almost sees miracles
    But misery.° I know 'tis from Cordelia,
170   Who hath most fortunately been informed
    Of my obscurèd° course. And shall find time
    From this enormous state, seeking to give
    Losses their remedies.° All weary and o'erwatched,
    Take vantage,° heavy eyes, not to behold
175   This shameful lodging. Fortune, good night;
    Smile once more, turn thy wheel.°

                                 Sleeps.

---

156 *disposition* inclination 157 *rubbed* diverted (metaphor from the
game of bowls) 158 *watched* gone without sleep 160 *A . . . heels*
even a good man may have bad fortune 161 *Give* God give 162 *taken*
received 163 *approve* confirm 163 *saw* proverb 164-65 *Thou . . . sun*
i.e., Lear goes from better to worse, from Heaven's blessing or shelter
to lack of shelter 166 *beacon . . . globe* i.e., the sun, whose rising
Kent anticipates 167 *comfortable* comforting 168-69 *Nothing . . .
misery* i.e., true perception belongs only to the wretched 171 *obscurèd*
disguised 171-73 *shall . . . remedies* (a possible reading: Cordelia,
away from this monstrous state of things, will find occasion to right
the wrongs we suffer) 174 *vantage* advantage (of sleep) 176 *turn thy
wheel* i.e., so that Kent, who is at the bottom, may climb upward

[Scene III. *A wood.*]

Enter Edgar.

Edgar. I heard myself proclaimed,
  And by the happy° hollow of a tree
  Escaped the hunt. No port is free, no place
  That guard and most unusual vigilance
  Does not attend my taking.° Whiles I may 'scape,   *5*
  I will preserve myself; and am bethought°
  To take the basest and most poorest shape
  That ever penury, in contempt of man,
  Brought near to beast;° my face I'll grime with filth,
  Blanket° my loins, elf° all my hairs in knots,   *10*
  And with presented° nakedness outface°
  The winds and persecutions of the sky.
  The country gives me proof° and precedent
  Of Bedlam° beggars, who, with roaring voices,
  Strike° in their numbed and mortified° bare arms   *15*
  Pins, wooden pricks,° nails, sprigs of rosemary;
  And with this horrible object,° from low° farms,
  Poor pelting° villages, sheepcotes, and mills,
  Sometimes with lunatic bans,° sometime with
      prayers,
  Enforce their charity. Poor Turlygod, Poor Tom,°   *20*
  That's something yet: Edgar I nothing am.° *Exit.*

II.iii. ² *happy* lucky ⁵ *attend my taking* watch to capture me ⁶ *am bethought* have decided ⁸⁻⁹ *penury . . . beast* poverty, to show how contemptible man is, reduced to the level of a beast ¹⁰ *Blanket* cover only with a blanket ¹⁰ *elf* tangle (into "elflocks," supposed to be caused by elves) ¹¹ *presented* the show of ¹¹ *outface* brave ¹³ *proof* example ¹⁴ *Bedlam* (see I.ii.r. ¹⁴⁰⁻⁴ᵗ) ¹⁵ *strike* stick ¹⁵ *mortified* not alive to pain ¹⁶ *pricks* skewers ¹⁷ *object* spectacle ¹⁷ *low* humble ¹⁸ *pelting* paltry ¹⁹ *bans* curses ²⁰ *Poor . . . Tom* (Edgar recites the names a Bedlam beggar gives himself) ²¹ *That's . . . am* there's a chance for me in that I am no longer known for myself

[Scene IV.   *Before Gloucester's castle. Kent in
the stocks.*]

Enter Lear, Fool, and Gentleman.

Lear. 'Tis strange that they should so depart from
home,
And not send back my messenger.

Gentleman.   As I learned,
The night before there was no purpose° in them
Of this remove.°

Kent.   Hail to thee, noble master.

5 *Lear.* Ha!
Mak'st thou this shame thy pastime?°

Kent.   No, my lord.

Fool. Ha, ha, he wears cruel° garters. Horses are tied
by the heads, dogs and bears by th' neck, monkeys
by th' loins, and men by th' legs. When a man's over-
10 'lusty at legs,° then he wears wooden netherstocks.°

Lear. What's he that hath so much thy place mistook
To set thee here?

Kent.   It is both he and she,
Your son and daughter.

Lear. No.

15 *Kent.* Yes.

Lear. No, I say.

Kent. I say yea.

II.iv. 3 *purpose* intention   4 *remove* removal   6 *Mak'st . . . pastime* i.e.,
are you doing this to amuse yourself 7 *cruel* (1) painful (2)
"crewel," a worsted yarn used in garters 9-10 *overlusty at legs* (1) a
vagabond (2) ? sexually promiscuous 10 *netherstocks* stockings (as
opposed to knee breeches or upperstocks)

Lear. No, no, they would not.

Kent. Yes, they have.

Lear. By Jupiter, I swear no!   20

Kent. By Juno, I swear ay!

Lear.   They durst not do't;
  They could not, would not do't. 'Tis worse than
      murder
  To do upon respect° such violent outrage.
  Resolve° me with all modest° haste which way
  Thou mightst deserve or they impose this usage,   25
  Coming from us.

Kent.   My lord, when at their home
  I did commend° your Highness' letters to them,
  Ere I was risen from the place that showed
  My duty kneeling, came there a reeking post,°
  Stewed° in his haste, half breathless, panting forth   30
  From Goneril his mistress salutations,
  Delivered letters, spite of intermission,°
  Which presently° they read; on° whose contents
  They summoned up their meiny,° straight took
      horse,
  Commanded me to follow and attend   35
  The leisure of their answer, gave me cold looks,
  And meeting here the other messenger,
  Whose welcome I perceived had poisoned mine,
  Being the very fellow which of late
  Displayed° so saucily against your Highness,   40
  Having more man than wit° about me, drew;
  He raised° the house, with loud and coward cries.
  Your son and daughter found this trespass worth°
  The shame which here it suffers.

²³ *upon respect* (1) on the respect due to the King (2) deliberately
²⁴ *Resolve* inform ²⁴ *modest* becoming ²⁷ *commend* deliver ²⁹ *reeking post* sweating messenger ³⁰ *stewed* steaming ³² *spite of intermission* in spite of the interrupting of my business ³³ *presently* at once
³³ *on* on the strength of ³⁴ *meiny* retinue ⁴⁰ *Displayed* showed off
⁴¹ *more man than wit* more manhood than sense ⁴² *raised* aroused
⁴³ *worth* deserving

45   *Fool.* Winter's not gone yet, if the wild geese fly that
                way.°
                        Fathers that wear rags
                            Do make their children blind,°
                        But fathers that bear bags°
50   Shall see their children kind.
                        Fortune, that arrant whore,
                            Ne'er turns the key° to th' poor.
                But for all this, thou shalt have as many dolors° for
                thy daughters as thou canst tell° in a year.

55   *Lear.* O, how this mother° swells up toward my heart!
                Hysterica passio,° down, thou climbing sorrow,
                Thy element's° below. Where is this daughter?

        Kent. With the Earl, sir, here within.

        Lear.   Follow me not;
                Stay here.   *Exit.*

        Gentleman. Made you no more offense but what you
60   speak of?

        Kent. None.
                How chance° the King comes with so small a
                number?

        Fool. And° thou hadst been set i' th' stocks for that
                question, thou'dst well deserved it.

65   *Kent.* Why, Fool?

        Fool. We'll set thee to school to an ant, to teach thee
                there's no laboring i' th' winter.° All that follow

---

45-46 *Winter's . . . way* i.e., more trouble is to come, since Cornwall
and Regan act so ("geese" is used contemptuously, as in Kent's quarrel with Oswald, II.ii. 85-6)   48 *blind* i.e., indifferent   49 *bags* money-
bags   52 *turns the key* i.e., opens the door   53 *dolors* (1) sorrows (2)
dollars (English name for Spanish and German coins)   54 *tell* (1) tell
about (2) count   55-56 *mother . . . Hysterica passio* hysteria, causing
suffocation or choking   57 *element* proper place   62 *How chance* how
does it happen that   63 *And* if   66-67 *We'll . . . winter* (in the popular
fable the ant, unlike the improvident grasshopper, anticipates the winter
when none can labor by laying up provisions in the summer. Lear,
trusting foolishly to summer days, finds himself unprovided for, and
unable to provide, now that "winter" has come)

their noses are led by their eyes but blind men,
and there's not a nose among twenty but can smell
him that's stinking.° Let go thy hold when a great   70
wheel runs down a hill, lest it break thy neck with
following. But the great one that goes upward,
let him draw thee after. When a wise man gives
thee better counsel, give me mine again. I would
have none but knaves follow it since a Fool gives   75
it.

> That sir, which serves and seeks for gain,
>   And follows but for form,°
> Will pack,° when it begins to rain,
>   And leave thee in the storm.   80
> But I will tarry; the Fool will stay,
>   And let the wise man fly.
> The knave turns Fool that runs away,
>   The Fool no knave,° perdy.°

Kent. Where learned you this, Fool?   85

Fool. Not i' th' stocks, fool.

Enter Lear and Gloucester.

Lear. Deny° to speak with me? They are sick, they
    are weary,
They have traveled all the night? Mere fetches,°
The images° of revolt and flying off!°
Fetch me a better answer.

Gloucester.   My dear lord,   90
You know the fiery quality° of the Duke,
How unremovable and fixed he is
In his own course.

Lear.   Vengeance, plague, death, confusion!
Fiery? What quality? Why, Gloucester, Gloucester,
I'd speak with the Duke of Cornwall and his wife.   95

67-70 *All . . . stinking* i.e., all can smell out the decay of Lear's fortunes   78 *form* show   79 *pack* be off   83-84 *The . . . knave* i.e., the
faithless man is the true fool, for wisdom requires fidelity. Lear's Fool,
who remains faithful, is at least no knave   84 *perdy* by God (Fr. *par
Dieu*)   87 *Deny* refuse   88 *fetches* subterfuges, acts of tacking (nautical
metaphor)   89 *images* exact likenesses   89 *flying off* desertion   91 *quality* temperament

Gloucester. Well, my good lord, I have informed them so.

Lear. Informed them? Dost thou understand me, man?

Gloucester. Ay, my good lord.

Lear. The King would speak with Cornwall. The dear father
Would with his daughter speak, commands——tends°
100 ——service.
Are they informed of this? My breath and blood!
Fiery? The fiery Duke, tell the hot Duke that——
No, but not yet. May be he is not well.
Infirmity doth still neglect all office
Whereto our health is bound.° We are not
105 ourselves
When nature, being oppressed, commands the mind
To suffer with the body. I'll forbear;
And am fallen out° with my more headier will°
To take the indisposed and sickly fit
For the sound man. [*Looking on Kent*] Death on
110 my state!° Wherefore
Should he sit here? This act persuades me
That this remotion° of the Duke and her
Is practice° only. Give me my servant forth.°
Go tell the Duke and's wife I'd speak with them!
Now, presently!° Bid them come forth and hear
115 me,
Or at their chamber door I'll beat the drum
Till it cry sleep to death.°

Gloucester. I would have all well betwixt you.

Exit.

---

100 *tends* attends (i.e., awaits); with, possibly, an ironic second meaning, "tenders," or "offers"   105 *Whereto . . . bound* duties which we are required to perform, when in health   108 *fallen out* angry   108 *headier will* headlong inclination   110 *state* royal condition   112 *remotion* (1) removal (2) remaining aloof   113 *practice* pretense   113 *forth* i.e., out of the stocks   115 *presently* at once   117 *cry . . . death* follow sleep, like a cry or pack of hounds, until it kills it

Lear. O me, my heart, my rising heart! But down!

Fool. Cry to it, Nuncle, as the cockney° did to 120
the eels when she put 'em i' th' paste° alive. She
knapped° 'em o' th' coxcombs° with a stick and
cried, "Down, wantons,° down!" 'Twas her brother
that, in pure kindness to his horse, buttered his
hay.°   125

Enter Cornwall, Regan, Gloucester, Servants.

Lear. Good morrow to you both.

Cornwall.   Hail to your Grace.

                                    Kent here set at liberty.

Regan. I am glad to see your Highness.

Lear. Regan, I think you are. I know what reason
I have to think so. If thou shouldst not be glad,
I would divorce me from thy mother's tomb,   130
Sepulchring an adultress.° [*To Kent*] O, are you
      free?
Some other time for that. Beloved Regan,
Thy sister's naught.° O Regan, she hath tied
Sharp-toothed unkindness, like a vulture, here.

                              [*Points to his heart.*]

I can scarce speak to thee. Thou'lt not believe   135
With how depraved a quality°—O Regan!

Regan. I pray you, sir, take patience. I have hope
You less know how to value her desert
Than she to scant her duty.°

Lear.   Say? how is that?

---

120 *cockney* Londoner (ignorant city dweller)   121 *paste* pastry pie
122 *knapped* rapped   122 *coxcombs* heads   123 *wantons* i.e., playful
things (with a sexual implication)   125 *buttered his hay* i.e., the city
dweller does from ignorance what the dishonest ostler does from craft:
greases the hay the traveler has paid for, so that the horse will not
eat   130-31 *divorce . . . adultress* i.e., repudiate your dead mother as
having conceived you by another man   133 *naught* wicked   136 *quality*
nature   137-39 *I . . . duty* (despite the double negative, the passage
means, "I believe that you fail to give Goneril her due, rather than
that she fails to fulfill her duty")

140 *Regan.* I cannot think my sister in the least
　　　　Would fail her obligation. If, sir, perchance
　　　　She have restrained the riots of your followers,
　　　　'Tis on such ground, and to such wholesome end,
　　　　As clears her from all blame.

Lear. My curses on her!

145 *Regan.*　　　　　　　　　　O, sir, you are old,
　　　　Nature in you stands on the very verge
　　　　Of his confine.° You should be ruled, and led
　　　　By some discretion that discerns your state
　　　　Better than you yourself.° Therefore I pray you
150　　　That to our sister you do make return,
　　　　Say you have wronged her.

Lear.　　　　　　　　　　Ask her forgiveness?
　　　　Do you but mark how this becomes the house:°
　　　　"Dear daughter, I confess that I am old.

　　　　　　　　　　　　　　　　　　[*Kneeling.*]

　　　　Age is unnecessary. On my knees I beg
155　　　That you'll vouchsafe me raiment, bed, and food."

Regan. Good sir, no more. These are unsightly tricks.
　　　　Return you to my sister.

Lear.　　　　　　　　　[*Rising*] Never, Regan.
　　　　She hath abated° me of half my train,
　　　　Looked black upon me, struck me with her tongue,
160　　　Most serpentlike, upon the very heart.
　　　　All the stored vengeances of heaven fall
　　　　On her ingrateful top!° Strike her young bones,°
　　　　You taking° airs, with lameness.

Cornwall.　　　　　　　　　Fie, sir, fie!

Lear. You nimble lightnings, dart your blinding flames
165　　　Into her scornful eyes! Infect her beauty,

146-47 *Nature . . . confine* i.e., you are nearing the end of your life
148-49 *some . . . yourself* some discreet person who understands your
condition more than you do　152 *becomes the house* suits my royal and
paternal position　158 *abated* curtailed　162 *top* head　162 *young bones*
(the reference may be to unborn children, rather than to Goneril herself)　163 *taking* infecting

You fen-sucked° fogs, drawn by the pow'rful sun,
To fall and blister° her pride.

Regan.   O the blest gods!
So will you wish on me when the rash mood is on.

Lear. No, Regan, thou shalt never have my curse.
Thy tender-hefted° nature shall not give   170
Thee o'er to harshness. Her eyes are fierce, but thine
Do comfort, and not burn. 'Tis not in thee
To grudge my pleasures, to cut off my train,
To bandy° hasty words, to scant my sizes,°
And, in conclusion, to oppose the bolt°   175
Against my coming in. Thou better know'st
The offices of nature, bond of childhood,°
Effects° of courtesy, dues of gratitude.
Thy half o' th' kingdom hast thou not forgot,
Wherein I thee endowed.

Regan.   Good sir, to th' purpose.°   180

                              Tucket within.

Lear. Who put my man i' th' stocks?

Cornwall.   What trumpet's that?

Regan. I know't—my sister's. This approves° her
     letter,
That she would soon be here.

                    Enter Oswald.

                              Is your lady come?

Lear. This is a slave, whose easy borrowed° pride
Dwells in the fickle grace° of her he follows.   185
Out, varlet,° from my sight.

Cornwall.   What means your Grace?

---

166 *fen-sucked* drawn up from swamps by the sun   167 *fall and blister*
fall upon and raise blisters   170 *tender-hefted* gently framed   174 *bandy*
volley (metaphor from tennis)   174 *scant my sizes* reduce my allow-
ances   175 *oppose the bolt* i.e., bar the door   177 *offices . . . childhood*
natural duties, a child's duty to its parent   178 *Effects* manifestations
180 *to th' purpose* come to the point   182 *approves* confirms   184 *easy
borrowed* (1) facile and taken from another (2) acquired without anything to back it up (like money borrowed without security)   185 *grace*
favor   186 *varlet* base fellow

Lear. Who stocked my servant? Regan, I have good
    hope
Thou didst not know on't.

Enter Goneril.

             Who comes here? O heavens!
If you do love old men, if your sweet sway
190   Allow° obedience, if you yourselves are old,
Make it° your cause. Send down, and take my part.
[*To Goneril*] Art not ashamed to look upon
    this beard?
O Regan, will you take her by the hand?

Goneril. Why not by th' hand, sir? How have I
    offended?
195   All's not offense that indiscretion finds°
And dotage terms so.

Lear.   O sides,° you are too tough!
Will you yet hold? How came my man i' th' stocks?

Cornwall. I set him there, sir; but his own disorders°
Deserved much less advancement.°

Lear.   You? Did you?

200 *Regan.* I pray you, father, being weak, seem so.°
If till the expiration of your month
You will return and sojourn with my sister,
Dismissing half your train, come then to me.
I am now from home, and out of that provision
205   Which shall be needful for your entertainment.°

Lear. Return to her, and fifty men dismissed?
No, rather I abjure all roofs, and choose
To wage° against the enmity o' th' air,
To be a comrade with the wolf and owl,
210   Necessity's sharp pinch.° Return with her?
Why, the hot-blooded° France, that dowerless
    took

---

190 *Allow* approve of   191 *it* i.e., my cause   195 *finds* judges   196 *sides*
breast   198 *disorders* misconduct   199 *advancement* promotion   200 *seem
so* i.e., act weak   205 *entertainment* maintenance   208 *wage* fight
210 *Necessity's sharp pinch* (a summing up of the hard choice he has
just announced)   211 *hot-blooded* passionate

Our youngest born, I could as well be brought
To knee° his throne, and, squirelike,° pension beg
To keep base life afoot. Return with her?
Persuade me rather to be slave and sumpter°   215
To this detested groom. [*Pointing at Oswald.*]

Goneril.   At your choice, sir.

Lear. I prithee, daughter, do not make me mad.
I will not trouble thee, my child; farewell.
We'll no more meet, no more see one another.
But yet thou art my flesh, my blood, my daughter,   220
Or rather a disease that's in my flesh,
Which I must needs call mine. Thou art a boil,
A plague-sore, or embossèd carbuncle°
In my corrupted blood. But I'll not chide thee.
Let shame come when it will, I do not call it.   225
I do not bid the Thunder-bearer° shoot,
Nor tell tales of thee to high-judging° Jove.
Mend when thou canst, be better at thy leisure,
I can be patient, I can stay with Regan,
I and my hundred knights.

Regan.   Not altogether so.   230
I looked not for you yet, nor am provided
For your fit welcome. Give ear, sir, to my sister,
For those that mingle reason with your passion°
Must be content to think you old, and so—
But she knows what she does.

Lear.   Is this well spoken?   235

Regan. I dare avouch° it, sir. What, fifty followers?
Is it not well? What should you need of more?
Yea, or so many, sith that° both charge° and
    danger
Speak 'gainst so great a number? How in one house

---

²¹³ *knee* kneel before ²¹³ *squirelike* like a retainer ²¹⁵ *sumpter* pack
horse ²²³ *embossèd carbuncle* swollen boil ²²⁶ *Thunder-bearer* i.e.,
Jupiter ²²⁷ *high-judging* (1) supreme (2) judging from heaven
²³³ *mingle . . . passion* i.e., consider your turbulent behavior coolly
and reasonably ²³⁶ *avouch* swear by ²³⁸ *sith that* since ²³⁸ *charge*
expense

240 Should many people, under two commands,
    Hold° amity? 'Tis hard, almost impossible.

Goneril. Why might not you, my lord, receive
        attendance
    From those that she calls servants, or from mine?

Regan. Why not, my lord? If then they chanced to
        slack° ye,
245 We could control them. If you will come to me
    (For now I spy a danger), I entreat you
    To bring but five-and-twenty. To no more
    Will I give place or notice.°

Lear. I gave you all.

Regan.   And in good time you gave it.

250 *Lear.* Made you my guardians, my depositaries,°
    But kept a reservation° to be followed
    With such a number. What, must I come to you
    With five-and-twenty? Regan, said you so?

Regan. And speak't again, my lord. No more with me.

Lear. Those wicked creatures yet do look well-
255   favored°
    When others are more wicked; not being the worst
    Stands in some rank of praise.° [*To Goneril*] I'll
        go with thee.
    Thy fifty yet doth double five-and-twenty,
    And thou art twice her love.°

Goneril.   Hear me, my lord.
260 What need you five-and-twenty? ten? or five?
    To follow° in a house where twice so many
    Have a command to tend you?

Regan.   What need one?

Lear. O reason° not the need! Our basest beggars

---

241 *hold* preserve   244 *slack* neglect   248 *notice* recognition   250 *depositaries* trustees   251 *reservation* condition   255 *well-favored* handsome
256-57 *not . . . praise* i.e., that Goneril is not so bad as Regan is one
thing in her favor   259 *her love* i.e., as loving as she   261 *follow* attend
on you   263 *reason* scrutinize

Are in the poorest thing superfluous.°
Allow not nature more than nature needs,° 265
Man's life is cheap as beast's. Thou art a lady:
If only to go warm were gorgeous,
Why, nature needs not what thou gorgeous wear'st,
Which scarcely keeps thee warm.° But, for true
  need—
You heavens, give me that patience, patience I
  need. 270
You see me here, you gods, a poor old man,
As full of grief as age, wretched in both.
If it be you that stirs these daughters' hearts
Against their father, fool° me not so much
To bear° it tamely; touch me with noble anger, 275
And let not women's weapons, water drops,
Stain my man's cheeks. No, you unnatural hags!
I will have such revenges on you both
That all the world shall—I will do such things—
What they are, yet I know not; but they shall be 280
The terrors of the earth. You think I'll weep.
No, I'll not weep.

                              Storm and tempest.

I have full cause of weeping, but this heart
Shall break into a hundred thousand flaws°
Or ere° I'll weep. O Fool, I shall go mad! 285

            Exeunt Lear, Gloucester, Kent, and Fool.

Cornwall. Let us withdraw, 'twill be a storm.

Regan. This house is little; the old man and's people
  Cannot be well bestowed.°

Goneril. 'Tis his own blame; hath° put himself from
  rest°
  And must needs taste his folly. 290

---

264 *Are . . . superfluous* i.e., have some trifle not absolutely necessary
265 *needs* i.e., to sustain life   267-69 *If . . . warm* i.e., if to satisfy the
need for warmth were to be gorgeous, you would not need the clothing you wear, which is worn more for beauty than warmth   274 *fool*
humiliate   275 *To bear* as to make me bear   284 *flaws* (1) pieces (2)
cracks (3) gusts of passion   285 *Or ere* before   288 *bestowed* lodged
289 *hath* he hath   289 *rest* (1) place of residence (2) repose of mind

Regan. For his particular,° I'll receive him gladly,
But not one follower.

Goneril.   So am I purposed.°
Where is my Lord of Gloucester?

Cornwall. Followed the old man forth.

Enter Gloucester.

                         He is returned.

Gloucester. The King is in high rage.

295 *Cornwall.*   Whither is he going?

Gloucester. He calls to horse, but will I know not
whither.

Cornwall. 'Tis best to give him way, he leads himself.°

Goneril. My lord, entreat him by no means to stay.

Gloucester. Alack, the night comes on, and the high
winds
300   Do sorely ruffle.° For many miles about
There's scarce a bush.

Regan.   O, sir, to willful men
The injuries that they themselves procure
Must be their schoolmasters. Shut up your doors.
He is attended with a desperate train,
305   And what they may incense° him to, being apt
To have his ear abused,° wisdom bids fear.

Cornwall. Shut up your doors, my lord; 'tis a wild
night.
My Regan counsels well. Come out o' th' storm.

                              Exeunt.

---

291 *his particular* himself personally   292 *purposed* determined   297 *give
. . . himself* let him go; he insists on his own way   300 *ruffle* rage
305 *incense* incite   305-06 *being . . . abused* he being inclined to harken
to bad counsel

ACT III

Scene I. [*A heath.*]

Storm still.° Enter Kent and a Gentleman
severally.

Kent. Who's there besides foul weather?

Gentleman. One minded like the weather most
unquietly.°

Kent. I know you. Where's the King?

Gentleman. Contending with the fretful elements;
Bids the wind blow the earth into the sea,   5
Or swell the curlèd waters 'bove the main,°
That things might change,° or cease; tears his white
hair,
Which the impetuous blasts, with eyeless° rage,
Catch in their fury, and make nothing of;
Strives in his little world of man° to outscorn   10
The to-and-fro-conflicting wind and rain.
This night, wherein the cub-drawn° bear would
couch,°
The lion, and the belly-pinchèd° wolf
Keep their fur dry, unbonneted° he runs,

III.i.s.d. *still* continually 2 *minded . . . unquietly* disturbed in mind,
like the weather 6 *main* land 7 *change* (1) be destroyed (2) be ex-
changed (i.e., turned upside down) (3) change for the better 8 *eye-*
less (1) blind (2) invisible 10 *little world of man* (the microcosm, as
opposed to the universe or macrocosm, which it copies in little)
12 *cub-drawn* sucked dry by her cubs, and so ravenously hungry
12 *couch* take shelter in its lair 13 *belly-pinchèd* starved 14 *unbonneted*
hatless

And bids what will take all.°

15   Kent.   But who is with him?
     Gentleman. None but the Fool, who labors to outjest
        His heart-struck injuries.

     Kent.   Sir, I do know you,
        And dare upon the warrant of my note°
        Commend a dear thing° to you. There is division,
20   Although as yet the face of it is covered
        With mutual cunning, 'twixt Albany and Cornwall;
        Who have—as who have not, that° their great
           stars
        Throned° and set high?—servants, who seem no
           less,°
        Which are to France the spies and speculations
25   Intelligent° of our state. What hath been seen,
        Either in snuffs and packings° of the Dukes,
        Or the hard rein which both of them hath borne°
        Against the old kind King, or something deeper,
        Whereof, perchance, these are but furnishings°—
30   But, true it is, from France there comes a power°
        Into this scattered° kingdom, who already,
        Wise in our negligence, have secret feet
        In some of our best ports, and are at point°
        To show their open banner. Now to you:
35   If on my credit you dare build° so far
        To make your speed to Dover, you shall find
        Some that will thank you, making° just° report
        Of how unnatural and bemadding° sorrow
        The King hath cause to plain.°
40   I am a gentleman of blood and breeding,°

---

¹⁵ *take all* (like the reckless gambler, staking all he has left)   ¹⁸ *warrant of my note* strength of what I have taken note (of you)   ¹⁹ *Commend . . . thing* entrust important business   ²² *that* whom   ²²⁻²³ *stars /Throned* destinies have throned   ²³ *seem no less* seem to be so   ²⁴⁻²⁵ *speculations/Intelligent* giving intelligence   ²⁶ *snuffs and packings* quarrels and plots   ²⁷ *hard . . . borne* close and cruel control they have exercised   ²⁹ *furnishings* excuses   ³⁰ *power* army   ³¹ *scattered* disunited   ³³ *at point* ready   ³⁵ *If . . . build* if you can trust me, proceed   ³⁶ *To* as to   ³⁷ *making* for making   ³⁷ *just* accurate   ³⁸ *bemadding* maddening   ³⁹ *plain* complain of   ⁴⁰ *blood and breeding* noble family

And from some knowledge and assurance° offer
This office° to you.

Gentleman. I will talk further with you.

Kent.   No, do not.
For confirmation that I am much more
Than my out-wall,° open this purse and take   45
What it contains. If you shall see Cordelia,
As fear not but you shall, show her this ring,
And she will tell you who that fellow° is
That yet you do not know. Fie on this storm!
I will go seek the King.   50

Gentleman. Give me your hand. Have you no more to
      say?

Kent. Few words, but, to effect,° more than all yet:
That when we have found the King—in which your
      pain°
That way, I'll this—he that first lights on 'him,
Holla the other.   *Exeunt* [*severally*].   55

Scene II.   [*Another part of the heath.*]

Storm still.

Enter Lear and Fool.

Lear. Blow, winds, and crack your cheeks. Rage, blow!
You cataracts and hurricanoes,° spout
Till you have drenched our steeples, drowned the
      cocks.°

---

41 *knowledge and assurance* sure and trustworthy information   42 *office*
service (i.e., the trip to Dover)   45 *out-wall* superficial appearance
48 *fellow* companion   52 *to effect* in their importance   53 *pain* labor
III.ii.   2 *hurricanoes* waterspouts   3 *cocks* weathercocks

You sulph'rous and thought-executing° fires,
5　　Vaunt-couriers° of oak-cleaving thunderbolts,
Singe my white head. And thou, all-shaking thunder,
Strike flat the thick rotundity° o' th' world,
Crack Nature's molds,° all germains spill° at once,
That makes ingrateful° man.

10　**Fool.** O Nuncle, court holy-water° in a dry house is
better than this rain water out o' door. Good
Nuncle, in; ask thy daughters blessing. Here's a
night pities neither wise man nor fools.

Lear. Rumble thy bellyful. Spit, fire. Spout, rain!
15　　Nor rain, wind, thunder, fire are my daughters.
I tax° not you, you elements, with unkindness.
I never gave you kingdom, called you children,
You owe me no subscription.° Then let fall
Your horrible pleasure.° Here I stand your slave,
20　　A poor, infirm, weak, and despised old man.
But yet I call you servile ministers,°
That will with two pernicious daughters join
Your high-engendered battles° 'gainst a head
So old and white as this. O, ho! 'tis foul.

25　**Fool.** He that has a house to put 's head in has a good
headpiece.°
　　　　　　The codpiece° that will house
　　　　　　Before the head as any,
　　　　　　The head and he° shall louse:
30　　　　　　So beggars marry many.°
　　　　　　The man that makes his toe

---

4 *thought-executing* (1) doing execution as quick as thought (2) exe-
cuting or carrying out the thought of him who hurls the lightning
5 *Vaunt-couriers* heralds, scouts who range before the main body of the
army　7 *rotundity* i.e., not only the sphere of the globe, but the round-
ness of gestation (Delius)　8 *Nature's molds* the molds or forms in
which men are made　8 *all germains spill* destroy the basic seeds of
life　9 *ingrateful* ungrateful　10 *court holy-water* flattery　16 *tax* accuse
18 *subscription* allegiance, submission　19 *pleasure* will　21 *ministers*
agents　23 *high-engendered battles* armies formed in the heavens
26 *headpiece* (1) helmet (2) brain　27 *codpiece* penis (lit., padding
worn at the crotch of a man's hose)　29 *he* it　30 *many* i.e., lice
27-30 *The . . . many* i.e., the man who gratifies his sexual appetites
before he has a roof over his head will end up a lousy beggar

What he his heart should make
 Shall of a corn cry woe,
  And turn his sleep to wake.°
For there was never yet fair woman but she made *35*
mouths in a glass.°

Enter Kent.

Lear. No, I will be the pattern of all patience,
I will say nothing.

Kent. Who's there?

Fool. Marry,° here's grace and a codpiece; that's a *40*
wise man and a fool.°

Kent. Alas, sir, are you here? Things that love night
Love not such nights as these. The wrathful skies
Gallow° the very wanderers of the dark
And make them keep° their caves. Since I was man, *45*
Such sheets of fire, such bursts of horrid° thunder,
Such groans of roaring wind and rain, I never
Remember to have heard. Man's nature cannot
 carry°
Th' affliction nor the fear.

Lear.   Let the great gods
That keep this dreadful pudder° o'er our heads *50*
Find out their enemies now.° Tremble, thou wretch,
That hast within thee undivulgèd crimes
Unwhipped of justice. Hide thee, thou bloody
 hand,
Thou perjured,° and thou simular° of virtue

81-34 *The . . . wake* i.e., the man who, ignoring the fit order of things,
elevates what is base above what is noble, will suffer for it as Lear
has, in banishing Cordelia and enriching her sisters **35-36** *made mouths
in a glass* posed before a mirror (irrelevant nonsense, except that it
calls to mind the general theme of vanity and folly) **40** *Marry* by the
Virgin Mary **40-41** *here's . . . fool* (Kent's question is answered: The
King ("grace") is here, and the Fool—who customarily wears an ex-
aggerated codpiece. But which is which is left ambiguous, since Lear
has previously been called a codpiece) **44** *Gallow* frighten **45** *keep*
remain inside **46** *horrid* horrible **48** *carry* endure **50** *pudder* turmoil
51 *Find . . . now* i.e., discover sinners by the terror they reveal
54 *perjured* perjurer **54** *simular* counterfeiter

55 That art incestuous. Caitiff,° to pieces shake,
    That under covert and convenient seeming°
    Has practiced on° man's life. Close° pent-up guilts,
    Rive° your concealing continents° and cry
    These dreadful summoners grace.° I am a man
    More sinned against than sinning.

60 *Kent.*   Alack, bareheaded?
    Gracious my lord,° hard by here is a hovel;
    Some friendship will it lend you 'gainst the
        tempest.
    Repose you there, while I to this hard house
    (More harder than the stones whereof 'tis raised,
65 Which even but now, demanding after° you,
    Denied me to come in) return, and force
    Their scanted° courtesy.

    Lear.   My wits begin to turn.
    Come on, my boy. How dost, my boy? Art cold?
    I am cold myself. Where is this straw, my fellow?
70 The art° of our necessities is strange,
    That can make vile things precious. Come, your
        hovel.
    Poor Fool and knave, I have one part in my heart
    That's sorry yet for thee.

    Fool. [*Singing*]
        He that has and a little tiny wit,
75   With heigh-ho, the wind and the rain,
        Must make content with his fortunes fit,°
        Though the rain it raineth every day.

    Lear. True, my good boy. Come, bring us to this hovel.
                                    Exit [*with Kent*].

---

55 *Caitiff* wretch   56 *seeming* hypocrisy   57 *practiced on* plotted against
57 *Close* hidden   58 *Rive* split open   58 *continents* containers   58-59 *cry
. . . grace* beg mercy from the vengeful gods (here figured as officers
who summoned a man charged with immorality before the ecclesiastical
court)   61 *Gracious my lord* my gracious lord   65 *demanding after*
asking for   67 *scanted* stinted   70 *art* magic powers of the alchemists,
who sought to transmute base metals into precious   76 *Must . . . fit*
must be satisfied with a fortune as tiny as his wit

Fool. This is a brave° night to cool a courtesan. I'll
   speak a prophecy ere I go: 80

    When priests are more in word than matter;
    When brewers mar their malt with water;
    When nobles are their tailors' tutors,
    No heretics burned, but wenches' suitors;°
    When every case in law is right,   85
    No squire in debt nor no poor knight;
    When slanders do not live in tongues;
    Nor cutpurses come not to throngs;
    When usurers tell their gold i' th' field,°
    And bawds and whores do churches build,°   90
    Then shall the realm of Albion°
    Come to great confusion.
    Then comes the time, who lives to see't,
    That going shall be used with feet.°

   This prophecy Merlin° shall make, for I live before   95
   his time.   *Exit.*

Scene III.   [*Gloucester's castle.*]

Enter Gloucester and Edmund.

Gloucester. Alack, alack, Edmund, I like not this unnatural dealing. When I desired their leave that I
   might pity° him, they took from me the use of mine

---

79 *brave* fine 81-84 *When . . . suitors* (the first four prophecies are
fulfilled already, and hence "confusion" has come to England. The
priest does not suit his action to his words. The brewer adulterates
his beer. The nobleman is subservient to his tailor [i.e., cares only for
fashion]. Religious heretics escape, and only those burn [i.e., suffer]
who are afflicted with venereal disease) 89 *tell . . . field* count their
money in the open 85-90 *When . . . build* (the last six prophecies, as
they are Utopian, are meant ironically. They will never be fulfilled)
91 *Albion* England 94 *going . . . feet* people will walk on their feet
95 *Merlin* King Arthur's great magician who, according to Holinshed's
Chronicles, lived later than Lear III.iii. 3 *pity* show pity to

own house, charged me on pain of perpetual dis-
5   pleasure neither to speak of him, entreat for him,
or any way sustain° him.

Edmund. Most savage and unnatural.

Gloucester. Go to; say you nothing. There is division°
between the Dukes, and a worse° matter than that.
10   I have received a letter this night—'tis dangerous
to be spoken°—I have locked the letter in my
closet.° These injuries the King now bears will be
revenged home;° there is part of a power° already
footed;° we must incline to° the King. I will look°
15   him and privily° relieve him. Go you and maintain
talk with the Duke, that my charity be not of° him
perceived. If he ask for me, I am ill and gone to
bed. If I die for it, as no less is threatened me, the
King my old master must be relieved. There is
20   strange things toward,° Edmund; pray you be careful.   *Exit.*

Edmund. This courtesy forbid° thee shall the Duke
Instantly know, and of that letter too.
This seems a fair deserving,° and must draw me
25   That which my father loses—no less than all.
The younger rises when the old doth fall.
                                              Exit.

III.iii. 6 *sustain* care for 8 *division* falling out 9 *worse* more serious
(i.e., the French invasion) 11 *spoken* spoken of 12 *closet* room
13 *home* to the utmost 13 *power* army 14 *footed* landed 14 *incline to*
take the side of 14 *look* search for 15 *privily* secretly 16 *of* by
20 *toward* impending 22 *courtesy forbid* kindness forbidden (i.e., to
Lear) 24 *fair deserving* an action deserving reward

Scene IV. [*The heath. Before a hovel.*]

Enter Lear, Kent, and Fool.

Kent. Here is the place, my lord. Good my lord,
     enter.
The tyranny of the open night's too rough
For nature to endure.

                                        Storm still.

Lear.   Let me alone.

Kent. Good my lord, enter here.

Lear.   Wilt break my heart?°

Kent. I had rather break mine own. Good my lord,
     enter.   5

Lear. Thou think'st 'tis much that this contentious
     storm
Invades us to the skin: so 'tis to thee;
But where the greater malady is fixed,°
The lesser is scarce felt. Thou'dst shun a bear;
But if thy flight lay toward the roaring sea,   10
Thou'dst meet the bear i' th' mouth.° When the
     mind's free,°
The body's delicate. The tempest in my mind
Doth from my senses take all feeling else,
Save what beats there. Filial ingratitude,
Is it not as° this mouth should tear this hand   15
For lifting food to't? But I will punish home.°
No, I will weep no more. In such a night
To shut me out! Pour on, I will endure.

III.iv. 4 *break my heart* i.e., by shutting out the storm which distracts
me from thinking 8 *fixed* lodged (in the mind) 11 *i' th' mouth* in the
teeth 11 *free* i.e., from care 15 *as* as if 16 *home* to the utmost

In such a night as this! O Regan, Goneril,
Your old kind father, whose frank° heart gave
20   all—
O, that way madness lies; let me shun that.
No more of that.

Kent.   Good my lord, enter here.

Lear. Prithee go in thyself; seek thine own ease.
This tempest will not give me leave to ponder
25 On things would hurt me more, but I'll go in.
[*To the Fool*] In, boy; go first. You houseless
          poverty°—
Nay, get thee in. I'll pray, and then I'll sleep.

                              Exit [*Fool*].

Poor naked wretches, wheresoe'er you are,
That bide° the pelting of this pitiless storm,
80 How shall your houseless heads and unfed sides,
Your looped and windowed° raggedness, defend
          you
From seasons such as these? O, I have ta'en
Too little care of this! Take physic, pomp;°
Expose thyself to feel what wretches feel,
85 That thou mayst shake the superflux° to them,
And show the heavens more just.

Edgar. [*Within*] Fathom and half, fathom and half!°
Poor Tom!

                    Enter Fool.

Fool. Come not in here, Nuncle, here's a spirit. Help
40 me, help me!

Kent. Give me thy hand. Who's there?

Fool. A spirit, a spirit. He says his name's Poor Tom.

Kent. What art thou that dost grumble there i' th'
          straw?
Come forth.

---

20 *frank* liberal (magnanimous) 26 *houseless poverty* (the unsheltered
poor, abstracted)   29 *bide* endure 31 *looped and windowed* full of
holes 33 *Take physic, pomp* take medicine to cure yourselves, you
great men 35 *superflux* superfluity 37 *Fathom and half* (Edgar, because of the downpour, pretends to take soundings)

Enter Edgar [disguised as a madman].

Edgar. Away! the foul fiend follows me. Through the   45
sharp hawthorn blows the cold wind.° Humh! Go
to thy cold bed, and warm thee.°

Lear. Didst thou give all to thy daughters? And art
thou come to this?

Edgar. Who gives anything to Poor Tom? Whom the   50
foul fiend hath led through fire and through flame,
through ford and whirlpool, o'er bog and quag-
mire; that hath laid knives under his pillow and
halters in his pew,° set ratsbane° by his porridge,°
made him proud of heart, to ride on a bay trotting   55
horse over four-inched bridges,° to course° his
own shadow for° a traitor. Bless thy five wits,°
Tom's a-cold. O, do, de, do, de, do, de. Bless thee
from whirlwinds, star-blasting,° and taking.° Do
Poor Tom some charity, whom the foul fiend vexes.   60
There could I have him now—and there—and
there again—and there.

                   Storm still.

Lear. What, has his daughters brought him to this
pass?°
Couldst thou save nothing? Wouldst thou give 'em
all?

Fool. Nay, he reserved a blanket,° else we had been   65
all shamed.

Lear. Now all the plagues that in the pendulous° air
Hang fated o'er° men's faults light on thy
daughters!

45-46 *Through . . . wind* (a line from the ballad of "The Friar of
Orders Gray")   46-47 *go . . . thee* (a reminiscence of *The Taming of
the Shrew,* Induction, 1.10)   53-54 *knives . . . halters . . . ratsbane* (the
fiend tempts Poor Tom to suicide)   54 *pew* gallery or balcony outside
a window   54 *porridge* broth   55-56 *ride . . . bridges* i.e., risk his life
56 *course* chase   57 *for* as   57 *five wits* i.e., common wit, imagination,
fantasy, estimation, memory   59 *star-blasting* the evil caused by malignant stars   59 *taking* pernicious influences   63 *pass* wretched condition
65 *blanket* i.e., to cover his nakedness   67 *pendulous* overhanging
68 *fated o'er* destined to punish

Kent. He hath no daughters, sir.

70 *Lear.* Death, traitor; nothing could have subdued°
nature
To such a lowness but his unkind daughters.
Is it the fashion that discarded fathers
Should have thus little mercy on° their flesh?
Judicious punishment—'twas this flesh begot
75 Those pelican° daughters.

Edgar. Pillicock sat on Pillicock Hill.° Alow, alow,
loo, loo!°

Fool. This cold night will turn us all to fools and
madmen.

80 *Edgar.* Take heed o' th' foul fiend; obey thy parents;
keep thy word's justice;° swear not; commit not°
with man's sworn spouse; set not thy sweet heart
on proud array. Tom's a-cold.

Lear. What hast thou been?

85 *Edgar.* A servingman, proud in heart and mind; that
curled my hair, wore gloves in my cap;° served the
lust of my mistress' heart, and did the act of darkness with her; swore as many oaths as I spake
words, and broke them in the sweet face of
90 heaven. One that slept in the contriving of lust,
and waked to do it. Wine loved I deeply, dice
dearly; and in woman out-paramoured the Turk.°
False of heart, light of ear,° bloody of hand; hog
in sloth, fox in stealth, wolf in greediness, dog in
95 madness, lion in prey.° Let not the creaking° of
shoes nor the rustling of silks betray thy poor

---

70 *subdued* reduced   73 *on* i.e., shown to   75 *pelican* (supposed to feed
on its parent's blood)   76 *Pillicock . . . Hill* (probably quoted from a
nursery rhyme, and suggested by "pelican." *Pillicock* is a term of
endearment and the phallus)   76-77 *Alow . . . loo* (? a hunting call,
or the refrain of the song)   81 *keep . . . justice* i.e., do not break thy
word   81 *commit not* i.e., adultery   86 *gloves in my cap* i.e., as a pledge
from his mistress   92 *out-paramoured the Turk* had more concubines
than the Sultan   93 *light of ear* ready to hear flattery and slander
95 *prey* preying   95 *creaking* (deliberately cultivated, as fashionable)

heart to woman. Keep thy foot out of brothels, thy hand out of plackets,° thy pen from lenders' books,° and defy the foul fiend. Still through the hawthorn blows the cold wind; says suum, mun, nonny.° Dolphin° my boy, boy, sessa!° let him trot by.   100

Storm still.

Lear. Thou wert better in a grave than to answer° with thy uncovered body this extremity° of the skies. Is man no more than this? Consider him well. Thou ow'st° the worm no silk, the beast no hide, the sheep no wool, the cat° no perfume. Ha! here's three on's° are sophisticated.° Thou art the thing itself; unaccommodated° man is no more but such a poor, bare, forked° animal as thou art. Off, off, you lendings!° Come, unbutton here.   105   110

[*Tearing off his clothes.*]

Fool. Prithee, Nuncle, be contented, 'tis a naughty° night to swim in. Now a little fire in a wild° field were like an old lecher's heart—a small spark, all the rest on's body, cold. Look, here comes a walking fire.   115

Enter Gloucester, with a torch.

Edgar. This is the foul fiend Flibbertigibbet.° He begins at curfew,° and walks till the first cock.° He gives the web and the pin,° squints° the eye, and makes the harelip; mildews the white° wheat, and hurts the poor creature of earth.   120

---

⁹⁸ *plackets* openings in skirts   ⁹⁶⁻⁹⁹ *pen . . . books* i.e., do not enter your name in the moneylender's account book   ¹⁰⁰⁻⁰¹ *suum, mun, nonny* the noise of the wind   ¹⁰¹ *Dolphin* the Frênch Dauphin (identified by the English with the devil. Poor Tom is presumably quoting from a ballad)   ¹⁰¹ *sessa* an interjection: "Go on!"   ¹⁰³ *answer* confront, bear the brunt of   ¹⁰⁴ *extremity* extreme severity   ¹⁰⁶ *ow'st* have taken from   ¹⁰⁷ *cat* civet cat, whose glands yield perfume   ¹⁰⁸ *on's* of us   ¹⁰⁸ *sophisticated* adulterated, made artificial   ¹⁰⁹ *unaccommodated* uncivilized   ¹¹⁰ *forked* i.e., two-legged   ¹¹¹ *lendings* borrowed garments   ¹¹² *naughty* wicked   ¹¹³ *wild* barren   ¹¹⁷ *Flibbertigibbet* (a figure from Elizabethan demonology)   ¹¹⁸ *curfew:* 9 P.M.   ¹¹⁸ *first cock* midnight   ¹¹⁹ *web and the pin* cataract   ¹¹⁹ *squints* crosses   ¹²⁰ *white* ripening

Swithold footed thrice the old;°
He met the nightmare,° and her nine fold;°
   Bid her alight°
125   And her troth plight,°
And aroint° thee, witch, aroint thee!

Kent. How fares your Grace?

Lear. What's he?

Kent. Who's there? What is't you seek?

130 *Gloucester.* What are you there? Your names?

Edgar. Poor Tom, that eats the swimming frog, the
toad, the todpole, the wall-newt and the water;°
that in the fury of his heart, when the foul fiend
rages, eats cow-dung for sallets,° swallows the old
135   rat and the ditch-dog,° drinks the green mantle°
of the standing° pool; who is whipped from tithing°
to tithing, and stocked, punished, and imprisoned;
who hath had three suits to his back, six shirts to
his body,
140   Horse to ride, and weapon to wear,
      But mice and rats, and such small deer,°
      Have been Tom's food for seven long year.°
Beware my follower!° Peace, Smulkin,° peace,
thou fiend!

Gloucester. What, hath your Grace no better com-
145   pany?

Edgar. The Prince of Darkness is a gentleman.
Modo° he's called, and Mahu.°

Gloucester. Our flesh and blood, my Lord, is grown
    so vile
  That it doth hate what gets° it.

Edgar. Poor Tom's a-cold.   *150*

Gloucester. Go in with me. My duty cannot suffer°
  T' obey in all your daughters' hard commands.
  Though their injunction be to bar my doors
  And let this tyrannous night take hold upon you,
  Yet have I ventured to come seek you out   *155*
  And bring you where both fire and food is ready.

Lear. First let me talk with this philosopher.
  What is the cause of thunder?

Kent. Good my lord, take his offer; go into th' house.

Lear. I'll talk a word with this same learnèd Theban.°   *160*
  What is your study?°

Edgar. How to prevent° the fiend, and to kill vermin.

Lear. Let me ask you one word in private.

Kent. Importune him once more to go, my lord.
  His wits begin t' unsettle.

Gloucester.   Canst thou blame him?   *165*

                            Storm still.

  His daughters seek his death. Ah, that good Kent,
  He said it would be thus, poor banished man!
  Thou say'st the King grows mad—I'll tell thee,
    friend,
  I am almost mad myself. I had a son,
  Now outlawed from my blood;° he sought my life   *170*
  But lately, very late.° I loved him, friend,
  No father his son dearer. True to tell thee,
  The grief hath crazed my wits. What a night's this!

---

149 *gets* begets   151 *suffer* permit me   160 *Theban* i.e., Greek philosopher   161 *study* particular scientific study   162 *prevent* balk   170 *outlawed from my blood* disowned and tainted, like a carbuncle in the
corrupted blood   171 *late* recently

    I do beseech your Grace——

Lear.   O, cry you mercy,° sir.
175   Noble philosopher, your company.

Edgar. Tom's a-cold.

Gloucester. In, fellow, there, into th' hovel; keep thee
    warm.

Lear. Come, let's in all.

Kent.   This way, my lord.

Lear.   With him!
    I will keep still with my philosopher.

Kent. Good my lord, soothe° him; let him take the
180   fellow.

Gloucester. Take him you on.°

Kent. Sirrah, come on; go along with us.

Lear. Come, good Athenian.°

Gloucester. No words, no words! Hush.

185   *Edgar.* Child Rowland to the dark tower came;°
        His word was still,° "Fie, foh, and fum,
        I smell the blood of a British man."°   *Exeunt.*

---

174 *cry you mercy* I beg your pardon 180 *soothe* humor 181 *you on*
with you 183 *Athenian* i.e., philosopher (like "Theban") 185 *Child
. . . came* (? from a lost ballad; "child"=a candidate for knighthood;
Rowland was Charlemagne's nephew, the hero of *The Song of Roland*)
186 *His . . . still* his motto was always 186-87 *Fie . . . man* (a deliberately absurd linking of the chivalric hero with the nursery tale of
Jack the Giant-Killer)

Scene V.   [Gloucester's castle.]

Enter Cornwall and Edmund.

Cornwall. I will have my revenge ere I depart his
house.

Edmund. How, my lord, I may be censured,° that
nature thus gives way to loyalty, something fears°
me to think of.   *3*

Cornwall. I now perceive it was not altogether your
brother's evil disposition made him seek his death;
but a provoking merit, set a-work by a reprovable
badness in himself.°

Edmund. How malicious is my fortune that I must   *10*
repent to be just! This is the letter which he spoke
of, which approves° him an intelligent party°
to the advantages° of France. O heavens, that his
treason were not! or not I the detector!

Cornwall. Go with me to the Duchess.   *15*

Edmund. If the matter of this paper be certain, you
have mighty business in hand.

Cornwall. True or false, it hath made thee Earl of
Gloucester. Seek out where thy father is, that he
may be ready for our apprehension.°   *20*

Edmund. [*Aside*] If I find him comforting° the
King, it will stuff his suspicion more fully.—I will
persever° in my course of loyalty, though the conflict be sore between that and my blood.°

III.v. 3 *censured* judged   4 *something fears* somewhat frightens   8-9 *a
provoking . . . himself* a stimulating goodness in Edgar, brought into
play by a blamable badness in Gloucester   12 *approves* proves   12 *intelligent party* (1) spy (2) well-informed person   13 *to the advantages*
on behalf of   20 *apprehension* arrest   21 *comforting* supporting (a
legalism)   23 *persever* persevere   24 *blood* natural feelings

25   *Cornwall.* I will lay trust upon° thee, and thou
    shalt find a dearer father in my love.   *Exeunt.*

Scene VI.   [*A chamber in a farmhouse
adjoining the castle.*]

Enter Kent and Gloucester.

Gloucester. Here is better than the open air; take it
    thankfully. I will piece out the comfort with what
    addition I can. I will not be long from you.

Kent. All the power of his wits have given way to his
3   impatience.° The gods reward your kindness.
                      Exit [Gloucester].

Enter Lear, Edgar, and Fool.

Edgar. Frateretto° calls me, and tells me Nero° is
    an angler in the lake of darkness. Pray, innocent,°
    and beware the foul fiend.

Fool. Prithee, Nuncle, tell me whether a madman be a
10   gentleman or a yeoman.°

Lear. A king, a king.

Fool. No, he's a yeoman that has a gentleman to his
    son; for he's a mad yeoman that sees his son a gen-
    tleman before him.

15 *Lear.* To have a thousand with red burning spits
    Come hizzing° in upon 'em——

---

25 *lay trust upon* (1) trust (2) advance III.vi. 5 *impatience* raging
6 *Frateretto* Elizabethan devil, from Harsnett's *Declaration* 6 *Nero*
(who is mentioned by Harsnett, and whose angling is reported by
Chaucer in "The Monk's Tale") 7 *innocent* fool 10 *yeoman* farmer
(just below a gentleman in rank. The Fool asks what class of man has
most indulged his children, and thus been driven mad) 16 *hizzing*
hissing

Edgar. The foul fiend bites my back.

Fool. He's mad that trusts in the tameness of a wolf,
a horse's health, a boy's love, or a whore's oath.

Lear. It shall be done; I will arraign° them straight.°   *20*
[*To Edgar*] Come, sit thou here, most learned
justice.°
[*To the Fool*] Thou, sapient° sir, sit here. Now,
you she-foxes——

Edgar. Look, where he° stands and glares. Want'st
thou eyes at trial, madam?°
Come o'er the bourn,° Bessy, to me.   *25*

Fool. Her boat hath a leak,
    And she must not speak
      Why she dares not come over to thee.°

Edgar. The foul fiend haunts Poor Tom in the voice
of a nightingale.° Hoppedance° cries in Tom's belly   *30*
for two white herring.° Croak° not, black angel; I
have no food for thee.

Kent. How do you, sir? Stand you not so amazed.°
Will you lie down and rest upon the cushions?

Lear. I'll see their trial first. Bring in their evidence.   *85*
[*To Edgar*] Thou, robèd man of justice, take
thy place.
[*To the Fool*] And thou, his yokefellow of equity,°
Bench° by his side. [*To Kent*] You are o' th'
commission;°
Sit you too.

Edgar. Let us deal justly.   *40*

---

20 *arraign* bring to trial **20** *straight* straightaway **21** *justice* justicer, judge **22** *sapient* wise **23** *he* i.e., a fiend **23-24** *Want'st . . . madam* (to Goneril) i.e., do you want eyes to look at you during your trial? The fiend serves that purpose **25** *bourn* brook (Edgar quotes from a popular ballad) **26-28** *Her . . . thee* (the Fool parodies the ballad) **30** *nightingale* i.e., the Fool's singing **30** *Hoppedance* Hoberdidance (another devil from Harsnett's *Declaration*) **31** *white herring* unsmoked (? as against the black and sulfurous devil) **31** *Croak* rumble (because his belly is empty) **33** *amazed* astonished **35** *evidence* the evidence of witnesses against them **37** *yokefellow of equity* partner in justice **38** *Bench* sit on the bench **38** *commission* those commissioned as king's justices

Sleepest or wakest thou, jolly shepherd?
Thy sheep be in the corn;°
And for one blast of thy minikin° mouth
Thy sheep shall take no harm.°

45   Purr, the cat is gray.°

Lear. Arraign her first. 'Tis Goneril, I here take my
oath before this honorable assembly, she kicked
the poor King her father.

Fool. Come hither, mistress. Is your name Goneril?

50   *Lear.* She cannot deny it.

Fool. Cry you mercy, I took you for a joint stool.°

Lear. And here's another, whose warped looks
proclaim
What store° her heart is made on. Stop her there!
Arms, arms, sword, fire! Corruption in the place!°
55   False justicer, why hast thou let her 'scape?

Edgar. Bless thy five wits!

Kent. O pity! Sir, where is the patience now
That you so oft have boasted to retain?

Edgar. [*Aside*] My tears begin to take his part so
much
60   They mar my counterfeiting.°

Lear. The little dogs and all,
Tray, Blanch, and Sweetheart—see, they bark at
me.

Edgar. Tom will throw his head at them. Avaunt, you
curs.
Be thy mouth or black or° white,

41-44 *Sleepest . . . harm* (probably quoted or adapted from an Elizabethan song) **42** *corn* wheat **43** *minikin* shrill **45** *gray* (devils were
thought to assume the shape of a gray cat) **51** *Cry . . . joint stool*
(proverbial and deliberately impudent apology for overlooking a person. A joint stool was a low stool made by a joiner, perhaps here a
stage property to represent Goneril and in line 52, Regan. "Joint stool"
can also suggest the judicial bench; hence Goneril may be identified
by the Fool, ironically, with those in power, who judge) **53** *store*
stuff **54** *Corruption . . . place* bribery in the court **60** *counterfeiting*
i.e., feigned madness **64** *or . . . or* either . . . or

Tooth that poisons if it bite;   65
Mastiff, greyhound, mongrel grim,
Hound or spaniel, brach° or lym,°
Or bobtail tike, or trundle-tail°—
Tom will make him weep and wail;
For, with throwing° thus my head,   70
Dogs leaped the hatch,° and all are fled.
  Do, de, de, de. Sessa!° Come, march to wakes°
and fairs and market towns. Poor Tom, thy horn°
is dry.

Lear. Then let them anatomize Regan. See what breeds   75
about her heart.° Is there any cause in nature that
make° these hard hearts? [*To Edgar*] You, sir,
I entertain° for one of my hundred;° only I do not
like the fashion of your garments. You will say
they are Persian;° but let them be changed.   80

Kent. Now, good my lord, lie here and rest awhile.

Lear. Make no noise, make no noise; draw the
    curtains.°
  So, so. We'll go to supper i' th' morning.

Fool. And I'll go to bed at noon.°

Enter Gloucester.

Gloucester. Come hither, friend. Where is the King
    my master?   85

Kent. Here, sir, but trouble him not; his wits are gone.

Gloucester. Good friend, I prithee take him in thy
    arms.

---

67 *brach* bitch   67 *lym* bloodhound (from the liam or leash with
which he was led)   68 *bobtail . . . trundle-tail* short-tailed or long-
tailed cur   70 *throwing* jerking (as a hound lifts its head from the
ground, the scent having been lost)   71 *leaped the hatch* leaped over
the lower half of a divided door (i.e., left in a hurry)   72 *Sessa* be off
72 *wakes* feasts attending the dedication of a church   73 *horn* horn
bottle which the Bedlam used in begging a drink (Edgar is suggesting that he is unable to play his role any longer)   75-76 *Then . . .
heart* i.e., if the Bedlam's horn is dry, let Regan, whose heart has
become as hard as horn, be dissected   77 *make* (subjunctive)   78 *enter-
tain* engage   78 *hundred* i.e., Lear's hundred knights   80 *Persian*
gorgeous (ironically of Edgar's rags)   82 *curtains* (Lear imagines
himself in bed)   84 *And . . . noon* (the Fool's last words)

I have o'erheard a plot of death upon him.
There is a litter ready; lay him in't
And drive toward Dover, friend, where thou shalt
90   meet
Both welcome and protection. Take up thy master.
If thou shouldst dally half an hour, his life,
With thine and all that offer to defend him,
Stand in assurèd loss. Take up, take up,
95   And follow me, that will to some provision°
Give thee quick conduct.°

Kent.   Oppressèd nature sleeps.
This rest might yet have balmed thy broken
        sinews,°
Which, if convenience° will not allow,
Stand in hard cure.° [*To the Fool*] Come, help
        to bear thy master.
Thou must not stay behind.

100 *Gloucester.*   Come, come, away!
                        Exeunt [*all but Edgar*].

Edgar. When we our betters see bearing our woes,
We scarcely think our miseries our foes.°
Who alone suffers suffers most i' th' mind,
Leaving free° things and happy shows° behind;
105   But then the mind much sufferance° doth o'erskip
When grief hath mates, and bearing fellowship.°
How light and portable° my pain seems now,
When that which makes me bend makes the
        King bow.
He childed as I fathered. Tom, away.
110   Mark the high noises,° and thyself bewray°
When false opinion, whose wrong thoughts° defile
        thee,

---

95 *provision* maintenance   96 *conduct* direction   97 *balmed thy broken
sinews* soothed thy racked nerves   98 *convenience* fortunate occasion
99 *Stand . . . cure* will be hard to cure   102 *our foes* enemies peculiar
to ourselves   104 *free* carefree   104 *shows* scenes   105 *sufferance* suffering   106 *bearing fellowship* suffering has company   107 *portable* able to
be supported or endured   110 *Mark the high noises* observe the rumors
of strife among those in power   110 *bewray* reveal   111 *wrong thoughts*
misconceptions

In thy just proof repeals and reconciles thee.°
What will hap more° tonight, safe 'scape the King!
Lurk,° lurk.   *[Exit.]*

Scene VII.   *[Gloucester's castle.]*

Enter Cornwall, Regan, Goneril, Edmund, and
Servants.

Cornwall. *[To Goneril]* Post speedily to my Lord
your husband; show him this letter. The army of
France is landed. *[To Servants]* Seek out the
traitor Gloucester. *[Exeunt some of the Servants.]*

Regan. Hang him instantly.   *5*

Goneril. Pluck out his eyes.

Cornwall. Leave him to my displeasure. Edmund, keep
you our sister company. The revenges we are
bound° to take upon your traitorous father are not
fit for your beholding. Advise the Duke where you   *10*
are going, to a most festinate° preparation. We are
bound to the like. Our posts° shall be swift and
intelligent° betwixt us. Farewell, dear sister; farewell, my Lord of Gloucester.°

Enter Oswald.

How now? Where's the King?   *15*

Oswald. My Lord of Gloucester hath conveyed him
hence.

---

112 *In . . . thee* on the manifesting of your innocence recalls you
from outlawry and restores amity between you and your father
113 *What . . . more* whatever else happens   114 *Lurk* hide III.vii.
9 *bound* (1) forced (2) purposing to   11 *festinate* speedy   12 *posts*
messengers   13 *intelligent* full of information   14 *Lord of Gloucester*
i.e., Edmund, now elevated to the title

Some five or six and thirty of his knights,
Hot questrists° after him, met him at gate;
Who, with some other of the lords dependants,°
Are gone with him toward Dover, where they
20   boast
To have well-armèd friends.

Cornwall.   Get horses for your mistress.
                            [Exit Oswald.]

Goneril. Farewell, sweet lord, and sister.

Cornwall. Edmund, farewell.
                    [Exeunt Goneril and Edmund.]
            Go seek the traitor Gloucester,
Pinion him like a thief, bring him before us.
                    [Exeunt other Servants.]
25   Though well we may not pass upon° his life
Without the form of justice, yet our power
Shall do a court'sy to° our wrath, which men
May blame, but not control.

    Enter Gloucester, brought in by two or three.

                        Who's there, the traitor?

Regan. Ingrateful fox, 'tis he.

30   Cornwall. Bind fast his corky° arms.

Gloucester. What means your Graces? Good my
    friends, consider
    You are my guests. Do me no foul play, friends.

Cornwall. Bind him, I say.

                        [Servants bind him.]

Regan.   Hard, hard! O filthy traitor.

Gloucester. Unmerciful lady as you are, I'm none.

Cornwall. To this chair bind him. Villain, thou shalt
35   find——

18 *questrists* searchers 19 *lords dependants* attendant lords (members of Lear's retinue) 25 *pass upon* pass judgment on 27 *do a
court'sy to* indulge 30 *corky* sapless (because old)

[Regan plucks his beard.°]

Gloucester. By the kind gods, 'tis mostly ignobly done
  To pluck me by the beard.

Regan. So white, and such a traitor?

Gloucester.   Naughty° lady,
  These hairs which thou dost ravish from my chin
  Will quicken° and accuse thee. I am your host.   *40*
  With robber's hands my hospitable favors°
  You should not ruffle° thus. What will you do?

Cornwall. Come, sir, what letters had you late° from
  France?

Regan. Be simple-answered,° for we know the truth.

Cornwall. And what confederacy have you with the
  traitors   *45*
  Late footed in the kingdom?

Regan. To whose hands you have sent the lunatic
  King:
  Speak.

Gloucester. I have a letter guessingly° set down,
  Which came from one that's of a neutral heart,
  And not from one opposed.

Cornwall.   Cunning.

Regan.   And false.   *50*

Cornwall. Where hast thou sent the King?

Gloucester. To Dover.

Regan. Wherefore to Dover? Wast thou not charged
  at peril°———

Cornwall. Wherefore to Dover? Let him answer that.

---

85 s.d. *plucks his beard* (a deadly insult) 38 *Naughty* wicked 40 *quicken* come to life 41 *hospitable favors* face of your host 42 *ruffle* tear at violently 43 *late* recently 44 *simple-answered* straightforward in answering 48 *guessingly* without certain knowledge 53 *charged at peril* ordered under penalty

Gloucester. I am tied to th' stake, and I must stand
55   the course.°

Regan. Wherefore to Dover?

Gloucester. Because I would not see thy cruel nails
Pluck out his poor old eyes; nor thy fierce sister
In his anointed° flesh rash° boarish fangs.
60   The sea, with such a storm as his bare head
In hell-black night endured, would have buoyed° up
And quenched the stellèd° fires.
Yet, poor old heart, he holp° the heavens to rain.
If wolves had at thy gate howled that dearn° time,
Thou shouldst have said, "Good porter, turn the
65   key."°
All cruels else subscribe.° But I shall see
The wingèd° vengeance overtake such children.

Cornwall. See't shalt thou never. Fellows, hold the
chair.
Upon these eyes of thine I'll set my foot.

Gloucester. He that will think° to live till he be
70   old,
Give me some help. —O cruel! O you gods!

Regan. One side will mock° another. Th' other too.

Cornwall. If you see vengeance——

First Servant.   Hold your hand, my lord!
I have served you ever since I was a child;
75   But better service have I never done you
Than now to bid you hold.

Regan.   How now, you dog?

First Servant. If you did wear a beard upon your chin,

---

55 *course* coursing (in which a relay of dogs baits a bull or bear
tied in the pit)   59 *anointed* holy (because king)   59 *rash* strike with
the tusk, like a boar   61 *buoyed* risen   62 *stellèd* (1) fixed (as opposed to the planets or wandering stars)   (2) starry   63 *holp* helped
64 *dearn* dread   65 *turn the key* i.e., unlock the gate   66 *All cruels else
subscribe* all cruel creatures but man are compassionate   67 *wingèd*
(1) heavenly   (2) swift   70 *will think* expects   72 *mock* make ridic-
ulous (because of the contrast)

I'd shake it° on this quarrel. What do you mean!°

Cornwall. My villain!°

Draw and fight.

First Servant. Nay, then, come on, and take the
chance of anger.   80

Regan. Give me thy sword. A peasant stand up thus?

She takes a sword and runs at him behind,
kills him.

First Servant. O, I am slain! my lord, you have one
eye left
To see some mischief° on him. O!

Cornwall. Lest it see more, prevent it. Out, vile jelly.
Where is thy luster now?   85

Gloucester. All dark and comfortless. Where's my son
Edmund?
Edmund, enkindle all the sparks of nature°
To quit° this horrid act.

Regan.   Out, treacherous villain,
Thou call'st on him that hates thee. It was he
That made the overture° of thy treasons to us;   90
Who is too good to pity thee.

Gloucester. O my follies! Then Edgar was abused.°
Kind gods, forgive me that, and prosper him.

Regan. Go thrust him out at gates, and let him smell
His way to Dover.   *Exit [one] with Gloucester.*
How is't, my lord? How look you?°   95

Cornwall. I have received a hurt. Follow me, lady.
Turn out that eyeless villain. Throw this slave
Upon the dunghill. Regan, I bleed apace.

---

78 *shake it* (an insult comparable to Regan's plucking of Gloucester's
beard)   78 *What . . . mean* i.e., what terrible thing are you doing
79 *villain* serf (with a suggestion of the modern meaning)   83 *mischief* injury   87 *enkindle . . . nature* fan your natural feeling into
flame   88 *quit* requite   90 *overture* disclosure   92 *abused* wronged
95 *How look you* how are you

Untimely comes this hurt. Give me your arm.
                                    Exeunt.

100   *Second Servant.* I'll never care what wickedness I do,
         If this man come to good.

      Third Servant.   If she live long,
         And in the end meet the old course of death,°
         Women will all turn monsters.

      Second Servant. Let's follow the old Earl, and get the
         Bedlam
105   To lead him where he would. His roguish madness
         Allows itself to anything.°

      Third Servant. Go thou. I'll fetch some flax and
         whites of eggs
         To apply to his bleeding face. Now heaven help
         him.   [*Exeunt severally.*]

102 *meet . . . death* die the customary death of old age   105-6 *His
. . . anything* his lack of all self-control leaves him open to any
suggestion

ACT IV

Scene I.　[*The heath.*]

Enter Edgar.

Edgar. Yet better thus, and known to be contemned,°
　　Than still contemned and flattered. To be worst,
　　The lowest and most dejected° thing of fortune,
　　Stands still in esperance,° lives not in fear:
　　The lamentable change is from the best,　　　　　　　　5
　　The worst returns to laughter.° Welcome then,
　　Thou unsubstantial air that I embrace!
　　The wretch that thou hast blown unto the worst
　　Owes° nothing to thy blasts.

　　　　　Enter Gloucester, led by an Old Man.

　　　　　　　　　　　　But who comes here?
　　My father, poorly led?° World, world, O world!　　10
　　But that thy strange mutations make us hate thee,
　　Life would not yield to age.°

Old Man. O, my good lord, I have been your tenant,
　　and your father's tenant, these fourscore years.

Gloucester. Away, get thee away; good friend, be
　　gone:　　　　　　　　　　　　　　　　　　　15

IV.i. 1 *known to be contemned* conscious of being despised　3 *dejected*
abased　4 *esperance* hope　6 *returns to laughter* changes for the better
9 *Owes* is in debt for　10 *poorly led* (1) led like a poor man, with
only one attendant (2) led by a poor man　11-12 *But . . . age* we
should not agree to grow old and hence die, except for the hateful
mutability of life

Thy comforts° can do me no good at all;
Thee they may hurt.°

Old Man.   You cannot see your way.

Gloucester. I have no way and therefore want° no
        eyes;
    I stumbled when I saw. Full oft 'tis seen,
20 Our means secure us, and our mere defects
    Prove our commodities.° Oh, dear son Edgar,
    The food° of thy abusèd° father's wrath!
    Might I but live to see thee in° my touch,
    I'd say I had eyes again!

Old Man.   How now! Who's there?

Edgar. [*Aside*] O gods! Who is 't can say "I am a
25   the worst"?
    I am worse than e'er I was.

Old Man.   'Tis poor mad Tom.

Edgar. [*Aside*] And worse I may be yet: the worst
        is not
    So long as we can say "This is the worst."°

Old Man. Fellow, where goest?

Gloucester.   Is it a beggar-man?

30 *Old Man.* Madman and beggar too.

Gloucester. He has some reason,° else he could not
            beg.
    I' th' last night's storm I such a fellow saw,
    Which made me think a man a worm. My son
    Came then into my mind, and yet my mind
    Was then scarce friends with him. I have heard
35   more since.
    As flies to wanton° boys, are we to th' gods,

---

16 *comforts* ministrations 17 *hurt* injure 18 *want* require 20-21 *Our
. . . commodities* our resources make us overconfident, while our
afflictions make for our advantage 22 *food* i.e., the object on which
Gloucester's anger fed 22 *abused* deceived 23 *in* i.e., with, by means
of 27-28 *the . . . worst* so long as a man continues to suffer (i.e., is
still alive), even greater suffering may await him 31 *reason* faculty
of reasoning 36 *wanton* (1) playful (2) reckless

They kill us for their sport.

Edgar. [*Aside*]   How should this be?°
　Bad is the trade that must play fool to sorrow,
　Ang'ring° itself and others. Bless thee, master!

Gloucester. Is that the naked fellow?

Old Man.   Ay, my lord.   40

Gloucester. Then, prithee, get thee gone: if for my
　　sake
　Thou wilt o'ertake us hence a mile or twain
　I' th' way toward Dover, do it for ancient° love,
　And bring some covering for this naked soul,
　Which I'll entreat to lead me.

Old Man.   Alack, sir, he is mad.   45

Gloucester. 'Tis the times' plague,° when madmen
　　lead the blind.
　Do as I bid thee, or rather do thy pleasure;°
　Above the rest,° be gone.

Old Man. I'll bring him the best 'parel° that I have,
　Come on 't what will.   *Exit.*   50

Gloucester. Sirrah, naked fellow——

Edgar. Poor Tom's a-cold. [*Aside*] I cannot daub
　it° further.

Gloucester. Come hither, fellow.

Edgar. [*Aside*] And yet I must. —Bless thy sweet
　eyes, they bleed.   55

Gloucester. Know'st thou the way to Dover?　·

Edgar. Both stile and gate, horse-way and footpath.
　Poor Tom hath been scared out of his good wits.
　Bless thee, good man's son, from the foul fiend!
　Five fiends have been in Poor Tom at once; of lust,   60

37 *How should this be* i.e., how can this horror be? 39 *Ang'ring*
offending　43 *ancient* (1) the love the Old Man feels, by virtue of
his long tenancy (2) the love that formerly obtained between master
and man　46 *times' plague* characteristic disorder of this time　47 *thy
pleasure* as you like　48 *the rest* all　49 *'parel* apparel　52-53 *daub
it* lay it on (figure from plastering mortar)

as Obidicut;° Hobbididence, prince of dumbness;° Mahu, of stealing; Modo, of murder; Flibbertigibbet, of mopping and mowing;° who since
possesses chambermaids and waiting-women. So,
65　bless thee, master!

Gloucester. Here, take this purse, thou whom the
　　heavens' plagues
Have humbled to all strokes:° that I am wretched
Makes thee the happier. Heavens, deal so still!
Let the superfluous° and lust-dieted° man,
70　That slaves° your ordinance,° that will not see
Because he does not feel, feel your pow'r quickly;
So distribution should undo excess,°
And each man have enough. Dost thou know
　　Dover?

Edgar. Ay, master.

Gloucester. There is a cliff whose high and bending°
75　head
Looks fearfully° in the confinèd deep:°
Bring me but to the very brim of it,
And I'll repair the misery thou dost bear
With something rich about me: from that place
I shall no leading need.

80　*Edgar.*　　　　　　　　　Give me thy arm:
Poor Tom shall lead thee.　　　　　　*Exeunt.*

---

61 *Obidicut* Hoberdicut, a devil (like the four that follow, from Harsnett's *Declaration*)　61-62 *dumbness* muteness (like the crimes and
afflictions in the next lines, the result of diabolic possession)
63 *mopping and mowing* grimacing and making faces　67 *humbled to
all strokes* brought so low as to bear anything humbly　69 *superfluous*
possessed of superfluities　69 *lust-dieted* whose lust is gratified (like
Gloucester's)　70 *slaves* (1) tramples, spurns like a slave (2) ?
tears, rends (Old English *slaefan*)　70 *ordinance* law　72 *So . . . excess*
then the man with too much wealth would distribute it among those
with too little　75 *bending* overhanging　76 *fearfully* occasioning fear
76 *confinèd deep* the sea, hemmed in below

Scene II.   [*Before the Duke of Albany's palace.*]

Enter Goneril and Edmund.

Goneril. Welcome, my lord: I marvel our mild husband
　　Not met° us on the way.

　　　　　　　　Enter Oswald.

　　　　　　　　　　Now, where's your master?

Oswald. Madam, within; but never man so changed.
　　I told him of the army that was landed:
　　He smiled at it. I told him you were coming;　　　*5*
　　His answer was, "The worse." Of Gloucester's treachery,
　　And of the loyal service of his son
　　When I informed him, then he called me sot,°
　　And told me I had turned the wrong side out:
　　What most he should dislike seems pleasant to him;　*10*
　　What like,° offensive.

Goneril. [*To Edmund*] Then shall you go no further.
　　It is the cowish° terror of his spirit,
　　That dares not undertake:° he'll not feel wrongs,
　　Which tie him to an answer.° Our wishes on the way
　　May prove effects.° Back, Edmund, to my brother;　　*15*
　　Hasten his musters° and conduct his pow'rs.°

IV.ii. 2 *Not met* did not meet 8 *sot* fool 11 *What like* what he should like 12 *cowish* cowardly 13 *undertake* venture 14 *tie him to an answer* oblige him to retaliate 14-15 *Our . . . effects* our desires (that you might be my husband), as we journeyed here, may be fulfilled 16 *musters* collecting of troops 16 *conduct his pow'rs* lead his army

I must change names° at home and give the
    distaff°
Into my husband's hands. This trusty servant
Shall pass between us: ere long you are like to hear,
20 If you dare venture in your own behalf,
A mistress's° command. Wear this; spare speech;

                        [*Giving a favor*]

Decline your head.° This kiss, if it durst speak,
Would stretch thy spirits up into the air:
Conceive,° and fare thee well.

Edmund. Yours in the ranks of death.

25 *Goneril.*   My most dear Gloucester!
                        Exit [*Edmund*].

O, the difference of man and man!
To thee a woman's services are due:
My fool usurps my body.°

Oswald.   Madam, here comes my lord.
                        Exit.

                Enter Albany.

Goneril. I have been worth the whistle.°

Albany.   O Goneril!
30 You are not worth the dust which the rude wind
Blows in your face. I fear your disposition:°
That nature which contemns° its origin
Cannot be bordered certain in itself;°
She that herself will sliver and disbranch°

---

17 *change names* i.e., exchange the name of "mistress" for that of
"master"   17 *distaff* spinning stick (wifely symbol)   21 *mistress's* lov-
er's (and also, Albany having been disposed of, lady's or wife's)
22 *Decline your head* i.e., that Goneril may kiss him   24 *Conceive*
understand (with a sexual implication, that includes "stretch thy
spirits," l. 23; and "death," l. 25: "to die," meaning "to experience
sexual intercourse")   28 *My fool usurps body* my husband wrong-
fully enjoys me   29 *I . . . whistle* i.e., once you valued me (the
proverb is implied, "It is a poor dog that is not worth the whistling")
31 *disposition* nature   32 *contemns* despises   33 *bordered . . . itself*
kept within its normal bounds   34 *sliver and disbranch* cut off

From her material sap,° perforce must wither   35
And come to deadly use.°

Goneril. No more; the text° is foolish.

Albany. Wisdom and goodness to the vile seem vile:
 Filths savor but themselves.° What have you done?
 Tigers, not daughters, what have you performed?   40
 A father, and a gracious agèd man,
 Whose reverence even the head-lugged bear°
  would lick,
 Most barbarous, most degenerate, have you
  madded.°
 Could my good brother suffer you to do it?
 A man, a prince, by him so benefited!   45
 If that the heavens do not their visible spirits°
 Send quickly down to tame these vile offenses,
 It will come,
 Humanity must perforce prey on itself,
 Like monsters of the deep.

Goneril.   Milk-livered° man!   50
 That bear'st a cheek for blows, a head for wrongs;
 Who hast not in thy brows an eye discerning
 Thine honor from thy suffering;° that not know'st
 Fools do those villains pity who are punished
 Ere they have done their mischief.° Where's thy
  drum?   55
 France spreads his banners in our noiseless°
  land,
 With plumèd helm° thy state begins to threat,°

---

³⁵ *material sap* essential and life-giving sustenance   ³⁶ *come to deadly use* i.e., be as a dead branch for the burning   ³⁷ *text* i.e., on which your sermon is based   ³⁹ *Filths savor but themselves* the filthy relish only the taste of filth   ⁴² *head-lugged bear* bear-baited by the dogs, and hence enraged   ⁴³ *madded* made mad   ⁴⁶ *visible spirits* avenging spirits in material form   ⁵⁰ *Milk-livered* lily-livered (hence cowardly, the liver being regarded as the seat of courage)   ⁵²⁻⁵³ *discerning . . . suffering* able to distinguish between insults that ought to be resented, and ordinary pain that is to be borne   ⁵⁴⁻⁵⁵ *Fools . . . mischief* only fools are sorry for criminals whose intended criminality is prevented by punishment   ⁵⁶ *noiseless* i.e., the drum, signifying preparation for war, is silent   ⁵⁷ *helm* helmet   ⁵⁷ *thy . . . threat* France begins to threaten Albany's realm

Whilst thou, a moral° fool, sits still and cries
"Alack, why does he so?"

Albany.   See thyself, devil!
60   Proper° deformity seems not in the fiend
So horrid as in woman.

Goneril.   O vain fool!

Albany. Thou changèd and self-covered° thing,
for shame,
Be-monster not thy feature.° Were 't my fitness°
To let these hands obey my blood,°
65   They are apt enough to dislocate and tear
Thy flesh and bones: howe'er° thou art a fiend,
A woman's shape doth shield thee.

Goneril. Marry,° your manhood mew°———

Enter a Messenger.

Albany. What news?

Messenger. O, my good lord, the Duke of Cornwall's
70   dead,
Slain by his servant, going to° put out
The other eye of Gloucester.

Albany.   Gloucester's eyes!

Messenger. A servant that he bred,° thrilled with
remorse,°
Opposed against the act, bending his sword
75   To his great master, who thereat enraged
Flew on him, and amongst them felled° him dead,
But not without that harmful stroke which since

---

⁵⁸ *moral* moralizing; but also with the implication that morality and
folly are one   ⁶⁰ *Proper* (1) natural (to a fiend) (2) fair-appearing
⁶² *changèd and self-covered* i.e., transformed, by the contorting of
her woman's face, on which appears the fiendish behavior she has
allowed herself. (Goneril has disguised nature by wickedness)   ⁶³ *Be-
monster not thy feature* do not change your appearance into a
fiend's   ⁶³ *my fitness* appropriate for me   ⁶⁴ *blood* passion   ⁶⁶ *howe'er*
but even if   ⁶⁸ *Marry* by the Virgin Mary   ⁶⁸ *your manhood mew*
(1) coop up or confine your (pretended) manhood (2) molt or shed
it, if that is what is supposed to "shield" me from you   ⁷¹ *going to*
as he was about to   ⁷³ *bred* reared   ⁷³ *thrilled with remorse* pierced
by compassion   ⁷⁶ *amongst them felled* others assisting, they felled

Hath plucked him after.°

Albany.   This shows you are above,
You justicers,° that these our nether° crimes
So speedily can venge.° But, O poor Gloucester!   80
Lost he his other eye?

Messenger.   Both, both, my lord.
This letter, madam, craves° a speedy answer;
'Tis from your sister.

Goneril.   [*Aside*] One way I like this well;
But being widow, and my Gloucester with her,
May all the building in my fancy pluck   85
Upon my hateful life.° Another way,°
The news is not so tart.°—I'll read, and answer.
                              Exit.

Albany. Where was his son when they did take his
          eyes?

Messenger. Come with my lady hither.

Albany.   He is not here.

Messenger. No, my good lord; I met him back° again.   90

Albany. Knows he the wickedness?

Messenger. Ay, my good lord; 'twas he informed
          against him,
And quit the house on purpose, that their punish-
          ment
Might have the freer course.

Albany.   Gloucester, I live
To thank thee for the love thou showed'st the
          King,   95
And to revenge thine eyes. Come hither, friend:
Tell me what more thou know'st.   *Exeunt.*

---

78 *plucked him after* i.e., brought Cornwall to death with his servant   79 *justicers* judges   79 *nether* committed below (on earth)   80 *venge* avenge   82 *craves* demands   85-86 *May . . . life* these things (1.84) may send my future hopes, my castles in air, crashing down upon the hateful (married) life I lead now   86 *Another way* looked at another way   87 *tart* sour   90 *back* going back

[Scene III.   *The French camp near Dover.*]

Enter Kent and a Gentleman.

Kent. Why the King of France is so suddenly gone
  back, know you no reason?

Gentleman. Something he left imperfect in the
  state,° which since his coming forth is thought of,
5 which imports° to the kingdom so much fear and
  danger that his personal return was most required
  and necessary.

Kent. Who hath he left behind him general?

Gentleman. The Marshal of France, Monsieur La Far.

10 *Kent.* Did your letters pierce° the queen to any dem-
  onstration of grief?

Gentleman. Ay, sir; she took them, read them in my
      presence,
  And now and then an ample tear trilled° down
  Her delicate cheek: it seemed she was a queen
15 Over her passion, who most rebel-like
  Sought to be king o'er her.

Kent.   O, then it moved her.

Gentleman. Not to a rage: patience and sorrow
      strove
  Who should express her goodliest.° You have seen
  Sunshine and rain at once: her smiles and tears
20 Were like a better way:° those happy smilets°
  That played on her ripe lip seemed not to know
  What guests were in her eyes, which parted thence

IV.iii. **3-4** *imperfect in the state* unsettled in his own kingdom   **5** *im-
ports* portends   **10** *pierce* impel   **13** *trilled* trickled   **18** *Who . . .
goodliest* which should give her the most becoming expression
20 *Were like a better way* i.e., improved on that spectacle   **20** *smilets*
little smiles

As pearls from diamonds dropped. In brief,
Sorrow would be a rarity most belovèd,
If all could so become it.°

Kent.   Made she no verbal question? 25

Gentleman. Faith, once or twice she heaved° the name
    of "father"
Pantingly forth, as if it pressed her heart;
Cried "Sisters! Sisters! Shame of ladies! Sisters!
Kent! Father! Sisters! What, i' th' storm? i' th'
    night?
Let pity not be believed!"° There she shook 30
The holy water from her heavenly eyes,
And clamor moistened:° then away she started
To deal with grief alone.

Kent.   It is the stars,
The stars above us, govern our conditions;°
Else one self mate and make could not beget 85
Such different issues.° You spoke not with her
    since?

Gentleman. No.

Kent. Was this before the King returned?

Gentleman.   No, since.

Kent. Well, sir, the poor distressèd Lear's i' th'
    town;
Who sometime in his better tune° remembers 40
What we are come about, and by no means
Will yield to see his daughter.

Gentleman.   Why, good sir?

Kent. A sovereign° shame so elbows° him: his own
    unkindness

24-25 *Sorrow . . . it* sorrow would be a coveted jewel if it became
others as it does her 26 *heaved* expressed with difficulty 30 *Let pity
not be believed* let it not be believed for pity 32 *clamor moistened*
moistened clamor, i.e., mixed (and perhaps assuaged) her outcries
with tears 34 *govern our conditions* determine what we are
35-36 *Else . . . issues* otherwise the same husband and wife could
not produce such different children 40 *better tune* composed, less
jangled intervals 43 *sovereign* overpowering 43 *elbows* jogs his elbow
i.e., reminds him

That stripped her from his benediction, turned her
45   To foreign casualties,° gave her dear rights
To his dog-hearted daughters: these things sting
His mind so venomously that burning shame
Detains him from Cordelia.

Gentleman.   Alack, poor gentleman!

Kent. Of Albany's and Cornwall's powers you heard
        not?

50   *Gentleman.* 'Tis so;° they are afoot.

Kent. Well, sir, I'll bring you to our master Lear,
        And leave you to attend him: some dear cause°
        Will in concealment wrap me up awhile;
        When I am known aright, you shall not grieve
55   Lending me this acquaintance. I pray you, go
        Along with me.   [*Exeunt.*]

[Scene IV.   *The same. A tent.*]

*Enter, with drum and colors, Cordelia, Doctor,
and Soldiers.*

Cordelia. Alack, 'tis he: why, he was met even now
        As mad as the vexed sea; singing aloud;
        Crowned with rank femiter and furrow-weeds,
        With hardocks, hemlock, nettles, cuckoo-flow'rs,
5   Darnel,° and all the idle weeds that grow
        In our sustaining corn.° A century° send forth;
        Search every acre in the high-grown field,

---

45 *casualties* chances   50 *'Tis so* i.e., I have heard of them   52 *dear
cause* important reason   IV.iv. 3-5 *femiter . . . Darnel: femiter* fumitory,
whose leaves and juice are bitter; *furrow-weeds* weeds that grow in the
furrow; or plowed land; *hardocks* ? hoar or white docks, burdocks, har-
locks; *hemlock* a poison; *nettles* plants which sting and burn; *cuckoo-
flow'rs* identified with a plant employed to remedy diseases of the brain;
Darnel tares, noisome weeds   6 *sustaining corn* life-maintaining wheat
6 *century* ? sentry; troop of a hundred soldiers

And bring him to our eye [*Exit an Officer.*] What
  can man's wisdom°
In the restoring his bereavèd° sense?
He that helps him take all my outward° worth.   10

Doctor. There is means, madam:
  Our foster-nurse° of nature is repose,
  The which he lacks: that to provoke° in him,
  Are many simples operative,° whose power
  Will close the eye of anguish.

Cordelia.   All blest secrets,   15
All you unpublished virtues° of the earth,
Spring with my tears! be aidant and remediate°
In the good man's distress! Seek, seek for him,
Lest his ungoverned rage dissolve the life
That wants the means to lead it.°

                Enter Messenger.

Messenger.   News, madam;   20
  The British pow'rs are marching hitherward.

Cordelia. 'Tis known before. Our preparation stands
In expectation of them. O dear father,
It is thy business that I go about;
Therefore° great France   25
My mourning and importuned° tears hath pitied.
No blown° ambition doth our arms incite,
But love, dear love, and our aged father's right:
Soon may I hear and see him!   *Exeunt.*

---

8 *What can man's wisdom* what can science accomplish 9 *bereavèd*
impaired 10 *outward* material 12 *foster-nurse* fostering nurse 13 *pro-
voke* induce 14 *simples operative* efficacious medicinal herbs 16 *unpublished virtues* i.e., secret remedial herbs 17 *remediate* remedial
20 *wants . . . it* i.e., lacks the reason to control the rage 25 *Therefore* because of that 26 *importuned* importunate 27 *blown* puffed up

[Scene V.   *Gloucester's castle.*]

Enter Regan and Oswald.

Regan. But are my brother's pow'rs set forth?

Oswald.   Ay, madam.

Regan. Himself in person there?

Oswald.   Madam, with much ado:°
    Your sister is the better soldier.

Regan. Lord Edmund spake not with your lord at
    home?

5 *Oswald.* No, madam.

Regan. What might import° my sister's letter to him?

Oswald. I know not, lady.

Regan. Faith, he is posted° hence on serious matter.
    It was great ignorance,° Gloucester's eyes being
    out,
10   To let him live. Where he arrives he moves
    All hearts against us: Edmund, I think, is gone,
    In pity of his misery, to dispatch
    His nighted° life; moreover, to descry
    The strength o' th' enemy.

Oswald. I must needs after him, madam, with my
15   letter.

Regan. Our troops set forth tomorrow: stay with us;
    The ways are dangerous.

Oswald.   I may not, madam:
    My lady charged my duty° in this business.

IV.v. 2 *ado* bother and persuasion   6 *import* purport, carry as its
message   8 *is posted* has ridden speedily   9 *ignorance* folly   13 *nighted*
(1) darkened, because blinded (2) benighted   18 *charged my duty*
ordered me as a solemn duty

Regan. Why should she write to Edmund? Might not
   you
   Transport her purposes° by word? Belike,°   20
   Some things I know not what. I'll love thee much,
   Let me unseal the letter.

Oswald.   Madam, I had rather——

Regan. I know your lady does not love her husband;
   I am sure of that: and at her late° being here
   She gave strange eliads° and most speaking looks   25
   To noble Edmund. I know you are of her bosom.°

Oswald. I, madam?

Regan. I speak in understanding: y'are; I know 't:
   Therefore I do advise you, take this note:°
   My lord is dead; Edmund and I have talked;   30
   And more convenient° is he for my hand
   Than for your lady's: you may gather more.°
   If you do find him, pray you, give him this;°
   And when your mistress hears thus much from you,
   I pray, desire her call° her wisdom to her.   35
   So, fare you well.
   If you do chance to hear of that blind traitor,
   Preferment° falls on him that cuts him off.

Oswald. Would I could meet him, madam! I should
   show
   What party I do follow.

Regan.   Fare thee well.   40

                        Exeunt.

---

20 *Transport her purposes* convey her intentions 20 *Belike* probably
24 *late* recently 25 *eliads* amorous looks 26 *of her bosom* in her
confidence 29 *take this note* take note of this 31 *convenient* fitting
32 *gather more* surmise more yourself 33 *this* this advice 35 *call*
recall 38 *Preferment* promotion

[Scene VI.   *Fields near Dover.*]

Enter Gloucester and Edgar.

Gloucester. When shall I come to th' top of that same
    hill?
Edgar. You do climb up it now. Look, how we labor.
Gloucester. Methinks the ground is even.
Edgar.   Horrible steep.
    Hark, do you hear the sea?
Gloucester.   No, truly.
5 *Edgar.* Why then your other senses grow imperfect
    By your eyes' anguish.°
Gloucester.   So may it be indeed.
    Methinks thy voice is altered, and thou speak'st
    In better phrase and matter than thou didst.
Edgar. Y'are much deceived: in nothing am I changed
    But in my garments.
10 *Gloucester.*   Methinks y'are better spoken.
Edgar. Come on, sir; here's the place: stand still. How
    fearful
    And dizzy 'tis to cast one's eyes so low!
    The crows and choughs° that wing the midway air°
    Show scarce so gross° as beetles. Half way down
15 Hangs one that gathers sampire,° dreadful trade!
    Methinks he seems no bigger than his head.
    The fishermen that walk upon the beach
    Appear like mice; and yond tall anchoring° bark
    Diminished to her cock;° her cock, a buoy

IV.vi.   °*anguish* pain   ¹³ *choughs* a kind of crow   ¹³ *midway air* i.e.,
halfway down the cliff   ¹⁴ *gross* large   ¹⁵ *sampire* samphire, an aromatic
herb associated with Dover Cliffs   ¹⁸ *anchoring* anchored   ¹⁹ *cock* cock-
boat, a small boat usually towed behind the ship

Almost too small for sight. The murmuring surge   20
That on th' unnumb'red idle pebble° chafes
Cannot be heard so high. I'll look no more,
Lest my brain turn and the deficient sight
Topple° down headlong.

Gloucester.   Set me where you stand.

Edgar. Give me your hand: you are now within a foot   25
Of th' extreme verge: for all beneath the moon
Would I not leap upright.°

Gloucester.   Let go my hand.
Here, friend, 's another purse; in it a jewel
Well worth a poor man's taking. Fairies° and gods
Prosper it with thee! Go thou further off;   30
Bid me farewell, and let me hear thee going.

Edgar. Now fare ye well, good sir.

Gloucester.   With all my heart.

Edgar. [*Aside*] Why I do trifle thus with his despair
Is done to cure it.°

Gloucester.   O you mighty gods!

                                        He kneels.

This world I do renounce, and in your sights   35
Shake patiently my great affliction off:
If I could bear it longer and not fall
To quarrel° with your great opposeless° wills,
My snuff° and loathèd part of nature should
Burn itself out. If Edgar live, O bless him!   40
Now, fellow, fare thee well.

                                        He falls.

Edgar.   Gone, sir, farewell.

21 *unnumb'red idle pebble* innumerable pebbles, moved to and fro
by the waves to no purpose   23-24 *the deficient sight/Topple* my failing
sight topple me   27 *upright* i.e., even up in the air, to say nothing
of forward, over the cliff   29 *Fairies* (who are supposed to guard
and multiply hidden treasure)   33-34 *Why . . . it* I play on his despair
in order to cure it   37-38 *fall/To quarrel with* rebel against   38 *oppose-
less* not to be, and not capable of being, opposed   39 *snuff* the gutter-
ing (and stinking) wick of a burnt-out candle

And yet I know not how° conceit° may rob
The treasury of life, when life itself
Yields to° the theft. Had he been where he thought,
By this had thought been past. Alive or dead?
Ho, you sir! friend! Hear you, sir! speak!
Thus might he pass° indeed: yet he revives.
What are you, sir?

Gloucester.   Away, and let me die.

Edgar. Hadst thou been aught but gossamer, feathers, air,
So many fathom down precipitating,°
Thou'dst shivered like an egg: but thou dost breathe;
Hast heavy substance; bleed'st not; speak'st; art sound.
Ten masts at each° make not the altitude
Which thou hast perpendicularly fell:
Thy life's° a miracle. Speak yet again.

Gloucester. But have I fall'n, or no?

Edgar. From the dread summit of this chalky bourn.°
Look up a-height;° the shrill-gorged° lark so far
Cannot be seen or heard: do but look up.

Gloucester. Alack, I have no eyes.
Is wretchedness deprived that benefit,
To end itself by death? 'Twas yet some comfort,
When misery could beguile° the tyrant's rage
And frustrate his proud will.

Edgar.   Give me your arm.
Up, so. How is 't? Feel you° your legs? You stand.

Gloucester. Too well, too well.

Edgar.   This is above all strangeness.
Upon the crown o' th' cliff, what thing was that

---

42 *how* but what   42 *conceit* imagination   44 *Yields to* allows   47 *pass* die   50 *precipitating* falling   53 *at each* one on top of the other   55 *life's* survival   57 *bourn* boundary   58 *a-height* on high   58 *gorged* throated, voiced   63 *beguile* cheat (i.e., by suicide)   65 *Feel you* have you any feeling in

Which parted from you?

Gloucester.   A poor unfortunate beggar.

Edgar. As I stood here below, methought his eyes
Were two full moons; he had a thousand noses,   *70*
Horns whelked° and waved like the enridgèd° sea:
It was some fiend; therefore, thou happy father,°
Think that the clearest° gods, who make them
    honors
Of men's impossibilities,° have preserved thee.

Gloucester. I do remember now: henceforth I'll bear   *75*
Affliction till it do cry out itself
"Enough, enough," and die. That thing you speak
    of,
I took it for a man; often 'twould say
"The fiend, the fiend"—he led me to that place.

Edgar. Bear free° and patient thoughts.
    *Enter Lear [fantastically dressed with wild
                        flowers].*

                        But who comes here?   *80*
The safer° sense will ne'er accommodate°
His master thus.

Lear. No, they cannot touch me for coining;° I am
the King himself.

Edgar. O thou side-piercing sight!   *85*

Lear. Nature's above art in that respect.° There's
your press-money.° That fellow handles his bow

---

⁷¹ *whelked* twisted ⁷¹ *enridgèd* i.e., furrowed into waves ⁷² *happy father* fortunate old man ⁷³ *clearest* purest ⁷³⁻⁷⁴ *who . . . impossibilities* who cause themselves to be honored and revered by performing miracles of which men are incapable ⁸⁰ *free* i.e., emancipated from grief and despair, which fetter the soul ⁸¹ *safer* sounder, saner ⁸¹ *accommodate* dress, adorn ⁸³ *touch me for coining* arrest me for minting coins (the king's prerogative) ⁸⁶ *Nature's . . . respect* i.e., a born king is superior to legal (and hence artificial) inhibition. There is also a glance here at the popular Renaissance debate, concerning the relative importance of nature (inspiration) and art (training) ⁸⁷ *press-money* (paid to conscripted soldiers)

like a crow-keeper;° draw me a clothier's yard.°
Look, look, a mouse! Peace, peace; this piece of
90   toasted cheese will do 't. There's my gauntlet;° I'll
prove it on° a giant. Bring up the brown bills.° O,
well flown,° bird! i' th' clout, i' th' clout:° hewgh!°
Give the word.°

Edgar. Sweet marjoram.°

95   *Lear.* Pass.

Gloucester. I know that voice.

Lear. Ha! Goneril, with a white beard! They flattered
me like a dog,° and told me I had white hairs
in my beard ere the black ones were there.° To
100   say "ay" and "no" to everything that I said! "Ay"
and "no" too was no good divinity.° When the
rain came to wet me once and the wind to make
me chatter; when the thunder would not peace at
my bidding; there I found 'em, there I smelt 'em
105   out. Go to, they are not men o' their words: they
told me I was everything; 'tis a lie, I am not ague-
proof.°

Gloucester. The trick° of that voice I do well remember: Is't not the king?

Lear.   Ay, every inch a king.

110   When I do stare, see how the subject quakes.
I pardon that man's life. What was thy cause?°

---

88 *crow-keeper* a farmer scaring away crows   88 *clothier's yard* (the
standard English arrow was a cloth-yard long. Here the injunction is
to draw the arrow back, like a powerful archer, a full yard to the ear)
90 *gauntlet* armored glove, thrown down as a challenge   91 *prove it on*
maintain my challenge even against   91 *brown bills* halberds varnished
to prevent rust (here the reference is to the soldiers who carry them)
92 *well flown* (falconer's cry; and perhaps a reference to the flight of
the arrow)   92 *clout* the target shot at   92 *hewgh* ? imitating the whizzing
of the arrow   93 *word* password   94 *Sweet marjoram* herb, used as a
remedy for brain disease   98 *like a dog* as a dog flatters   98-99 *I . . .
there* I was wise before I had even grown a beard   101 *no good divinity*
(bad theology, because contrary to the Biblical saying [II Corinthians
1:18], "Our word toward you was not yea and nay." See also James
5:12 "But let your yea be yea, and your nay, nay; lest ye fall into condemnation"; and Matthew 5:36-37)   106-07 *ague-proof* secure against
fever   108 *trick* intonation   111 *cause* offense

Adultery?
Thou shalt not die: die for adultery! No:
The wren goes to 't, and the small gilded fly
Does lecher° in my sight.   *115*
Let copulation thrive; for Gloucester's bastard son
Was kinder to his father than my daughters
Got° 'tween the lawful sheets.
To 't, luxury,° pell-mell! for I lack soldiers.°
Behold yond simp'ring dame,   *120*
Whose face between her forks presages snow,°
That minces° virtue and does shake the head
To hear of pleasure's name.°
The fitchew,° nor the soilèd° horse, goes to 't
With a more riotous appetite.   *125*
Down from the waist they are Centaurs,°
Though women all above:
But to the girdle° do the gods inherit,°
Beneath is all the fiend's.
There's hell, there's darkness, there is the
    sulphurous pit,   *130*
Burning, scalding, stench, consumption; fie, fie, fie!
pah, pah! Give me an ounce of civet;° good apothe-
cary, sweeten my imagination: there's money for thee.

Gloucester. O, let me kiss that hand!

Lear. Let me wipe it first; it smells of mortality.°   *135*

Gloucester. O ruined piece of nature! This great world
    Shall so wear out to nought.° Dost thou know me?

---

[115] *lecher* copulate [118] *Got* begot [119] *luxury* lechery [119] *for* . . .
soldiers i.e., ? (1) whom copulation will supply (2) and am therefore powerless [121] *Whose . . . snow* whose cold demeanor seems to
promise chaste behavior ("forks": legs) [122] *minces* squeamishly pretends to [123] *pleasure's name* the very name of sexual pleasure
[124] *fitchew* polecat (and slang for "prostitute") [124] *soilèd* put to
pasture, and hence wanton with feeding [126] *Centaurs* lustful creatures,
half man and half horse [128] *girdle* waist [128] *inherit* possess [132] *civet*
perfume [135] *mortality* (1) death (2) existence [136-37] *This . . . nought*
i.e., the universe (macrocosm) will decay to nothing in the same way
as the little world of man (microcosm)

Lear. I remember thine eyes well enough. Dost thou
squiny° at me? No, do thy worst, blind Cupid;° I'll
140   not love. Read thou this challenge;° mark but the
penning of it.

Gloucester. Were all thy letters suns, I could not see.

Edgar. I would not take° this from report: it is,
And my heart breaks at it.

145 *Lear.* Read.

Gloucester. What, with the case° of eyes?

Lear. O, ho, are you there with me?° No eyes in your
head, nor no money in your purse? Your eyes are
in a heavy case,° your purse in a light,° yet you
150   see how this world goes.

Gloucester. I see it feelingly.°

Lear. What, art mad? A man may see how this world
goes with no eyes. Look with thine ears: see how
yond justice rails upon yond simple° thief. Hark,
155   in thine ear: change places, and, handy-dandy,°
which is the justice, which is the thief? Thou hast
seen a farmer's dog bark at a beggar?

Gloucester. Ay, sir.

Lear. And the creature run from the cur? There thou
160   mightst behold the great image of authority:° a
dog's obeyed in office.°
Thou rascal beadle,° hold thy bloody hand!
Why dost thou lash that whore? Strip thy own
back;
Thou hotly lusts to use her in that kind°

---

¹³⁹ *squiny* squint, look sideways, like a prostitute ¹³⁹ *blind Cupid*
the sign hung before a brothel ¹⁴⁰ *challenge* a reminiscence of
ll. 89-90 ¹⁴³ *take* believe ¹⁴⁶ *case* empty sockets ¹⁴⁷ *are . . .
me* is that what you tell me ¹⁴⁹ *heavy case* sad plight (pun on l. 146)
¹⁴⁹ *light* i.e., empty ¹⁵¹ *feelingly* (1) by touch (2) by feeling pain
(3) with emotion ¹⁵⁴ *simple* common, of low estate ¹⁵⁵ *handy-dandy*
i.e., choose, guess (after the children's game—"Handy-dandy, prickly
prandy"—of choosing the right hand) ¹⁶⁰ *image of authority* symbol revealing the true meaning of authority ¹⁶⁰⁻⁶¹ *a . . . office* i.e.,
whoever has power is obeyed ¹⁶² *beadle* parish constable ¹⁶⁴ *kind*
i.e., sexual act

For which thou whip'st her. The usurer hangs the
    cozener.°   165
Through tattered clothes small vices do appear;
Robes and furred gowns° hide all. Plate sin with
    gold,
And the strong lance of justice hurtless° breaks;
Arm it in rags, a pygmy's straw does pierce it.
None does offend, none, I say, none; I'll able°
    'em: 170
Take that° of me, my friend, who have the power
To seal th' accuser's lips. Get thee glass eyes,°
And, like a scurvy politician,° seem
To see the things thou dost not. Now, now, now,
    now.
Pull off my boots: harder, harder: so.   175

Edgar. O, matter and impertinency° mixed!
    Reason in madness!

Lear. If thou wilt weep my fortunes, take my eyes.
    I know thee well enough; thy name is Gloucester:
    Thou must be patient; we came crying hither: 180
    Thou know'st, the first time that we smell the air
    We wawl and cry. I will preach to thee: mark.

Gloucester. Alack, alack the day!

Lear. When we are born, we cry that we are come
    To this great stage of fools. This'° a good block.° 185

164-65 *The usurer . . . cozener* i.e., the powerful moneylender, in his
role as judge, puts to death the petty cheat   167 *Robes and furred
gowns* (worn by a judge)   168 *hurtless* i.e., without hurting the sinner
170 *able* vouch for   171 *that* (the immunity just conferred) (l. 170)
172 *glass eyes* spectacles 173 *scurvy politician* vile politic man
176 *matter and impertinency* sense and nonsense 185 *This'* this is
185 *block* (various meanings have been suggested, for example, the
stump of a tree, on which Lear is supposed to climb; a mounting-
block, which suggests "horse" l. 187; a hat [which Lear or another
must be made to wear], from the block on which a felt hat is mold-
ed, and which would suggest a "felt" l. 187. The proposal here is
that "block" be taken to denote the quintain, whose function is to bear
blows, "a mere lifeless block" [*As You Like It*, I.ii.263], an object
shaped like a man and used for tilting practice. See also *Much Ado*,
II.i.246-7, "she misused me past the endurance of a block!" and, in
the same passage, the associated reference, "I stood like a man at
a mark [target]" [1. 253])

It were a delicate° stratagem, to shoe
A troop of horse with felt: I'll put 't in proof;°
And when I have stol'n upon these son-in-laws,
Then, kill, kill, kill, kill, kill, kill!

Enter a Gentleman [with Attendants].

190 *Gentleman.* O, here he is: lay hand upon him. Sir,
Your most dear daughter——

Lear. No rescue? What, a prisoner? I am even
The natural fool° of fortune. Use me well;
You shall have ransom. Let me have surgeons;
I am cut° to th' brains.

195 *Gentleman.*   You shall have anything.

Lear. No seconds?° all myself?
Why, this would make a man a man of salt,°
To use his eyes for garden water-pots,
Ay, and laying autumn's dust.

200 *Gentleman.* Good sir——

Lear. I will die bravely,° like a smug° bridegroom.°
What!
I will be jovial: come, come; I am a king;
Masters, know you that?

Gentleman. You are a royal one, and we obey you.

205 *Lear.* Then there's life in 't.° Come, and you get it,
you shall get it by running. Sa, sa, sa, sa.°

Exit [running; Attendants follow].

Gentleman. A sight most pitiful in the meanest wretch,
Past speaking of in a king! Thou hast one daughter
Who redeems nature from the general curse
210 Which twain have brought her to.°

---

186 *delicate* subtle 187 *put't in proof* test it 193 *natural fool* born
sport (with pun on "natural": "imbecile") 195 *cut* wounded 196 *seconds* supporters 197 *man of salt* i.e., all (salt) tears 201 *bravely* (1)
smartly attired (2) courageously 201 *smug* spick and span 201 *bridegroom* whose "brave" sexual feats are picked up in the pun on "die"
205 *there's life in't* there's still hope 206 *Sa . . . sa* hunting and
rallying cry; also an interjection of defiance 209-10 *general . . .
to* (1) universal condemnation which Goneril and Regan have made
for (2) damnation incurred by the original sin of Adam and Eve

Edgar. Hail, gentle° sir.

Gentleman.   Sir, speed° you: what's your will?

Edgar. Do you hear aught, sir, of a battle toward?°

Gentleman. Most sure and vulgar:° every one hears
    that,
  Which can distinguish sound.

Edgar.   But, by your favor,
  How near's the other army?   213

Gentleman. Near and on speedy foot; the main
    descry
  Stands on the hourly thought.°

Edgar.   I thank you, sir: that's all.

Gentleman. Though that the Queen on special cause
    is here,
  Her army is moved on.

Edgar.   I thank you, sir.

                              Exit [Gentleman].

Gloucester. You ever-gentle gods, take my breath
    from me;   220
  Let not my worser spirit° tempt me again
  To die before you please.

Edgar.   Well pray you, father.

Gloucester. Now, good sir, what are you?

Edgar. A most poor man, made tame° to fortune's
    blows;
  Who, by the art of known and feeling sorrows,°   225
  Am pregnant° to good pity. Give me your hand,
  I'll lead you to some biding.°

Gloucester.   Hearty thanks;

---

211 *gentle* noble   211 *speed* God speed   212 *toward* impending   213 *vulgar* common knowledge   216-17 *the . . . thought* we expect to see the main body of the army any hour   221 *worser spirit* bad angel, evil side of my nature   224 *tame* submissive   225 *art . . . sorrows* instruction of sorrows painfully experienced   226 *pregnant* disposed   227 *biding* place of refuge

The bounty and the benison° of heaven
To boot, and boot.°

Enter Oswald.

Oswald.   A proclaimed prize°! Most happy!°
230   That eyeless head of thine was first framed° flesh
To raise my fortunes. Thou old unhappy traitor,
Briefly thyself remember:° the sword is out
That must destroy thee.

Gloucester.   Now let thy friendly° hand
Put strength enough to 't.

[*Edgar interposes.*]

Oswald.   Wherefore, bold peasant,
235   Dar'st thou support a published° traitor? Hence!
Lest that th' infection of his fortune take
Like hold on thee. Let go his arm.

Edgar. Chill° not let go, zir, without vurther 'casion.°

Oswald. Let go, slave, or thou diest!

240   *Edgar.* Good gentleman, go your gait,° and let poor
volk° pass. And chud ha' bin zwaggered° out of my
life, 'twould not ha' bin zo long as 'tis by a vort-
night. Nay, come not near th' old man; keep out,
che vor' ye,° or I'se° try whether your costard°
245   or my ballow° be the harder: chill be plain with
you.

Oswald. Out, dunghill!

They fight.

---

²²⁸ *benison* blessing   ²²⁹ *To boot, and boot* also, and in the highest degree
²²⁹ *proclaimed prize* i.e., one with a price on his head   ²²⁹ *happy* fortunate (for Oswald)   ²³⁰ *framed* created   ²³² *thyself remember* i.e., pray
think of your sins   ²³³ *friendly* i.e., because it offers the death Gloucester
covets   ²³⁵ *published* proclaimed   ²³⁸ *Chill . . .* (Edgar speaks in rusti-
dialect)   ²³⁸ *Chill* I will   ²³⁸ *vurther 'casion* further occasion   ²⁴⁰ *gait*
way   ²⁴¹ *volk* folk   ²⁴¹ *And chud ha' bin zwaggered* if I could have been
swaggered   ²⁴⁴ *Che vor' ye* I warrant you   ²⁴⁴ *I'se* I shall   ²⁴⁴ *costard*
head (literally, "apple")   ²⁴⁵ *ballow* cudgel

Edgar. Chill pick your teeth,° zir: come; no matter
  vor your foins.°

                                     [*Oswald falls.*]

Oswald. Slave, thou hast slain me. Villain, take my
  purse: 250
  If ever thou wilt thrive, bury my body,
  And give the letters which thou find'st about° me
  To Edmund Earl of Gloucester; seek him out
  Upon the English party.° O, untimely death!
  Death!   255

                                         He dies.

Edgar. I know thee well. A serviceable° villain,
  As duteous° to the vices of thy mistress
  As badness would desire.

Gloucester.   What, is he dead?

Edgar. Sit you down, father; rest you.
  Let's see these pockets: the letters that he speaks
    of   260
  May be my friends. He's dead; I am only sorry
  He had no other deathsman.° Let us see:
  Leave,° gentle wax;° and, manners, blame us not:
  To know our enemies' minds, we rip their hearts;
  Their papers° is more lawful.   265

                       Reads the letter.

  "Let our reciprocal vows be remembered. You
have many opportunities to cut him off: if your
will want not,° time and place will be fruitfully
offered. There is nothing done, if he return the con-
queror: then am I the prisoner, and his bed my 270
jail; from the loathed warmth whereof deliver me,
and supply the place for your labor.
  "Your—wife, so I would° say—affectionate

---

²⁴⁸ *Chill pick your teeth* I will knock your teeth out   ²⁴⁹ *foins* thrusts
²⁵² *about* upon   ²⁵⁴ *party* side   ²⁵⁶ *serviceable* ready to be used   ²⁵⁷ *du-
teous* obedient   ²⁶² *deathsman* executioner   ²⁶³ *Leave* by your leave
²⁶³ *wax* (with which the letter is sealed)   ²⁶⁵ *Their papers* i.e., to rip
their papers   ²⁶⁷⁻⁶⁸ *if . . . not* if your desire (and lust) be not lacking
²⁷³ *would* would like to

servant, and for you her own for venture,°
275   'Goneril.' "

O indistinguished space of woman's will!°
A plot upon her virtuous husband's life;
And the exchange° my brother! Here in the sands
Thee I'll rake up,° the post unsanctified°
280 Of murderous lechers; and in the mature° time,
With this ungracious paper° strike° the sight
Of the death-practiced° Duke: for him 'tis well
That of thy death and business I can tell.

    Gloucester. The King is mad: how stiff° is my vile
       sense,°
285 That I stand up, and have ingenious° feeling
Of my huge sorrows! Better I were distract:°
So should my thoughts be severed from my griefs,
And woes by wrong imaginations° lose
The knowledge of themselves.
                               Drum afar off.

    Edgar.   Give me your hand:
290 Far off, methinks, I hear the beaten drum.
Come, father, I'll bestow° you with a friend.
                                  Exeunt.

Scene VII.   [*A tent in the French camp.*]

Enter Cordelia, Kent, Doctor, and Gentleman.

    Cordelia. O thou good Kent, how shall I live and
       work,

---

274 *and . . . venture* i.e., and one who holds her own for venturing
(Edmund had earlier been promised union by Goneril, "If you dare
venture in your own behalf," IV.ii.20).   276 *indistinguished . . . will*
unlimited range of woman's lust   278 *exchange* substitute   279 *rake up*
cover up, bury   279 *post unsanctified* unholy messenger   280 *mature* ripe
281 *ungracious paper* wicked letter   281 *strike* blast   282 *death-practiced*
whose death is plotted   284 *stiff* unbending   284 *vile sense* hateful capacity for feeling   285 *ingenious* conscious   286 *distract* distracted, mad
288 *wrong imaginations* delusions   291 *bestow* lodge

To match thy goodness? My life will be too short,
And every measure fail me.

Kent. To be acknowledged, madam, is o'erpaid.
All my reports go° with the modest truth,   *5*
Nor more nor clipped,° but so.

Cordelia.   Be better suited:°
These weeds° are memories° of those worser
    hours:
I prithee, put them off.

Kent.   Pardon, dear madam;
Yet to be known shortens my made intent:°
My boon I make it,° that you know me not   *10*
Till time and I think meet.°

Cordelia. Then be 't so, my good lord. [*To the Doctor.*] How does the King?

Doctor. Madam, sleeps still.

Cordelia. O you kind gods!
Cure this great breach in his abusèd° nature.   *15*
Th' untuned and jarring senses, O, wind up°
Of this child-changèd° father.

Doctor.   So please your Majesty
That we may wake the King: he hath slept long.

Cordelia. Be governed by your knowledge, and
    proceed
I' th' sway of° your own will. Is he arrayed?   *20*

      Enter Lear in a chair carried by Servants.

IV.vii. *5 go* conform *6 clipped* curtailed *6 suited* attired *7 weeds*
clothes *7 memories* reminders *9 Yet . . . intent* to reveal myself just
yet interferes with the plan I have made *10 My boon I make it* I ask
this reward *11 meet* fitting *15 abusèd* disturbed *16 wind up* tune
17 child-changèd changed, deranged (and also, reduced to a child) by
the cruelty of his children *20 I' th' sway of* according to

Gentleman. Ay, madam; in the heaviness of sleep
　　We put fresh garments on him.

Doctor. Be by, good madam, when we do awake him;
　　I doubt not of his temperance.°

Cordelia.　　　　　　　　　　Very well.

Doctor. Please you, draw near. Louder the music
25　　　there!

Cordelia. O my dear father, restoration hang
　　Thy medicine on my lips, and let this kiss
　　Repair those violent harms that my two sisters
　　Have in thy reverence° made.

Kent.　　　　　　　　　　Kind and dear Princess.

Cordelia. Had you not been their father, these white
30　　　flakes°
　　Did challenge° pity of them. Was this a face
　　To be opposed against the warring winds?
　　To stand against the deep dread-bolted° thunder?
　　In the most terrible and nimble stroke
　　Of quick, cross° lightning to watch—poor
35　　　perdu!°—
　　With this thin helm?° Mine enemy's dog,
　　Though he had bit me, should have stood that night
　　Against my fire; and wast thou fain,° poor father,
　　To hovel thee with swine and rogues° forlorn,
40　　In short° and musty straw? Alack, alack!
　　'Tis wonder that thy life and wits at once
　　Had not concluded all.° He wakes; speak to him.

Doctor. Madam, do you; 'tis fittest.

24 *temperance* sanity　29 *reverence* revered person　30 *flakes* hairs (in
long strands)　31 *challenge* claim　33 *deep dread-bolted* deep-voiced
and furnished with the dreadful thunderbolt　35 *cross* zigzag　35 *perdu*
(1) sentry in a forlorn position (2) lost one　36 *helm* helmet (his
scanty hair)　38 *fain* pleased　39 *rogues* vagabonds　40 *short* (when
straw is freshly cut, it is long, and suitable for bedding, given its flexi-
bility and crispness. As it is used, it becomes musty, shreds into pieces,
is "short." In contemporary Maine usage, "short manure" refers to
dung mixed with straw that has been broken up; "long manure" to
dung mixed with coarse new straw)　42 *concluded all* come to a complete end

Cordelia. How does my royal lord? How fares your
 Majesty?

Lear. You do me wrong to take me out o' th' grave: *45*
 Thou art a soul in bliss; but I am bound
 Upon a wheel of fire,° that mine own tears
 Do scald like molten lead.

Cordelia.   Sir, do you know me?

Lear. You are a spirit, I know. Where did you die?

Cordelia. Still, still, far wide.°   *50*

Doctor. He's scarce awake: let him alone awhile.

Lear. Where have I been? Where am I? Fair daylight?
 I am mightily abused.° I should ev'n die with pity,
 To see another thus. I know not what to say.
 I will not swear these are my hands: let's see; *55*
 I feel this pin prick. Would I were assured
 Of my condition.

Cordelia.   O, look upon me, sir,
 And hold your hand in benediction o'er me.
 You must not kneel.

Lear.   Pray, do not mock me:
 I am a very foolish fond° old man,   *60*
 Fourscore and upward, not an hour more nor less;
 And, to deal plainly,
 I fear I am not in my perfect mind.
 Methinks I should know you and know this man,
 Yet I am doubtful; for I am mainly° ignorant *65*
 What place this is, and all the skill I have
 Remembers not these garments, nor I know not
 Where I did lodge last night. Do not laugh at me,
 For, as I am a man, I think this lady
 To be my child Cordelia.

Cordelia.   And so I am, I am. *70*

Lear. Be your tears wet? Yes, faith. I pray, weep not.
 If you have poison for me, I will drink it.

---

47 *wheel of fire* (torment associated by the Middle Ages with Hell,
where Lear thinks he is) 50 *wide* i.e., of the mark (of sanity)
53 *abused* deluded 60 *fond* in dotage 65 *mainly* entirely

I know you do not love me; for your sisters
Have, as I do remember, done me wrong.
You have some cause, they have not.

75 *Cordelia.*   No cause, no cause.

Lear. Am I in France?

Kent.   In your own kingdom, sir.

Lear. Do not abuse° me.

Doctor. Be comforted, good madam: the great rage,°
   You see, is killed in him: and yet it is danger
80 To make him even o'er° the time he has lost.
   Desire him to go in; trouble him no more
   Till further settling.°

Cordelia. Will 't please your Highness walk?°

Lear. You must bear with me. Pray you now, forget
85 and forgive. I am old and foolish.

               Exeunt. Mane[n]t° Kent and Gentleman.

Gentleman. Holds it true, sir, that the Duke of Cornwall was so slain?

Kent. Most certain, sir.

Gentleman. Who is conductor of his people?

90 *Kent.* As 'tis said, the bastard son of Gloucester.

Gentleman. They say Edgar, his banished son, is with
   the Earl of Kent in Germany.

Kent. Report is changeable.° 'Tis time to look about;
   the powers° of the kingdom approach apace.

95 *Gentleman.* The arbitrement° is like to be bloody.
   Fare you well, sir.   [*Exit.*]

Kent. My point and period will be throughly
      wrought,°
   Or well or ill, as this day's battle's fought.

                                        Exit.

---

77 *abuse* deceive 78 *rage* frenzy 80 *even o'er* smooth over by filling
in; and hence, "recollect" 82 *settling* calming 83 *walk* (perhaps in
the sense of "withdraw") 85 s.d. *Mane[n]t* remain 93 *Report is
changeable* rumors are unreliable 94 *powers* armies 95 *arbitrement*
deciding encounter 97 *My . . . wrought* the aim and end, the close of
my life will be completely worked out

ACT V

Scene I. [*The British camp near Dover.*]

*Enter, with drum and colors, Edmund, Regan,
Gentlemen, and Soldiers.*

Edmund. Know° of the Duke if his last purpose hold,°
Or whether since he is advised° by aught
To change the course: he's full of alteration
And self-reproving: bring his constant pleasure.°

        [*To a Gentleman, who goes out.*]

Regan. Our sister's man is certainly miscarried.°   *5*

Edmund. 'Tis to be doubted,° madam.

Regan.   Now, sweet lord,
You know the goodness I intend upon you:
Tell me, but truly, but then speak the truth,
Do you not love my sister?

Edmund.   In honored° love.

Regan. But have you never found my brother's way   *10*
To the forfended° place?

Edmund.   That thought abuses° you.

V.i. 1 *Know* learn   1 *last purpose hold* most recent intention (to fight)
be maintained   2 *advised* induced   4 *constant pleasure* fixed (final)
decision   5 *miscarried* come to grief   6 *doubted* feared   9 *honored*
honorable   11 *forfended* forbidden   11 *abuses* (1) deceives (2) de-
means, is unworthy of

Regan. I am doubtful that you have been conjunct
　　And bosomed with her, as far as we call hers.°

Edmund. No, by mine honor, madam.

15　*Regan.* I shall never endure her: dear my lord,
　　Be not familiar with her.

Edmund.　　　　　　　　　Fear° me not.—
　　She and the Duke her husband!

　　　*Enter, with drum and colors, Albany, Goneril
　　　　　　　[and] Soldiers.*

Goneril. [*Aside*] I had rather lose the battle than
　　that sister
　　Should loosen° him and me.

20　*Albany.* Our very loving sister, well be-met.°
　　Sir, this I heard, the King is come to his daughter,
　　With others whom the rigor of our state°
　　Forced to cry out. Where I could not be honest,°
　　I never yet was valiant: for this business,
25　It touches us, as° France invades our land,
　　Not bolds the King, with others, whom, I fear,
　　Most just and heavy causes make oppose.°

Edmund. Sir, you speak nobly.

Regan.　　　　　　　　Why is this reasoned?°

Goneril. Combine together 'gainst the enemy;
80　For these domestic and particular broils°
　　Are not the question° here.

Albany.　　　　　　　Let's then determine
　　With th' ancient of war° on our proceeding.

Edmund. I shall attend you presently at your tent.

12-13 *I . . . hers* I fear that you have united with her intimately, in the
fullest possible way　16 *Fear* distrust　19 *loosen* separate　20 *be-met* met
22 *rigor . . . state* tyranny of our government　23 *honest* honorable
25 *touches us, as* concerns me, only in that　26-27 *Not . . oppose* and
not in that France emboldens the King and others, who have been
led, by real and serious grievances, to take up arms against us
28 *reasoned* argued　30 *particular broils* private quarrels　31 *question*
issue　32 *th' ancient of war* experienced commanders

Regan. Sister, you'll go with us?°

Goneril. No.   35

Regan. 'Tis most convenient;° pray you, go with us.

Goneril. [*Aside*] O, ho, I know the riddle.°—I
    will go.

    Exeunt both the Armies. Enter Edgar [disguised].

Edgar. If e'er your Grace had speech with man so
        poor,
    Hear me one word.

Albany. [*To those going out*] I'll overtake you. [*To
    Edgar*] Speak.

                    Exeunt [all but Albany and Edgar].

Edgar. Before you fight the battle, ope this letter.   40
    If you have victory, let the trumpet sound
    For° him that brought it: wretched though I seem,
    I can produce a champion that will prove°
    What is avouchèd° there. If you miscarry,
    Your business of° the world hath so an end,   45
    And machination° ceases. Fortune love you.

Albany. Stay till I have read the letter.

Edgar.   .   I was forbid it.
    When time shall serve, let but the herald cry,
    And I'll appear again.

Albany. Why, fare thee well: I will o'erlook° thy
        paper.   *Exit [Edgar].*   50

                Enter Edmund.

Edmund. The enemy's in view: draw up your powers.
    Here is the guess° of their true strength and
        forces
    By diligent discovery;° but your haste

---

34 *us* me (rather than Edmund)   36 *convenient* fitting, desirable   37 *riddle* real reason (for Regan's curious request)   41-42 *sound/For* summon   43 *prove* i.e., by trial of combat   44 *avouchèd* maintained   45 *of* in   46 *machination* plotting   50 *o'erlook* read over   52 *guess* estimate   53 *By diligent discovery* obtained by careful reconnoitering

Is now urged on you.

Albany.   We will greet° the time.   *Exit.*

55 *Edmund.* To both these sisters have I sworn my love;
        Each jealous° of the other, as the stung
        Are of the adder. Which of them shall I take?
        Both? One? Or neither? Neither can be enjoyed,
        If both remain alive: to take the widow
60   Exasperates, makes mad her sister Goneril;
        And hardly° shall I carry out my side,°
        Her husband being alive. Now then, we'll use
        His countenance° for the battle; which being done,
        Let her who would be rid of him devise
65   His speedy taking off. As for the mercy
        Which he intends to Lear and to Cordelia,
        The battle done, and they within our power,
        Shall never see his pardon; for my state
        Stands on me to defend, not to debate.°   *Exit.*

Scene II.   [*A field between the two camps.*]

*Alarum° within. Enter, with drum and colors,
Lear, Cordelia, and Soldiers, over the stage; and
exeunt.*
            Enter Edgar and Gloucester.

Edgar. Here, father,° take the shadow of this tree
        For your good host; pray that the right may thrive.
        If ever I return to you again,
        I'll bring you comfort.

Gloucester.   Grace go with you, sir.
                                        Exit [Edgar].

---

54 *greet* i.e., meet the demands of   56 *jealous* suspicious   61 *hardly* with
difficulty   61 *carry . . . side* (1) satisfy my ambition (2) fulfill my
bargain (with Goneril)   63 *countenance* authority   68-69 *for . . . debate*
my position requires me to act, not to reason about right and wrong
V.ii. s.d. *Alarum* a trumpet call to battle   1 *father* i.e., venerable
old man (Edgar has not yet revealed his identity)

Alarum and retreat° within. [Re-]enter Edgar.

Edgar. Away, old man; give me thy hand; away!　　　*5*
　　King Lear hath lost, he and his daughter ta'en:°
　　Give me thy hand; come on.

Gloucester. No further, sir; a man may rot even here.

Edgar. What, in ill thoughts again? Men must endure
　　Their going hence, even as their coming hither:　　　*10*
　　Ripeness° is all. Come on.

Gloucester.　　　　　　　And that's true too.
　　　　　　　　　　　　　　　　Exeunt.

Scene III.　　*[The British camp near Dover.]*

*Enter, in conquest, with drum and colors, Ed-
mund; Lear and Cordelia, as prisoners; Soldiers,
Captain.*

Edmund. Some officers take them away: good guard,°
　　Until their greater pleasures° first be known
　　That are to censure° them.

Cordelia.　　　　　　　We are not the first
　　Who with best meaning° have incurred the worst.
　　For thee, oppressèd King, I am cast down;　　　*5*
　　Myself could else out-frown false fortune's frown.
　　Shall we not see these daughters and these sisters?

Lear. No, no, no, no! Come, let's away to prison:
　　We two alone will sing like birds i' th' cage:
　　When thou dost ask me blessing, I'll kneel down　　　*10*
　　And ask of thee forgiveness: so we'll live,
　　And pray, and sing, and tell old tales, and laugh

---

4 s.d. *retreat* (signaled by a trumpet)　6 *ta'en* captured　11 *Ripeness*
maturity, as of fruit that is ready to fall　V.iii.　1 *good guard* let there
be good guard　2 *their greater pleasures* the will of those in command,
the great ones　3 *censure* pass judgment on　4 *meaning* intentions

At gilded butterflies,° and hear poor rogues
Talk of court news; and we'll talk with them too,
15 Who loses and who wins, who's in, who's out;
And take upon's the mystery of things,
As if we were God's spies:° and we'll wear out,°
In a walled prison, packs and sects of great ones
That ebb and flow by th' moon.°

Edmund.   Take them away.

20 *Lear.* Upon such sacrifices, my Cordelia,
The gods themselves throw incense.° Have I caught
    thee?
He that parts us shall bring a brand from heaven,
And fire us hence like foxes.° Wipe thine eyes;
The good years° shall devour them,° flesh and fell,°
Ere they shall make us weep. We'll see 'em starved
25   first.
Come.   [*Exeunt Lear and Cordelia, guarded.*]

Edmund. Come hither, captain; hark.
Take thou this note: go follow them to prison:
One step I have advanced thee; if thou dost
30 As this instructs thee, thou dost make thy way
To noble fortunes: know thou this, that men
Are as the time is:° to be tender-minded
Does not become a sword:° thy great employment
Will not bear question;° either say thou'lt do 't,
Or thrive by other means.

85 *Captain.*   I'll do 't, my lord.

---

13 *gilded butterflies* i.e., gorgeously attired courtiers, fluttering after nothing 16-17 *take . . . spies* profess to read the riddle of existence, as if endowed with divine omniscience 17 *wear out* outlast 18-19 *packs . . . moon* intriguing and partisan cliques of those in high station, whose fortunes change every month 20-21 *Upon . . . incense* i.e., the gods approve our renunciation of the world 22-23 *He . . . foxes* no human agency can separate us, but only divine interposition, as of a heavenly torch parting us like foxes who are driven from their place of refuge by fire and smoke 24 *good years* plague and pestilence ("undefined malefic power or agency," *N.E.D.*) 24 *them* i.e., the enemies of Lear and Cordelia 24 *fell* skin 32 *as the time is* i.e., absolutely determined by the exigencies of the moment 33 *become a sword* befit a soldier 34 *bear question* admit of discussion

Edmund. About it; and write happy° when th' hast
    done.
  Mark; I say, instantly, and carry it so°
  As I have set it down.

Captain. I cannot draw a cart, nor eat dried oats;
  If it be man's work, I'll do 't.   *Exit Captain.*   *40*

    Flourish. Enter Albany, Goneril, Regan [another
                Captain, and] Soldiers.

Albany. Sir, you have showed today your valiant
    strain,°
  And fortune led you well: you have the captives
  Who were the opposites of° this day's strife:
  I do require them of you, so to use them
  As we shall find their merits° and our safety   *45*
  May equally determine.

Edmund.   Sir, I thought it fit
  To send the old and miserable King
  To some retention and appointed guard;°
  Whose° age had charms in it, whose title more,
  To pluck the common bosom on his side,°   *50*
  And turn our impressed lances in our eyes°
  Which do command them. With him I sent the
    Queen:
  My reason all the same; and they are ready
  Tomorrow, or at further space,° t' appear
  Where you shall hold your session.° At this time   *55*
  We sweat and bleed: the friend hath lost his friend;
  And the best quarrels, in the heat, are cursed
  By those that feel their sharpness.°
  The question of Cordelia and her father

---

36 *write happy* style yourself fortunate   37 *carry it so* manage the affair in exactly that manner (as if Cordelia had taken her own life) 41 *strain* (1) stock (2) character   43 *opposites of* opponents in   45 *merits* deserts   48 *retention . . . guard* confinement under duly appointed guard   49 *Whose* i.e., Lear's   50 *pluck . . . side* win the sympathy of the people to himself   51 *turn . . . eyes* turn our conscripted lancers against us   54 *further space* a later time   55 *session* trial   57-58 *the . . . sharpness* the worthiest causes may be judged badly by those who have been affected painfully by them, and whose passion has not yet cooled

Requires a fitter place.

60 *Albany.*   Sir, by your patience,
I hold you but a subject of° this war,
Not as a brother.

Regan.   That's as we list to grace° him.
Methinks our pleasure might have been demanded,
Ere you had spoke so far. He led our powers,
65 Bore the commission of my place and person;
The which immediacy may well stand up
And call itself your brother.°

Goneril.   Not so hot:
In his own grace he doth exalt himself
More than in your addition.°

Regan.   In my rights,
70 By me invested, he compeers° the best.

Goneril. That were the most,° if he should husband
you.°

Regan. Jesters do oft prove prophets.

Goneril.   Holla, holla!
That eye that told you so looked but a-squint.°

Regan. Lady, I am not well; else I should answer
75 From a full-flowing stomach.° General,
Take thou my soldiers, prisoners, patrimony;°
Dispose of them, of me; the walls is thine:°
Witness the world, that I create thee here
My lord, and master.

Goneril.   Mean you to enjoy him?

80 *Albany.* The let-alone° lies not in your good will.

---

61 *subject of* subordinate in 62 *list to grace* wish to honor 65-67 *Bore
. . . brother* was authorized, as my deputy, to take command; his
present status, as my immediate representative, entitles him to be considered your equal 69 *your addition* honors you have bestowed on
him 70 *compeers* equals 71 *most* most complete investing in your
rights 71 *husband you* become your husband 78 *a-squint* cross-eyed
75 *From . . . stomach* angrily 76 *patrimony* inheritance 77 *walls is
thine* i.e., Regan's person, which Edmund has stormed and won
80 *let-alone* power to prevent

Edmund. Nor in thine, lord.

Albany.   Half-blooded° fellow, yes.

Regan. [To Edmund] Let the drum strike, and prove
    my title thine.°

Albany. Stay yet; hear reason. Edmund, I arrest thee
    On capital treason; and in thy attaint°
    This gilded serpent [*pointing to Goneril*]. For
      your claim, fair sister,   85
    I bar it in the interest of my wife.
    'Tis she is subcontracted° to this lord,
    And I, her husband, contradict your banes.°
    If you will marry, make your loves° to me;
    My Lady is bespoke.°

Goneril.   An interlude!°   90

Albany. Thou art armed, Gloucester: let the trumpet
    sound:
    If none appear to prove upon thy person
    Thy heinous, manifest, and many treasons,
    There is my pledge° [*throwing down a glove*]:
      I'll make° it on thy heart,
    Ere I taste bread, thou art in nothing less   95
    Than I have here proclaimed thee.

Regan.   Sick, O, sick!

Goneril. [Aside] If not, I'll ne'er trust medicine.°

Edmund. [Throwing down a glove] There's my
    exchange:° what in the world he is
    That names me traitor, villain-like he lies:°
    Call by the trumpet:° he that dares approach,   100

---

81 *Half-blooded* bastard, and so only half noble 82 *prove . . . thine*
prove by combat your entitlement to my rights 84 *in thy attaint* as a
sharer in the treason for which you are impeached 87 *subcontracted*
pledged by a contract which is called into question by the existence
of a previous contract (Goneril's marriage) 88 *contradict your banes*
forbid your announced intention to marry (by citing the precontract)
89 *loves* love-suits 90 *bespoke* already pledged 90 *interlude* play
94 *pledge* gage 94 *make* prove 97 *medicine* poison 98 *exchange* (technical term, denoting the glove Edmund throws down) 99 *villain-like he
lies* (the lie direct, a challenge to mortal combat) 100 *trumpet* trumpeter

On him, on you—who not?—I will maintain
My truth and honor firmly.

Albany. A herald, ho!

Edmund.   A herald, ho, a herald!

Albany. Trust to thy single virtue;° for thy soldiers,
105   All levied in my name, have in my name
Took their discharge.

Regan.   My sickness grows upon me.

Albany. She is not well; convey her to my tent.

                              [*Exit Regan, led.*]

                    Enter a Herald.

Come hither, herald. Let the trumpet sound—
And read out this.

110   *Captain.* Sound, trumpet!

                    A trumpet sounds.

Herald. (*Reads.*) "If any man of quality or degree°
within the lists° of the army will maintain upon Edmund, supposed Earl of Gloucester, that he is a
manifold traitor, let him appear by the third sound
115   of the trumpet: he is bold in his defense."

Edmund. Sound!

                    First trumpet.

Herald. Again!

                    Second trumpet.

Herald. Again!

                    Third trumpet.

        *Trumpet answers within. Enter Edgar, at the
        third sound, armed, a trumpet before him.°*

Albany. Ask him his purposes, why he appears
Upon this call o' th' trumpet.

120   *Herald.*   What are you?

---

104 *single virtue* unaided valor   111 *quality or degree* rank or position
112 *lists* rolls   118 s.d. *trumpet before him* trumpeter preceding him

Your name, your quality,° and why you answer
This present summons?

Edgar.   Know, my name is lost;
By treason's tooth bare-gnawn and canker-bit:°
Yet am I noble as the adversary
I come to cope.°

Albany.   Which is that adversary?   125

Edgar. What's he that speaks for Edmund, Earl of
    Gloucester?

Edmund. Himself: what say'st thou to him?

Edgar.   Draw thy sword,
That if my speech offend a noble heart,
Thy arm may do thee justice: here is mine.
Behold it is my privilege,   130
The privilege of mine honors,
My oath, and my profession.° I protest,
Maugre° thy strength, place, youth, and eminence,
Despite thy victor sword and fire-new° fortune,
Thy valor and thy heart,° thou art a traitor,   135
False to thy gods, thy brother, and thy father,
Conspirant° 'gainst this high illustrious prince,
And from th' extremest upward° of thy head
To the descent and dust below thy foot,°
A most toad-spotted traitor.° Say thou "No,"   140
This sword, this arm and my best spirits are bent°
To prove upon thy heart, whereto I speak,°
Thou liest.

Edmund.   In wisdom° I should ask thy name,
But since thy outside looks so fair and warlike,

---

121 *quality* rank   123 *canker-bit* eaten by the caterpillar   125 *cope* encounter   130-32 *it . . . profession* my knighthood entitles me to challenge you, and to have my challenge accepted   133 *Maugre* despite
134 *fire-new* fresh from the forge or mint   135 *heart* courage   137 *Con-
spirant* conspiring, a conspirator   138 *extremest upward* the very top
139 *the . . . foot* your lowest part (sole) and the dust beneath it
140 *toad-spotted traitor* spotted with treason (and hence venomous, as
the toad is allegedly marked with spots that exude venom)   141 *bent* directed   142 *whereto I speak* (Edgar speaks from the heart, and speaks
to the heart of Edmund)   143 *wisdom* prudence (since he is not obliged
to fight with one of lesser rank)

And that thy tongue some say° of breeding
145   breathes,
What safe and nicely° I might well delay°
By rule of knighthood, I disdain and spurn:
Back do I toss these treasons° to thy head;
With the hell-hated° lie o'erwhelm thy heart;
150 Which for they yet glance by and scarcely bruise,
This sword of mine shall give them instant way,
Where they shall rest for ever.° Trumpets, speak!

Alarums. [*They*] *fight.* [*Edmund falls.*]

Albany. Save° him, save him!

Goneril.   This is practice,° Gloucester:
By th' law of war thou wast not bound to answer
155 An unknown opposite;° thou art not vanquished,
But cozened and beguiled.

Albany.   Shut your mouth, dame,
Or with this paper shall I stop it. Hold, sir;°
Thou° worse than any name, read thine own evil.
No tearing, lady; I perceive you know it.

160 *Goneril.* Say, if I do, the laws are mine, not thine:
Who can arraign me for 't?

Albany.   Most monstrous! O!
Know'st thou this paper?

Goneril.   Ask me not what I know.

                                Exit.

Albany. Go after her; she's desperate; govern° her.

Edmund. What you have charged me with, that have
      I done;
165   And more, much more; the time will bring it out.
'Tis past, and so am I. But what art thou

---

145 *say* assay (i.e., touch, sign)   146 *safe and nicely* cautiously and punctiliously   146 *delay* i.e., avoid   148 *treasons* accusations of treason   149 *hell-hated* hated like hell   150-52 *Which . . . ever* which accusations of treason, since as yet they do no harm, even though I have hurled them back, I now thrust upon you still more forcibly, with my sword, so that they may remain with you permanently   153 *Save* spare   153 *practice* trickery   155 *opposite* opponent   157 *Hold, sir* (to Edmund: "Just a moment!")   158 *Thou* (probably Goneril)   163 *govern* control

That hast this fortune on° me? If thou 'rt noble,
I do forgive thee.

Edgar.   Let's exchange charity.°
I am no less in blood° than thou art, Edmund;
If more,° the more th' hast wronged me.   *170*
My name is Edgar, and thy father's son.
The gods are just, and of our pleasant° vices
Make instruments to plague us:
The dark and vicious place° where thee he got°
Cost him his eyes.

Edmund.   Th' hast spoken right, 'tis true;   *175*
The wheel is come full circle; I am here.°

Albany. Methought thy very gait did prophesy°
A royal nobleness: I must embrace thee:
Let sorrow split my heart, if ever I
Did hate thee or thy father!

Edgar.   Worthy° Prince, I know 't.   *180*

Albany. Where have you hid yourself?
How have you known the miseries of your father?

Edgar. By nursing them, my lord. List a brief tale;
And when 'tis told, O, that my heart would burst!
The bloody proclamation to escape°   *185*
That followed me so near—O, our lives' sweetness,
That we the pain of death would hourly die
Rather than die at once!°—taught me to shift
Into a madman's rags, t' assume a semblance
That very dogs disdained: and in this habit°   *190*
Met I my father with his bleeding rings,°
Their precious stones new lost; became his guide,
Led him, begged for him, saved him from despair;

---

167 *fortune on* victory over   168 *charity* forgiveness and love   169 *blood* lineage   170 *If more* if I am more noble (since legitimate)   172 *of our pleasant* out of our pleasurable   174 *place* i.e., the adulterous bed   174 *got* begot   176 *Wheel . . . here* i.e., Fortune's wheel, on which Edmund ascended, has now, in its downward turning, deposited him at the bottom, whence he began   177 *gait did prophesy* carriage did promise   180 *Worthy* honorable   185 *to escape* (my wish) to escape the sentence of death   186-88 *O . . . once* how sweet is life, that we choose to suffer death every hour rather than make an end at once   190 *habit* attire   191 *rings* sockets

Never—O fault!—revealed myself unto him,
195 Until some half-hour past, when I was armed,
Not sure, though hoping, of this good success,
I asked his blessing, and from first to last
Told him our pilgrimage.° But his flawed° heart—
Alack, too weak the conflict to support—
200 'Twixt two extremes of passion, joy and grief,
Burst smilingly.

   Edmund.   This speech of yours hath moved me,
And shall perchance do good: but speak you on;
You look as you had something more to say.

   Albany. If there be more, more woeful, hold it in;
205 For I am almost ready to dissolve,°
Hearing of this.

   Edgar.   This would have seemed a period°
To such as love not sorrow; but another,
To amplify too much, would make much more,
And top extremity.
210 Whilst I was big in clamor,° came there in a man,
Who, having seen me in my worst estate,°
Shunned my abhorred° society; but then, finding
Who 'twas that so endured, with his strong arms
He fastened on my neck, and bellowed out
215 As he'd burst heaven; threw him on my father;
Told the most piteous tale of Lear and him
That ever ear received: which in recoûnting
His grief grew puissant,° and the strings of life
Began to crack: twice then the trumpets sounded,
And there I left him tranced.°

220 *Albany.*   But who was this?

   Edgar. Kent, sir, the banished Kent; who in disguise
Followed his enemy° king, and did him service
Improper for a slave.

---

198 *our pilgrimage* of our (purgatorial) journey   198 *flawed* cracked
205 *dissolve* i.e., into tears   206 *period* limit   207-09 *but . . . extremity*
just one woe more, described too fully, would go beyond the extreme
limit   210 *big in clamor* loud in lamentation   211 *estate* condition
212 *abhorred* abhorrent   218 *puissant* overmastering   220 *tranced* insensi-
ble   222 *enemy* hostile

Enter a Gentleman, with a bloody knife.

Gentleman. Help, help, O, help!

Edgar.   What kind of help?

Albany.   Speak, man.

Edgar. What means this bloody knife?

Gentleman.   'Tis hot, it smokes;°   *225*
   It came even from the heart of—O, she's dead!

Albany. Who dead? Speak, man.

Gentleman. Your lady, sir, your lady: and her
      sister
   By her is poisoned; she confesses it.

Edmund. I was contracted° to them both: all three   *230*
   Now marry° in an instant.

Edgar.   Here comes Kent.

Albany. Produce the bodies, be they alive or dead.

                         [Exit Gentleman.]

   This judgment of the heavens, that makes us
      tremble,
   Touches us not with pity.

                    Enter Kent.

                    O, is this he?
   The time will not allow the compliment°   *235*
   Which very manners° urges.

Kent.   I am come
   To bid my king and master aye° good night:
   Is he not here?

Albany.   Great thing of° us forgot!
   Speak, Edmund, where's the King? and where's
      Cordelia?
   Seest thou this object,° Kent?   *240*

   The bodies of Goneril and Regan are brought in.

Kent. Alack, why thus?

---

²²⁵ *smokes* steams ²³⁰ *contracted* betrothed ²³¹ *marry* i.e., unite in
death ²³⁵ *compliment* ceremony ²³⁶ *very manners* ordinary civility
²³⁷ *aye* forever ²³⁸ *thing of* matter by ²⁴⁰ *object* sight (the bodies
of Goneril and Regan)

Edmund.   Yet° Edmund was beloved:
   The one the other poisoned for my sake,
   And after slew herself.

Albany. Even so. Cover their faces.

245 *Edmund.* I pant for life:° some good I mean to do,
   Despite of mine own nature. Quickly send,
   Be brief in it, to th' castle; for my writ°
   Is on the life of Lear and on Cordelia:
   Nay, send in time.

Albany.   Run, run, O, run!

250 *Edgar.* To who, my lord? Who has the office?° Send
   Thy token of reprieve.°

Edmund. Well thought on: take my sword,
   Give it the captain.

Edgar.   Haste thee, for thy life.

                              [*Exit Messenger.*]

Edmund. He hath commission from thy wife and me
255   To hang Cordelia in the prison, and
   To lay the blame upon her own despair,
   That she fordid° herself.

Albany. The gods defend her! Bear him hence awhile.

                              [*Edmund is borne off.*]

   *Enter Lear, with Cordelia in his arms [Gentle-
            man, and others following].*

Lear. Howl, howl, howl, howl! O, you are men of
      stones:
260   Had I your tongues and eyes, I'd use them so
   That heaven's vault should crack. She's gone for
      ever.
   I know when one is dead and when one lives;
   She's dead as earth. Lend me a looking-glass;
   If that her breath will mist or stain the stone,°
   Why, then she lives.

241 *Yet* in spite of all   245 *pant for life* gasp for breath   247 *writ* con.
mand (ordering the execution)   250 *office* commission   251 *token of
reprieve* sign that they are reprieved   257 *fordid* destroyed   264 *stone*
i.e., the surface of the crystal looking glass

Kent.   Is this the promised end?°   265

Edgar. Or image° of that horror?

Albany.   Fall and cease.°

Lear. This feather stirs; she lives. If it be so,
   It is a chance which does redeem° all sorrows
   That ever I have felt.

Kent.   O my good master.

Lear. Prithee, away.

Edgar.   'Tis noble Kent, your friend.   270

Lear. A plague upon you, murderers, traitors all!
   I might have saved her; now she's gone for ever.
   Cordelia, Cordelia, stay a little. Ha,
   What is 't thou say'st? Her voice was ever soft,
   Gentle and low, an excellent thing in woman.   275
   I killed the slave that was a-hanging thee.

Gentleman. 'Tis true, my lords, he did.

Lear.   Did I not, fellow?
   I have seen the day, with my good biting falchion°
   I would have made them skip: I am old now,
   And these same crosses° spoil me.° Who are you?   280
   Mine eyes are not o' th' best: I'll tell you straight.°

Kent. If Fortune brag of two° she loved and hated,
   One of them we behold.

Lear. This is a dull sight.° Are you not Kent?

Kent.   The same,
   Your servant Kent. Where is your servant Caius?°   285

Lear. He's a good fellow, I can tell you that;
   He'll strike, and quickly too: he's dead and rotten.

Kent. No, my good lord; I am the very man.

---

265 *promised end* Doomsday 266 *image* exact likeness 266 *Fall and cease* i.e., let the heavens fall, and all things finish 268 *redeem* make good 278 *falchion* small curved sword 280 *crosses* troubles 280 *spoil me* i.e., my prowess as a swordsman 281 *tell you straight* recognize you straightway 282 *two* i.e., Lear, and some hypothetical second, who is also a prime example of Fortune's inconstancy ("loved and hated") 284 *dull sight* (1) melancholy spectacle (2) faulty eyesight (Lear's own, clouded by weeping) 285 *Caius* (Kent's name, in disguise)

Lear. I'll see that straight.°

290 *Kent.* That from your first of difference and decay°
       Have followed your sad steps.

Lear.   You are welcome hither.

Kent. Nor no man else:° all's cheerless, dark and
       deadly.
    Your eldest daughters have fordone° themselves,
    And desperately° are dead.

Lear.   Ay, so I think.

295 *Albany.* He knows not what he says, and vain is it
       That we present us to him.

Edgar.   Very bootless.°

                Enter a Messenger.

Messenger. Edmund is dead, my lord.

Albany.   That's but a trifle here.
    You lords and noble friends, know our intent.
    What comfort to this great decay may come°
300 Shall be applied. For us, we° will resign,
    During the life of this old majesty,
    To him our absolute power: [*To Edgar and Kent*]
       you, to your rights;
    With boot,° and such addition° as your honors
    Have more than merited. All friends shall taste
805 The wages of their virtue, and all foes
    The cup of their deservings. O, see, see!

Lear. And my poor fool° is hanged: no, no, no
       life?
    Why should a dog, a horse, a rat, have life,

---

289 *see that straight* attend to that in a moment   290 *your . . . decay*
beginning of your decline in fortune   292 *Nor no man else* no, I am
not welcome, nor is anyone else   293 *fordone* destroyed   294 *desperately* in despair   296 *bootless* fruitless   299 *What . . . come* whatever
aid may present itself to this great ruined man   300 *us, we* (the royal
"we")   303 *boot* good measure   303 *addition* additional titles and rights
307 *fool* Cordelia ("fool" being a term of endearment. But it is perfectly possible to take the word as referring also to the Fool)

And thou no breath at all? Thou'lt come no more,
Never, never, never, never, never.   310
Pray you, undo this button.° Thank you, sir.
Do you see this? Look on her. Look, her lips,
Look there, look there.

                                        He dies.

Edgar.   He faints. My lord, my lord!

Kent. Break, heart; I prithee, break.

Edgar.   Look up, my lord.

Kent. Vex not his ghost:° O, let him pass! He hates
     him   315
That would upon the rack° of this tough world
Stretch him out longer.°

Edgar.   He is gone indeed.

Kent. The wonder is he hath endured so long:
     He but usurped° his life.

Albany. Bear them from hence. Our present business   320
     Is general woe. [*To Kent and Edgar*] Friends of
          my soul, you twain,
     Rule in this realm and the gored state sustain.

Kent. I have a journey, sir, shortly to go;
     My master calls me, I must not say no.

Edgar. The weight of this sad time we must obey,°   325
     Speak what we feel, not what we ought to say.
     The oldest hath borne most: we that are young
     Shall never see so much, nor live so long.

                    Exeunt, with a dead march.

                    F I N I S

311 *undo this button* i.e., to ease the suffocation Lear feels   315 *Vex . . . ghost* do not trouble his departing spirit   316 *rack* instrument of torture, stretching the victim's joints to dislocation   317 *longer* (1) in time (2) in bodily length   319 *usurped* possessed beyond the allotted term   325 *obey* submit to

Textual Note

The earliest extant version of Shakespeare's *King Lear* is the First Quarto of 1608. This premier edition is known as the Pied Bull Quarto, after the sign which hung before the establishment of the printer. The title page reads as follows: "M. William Shak-speare: / HIS / True Chronicle Historie of the life and / death of King Lear and his three / Daughters. / *With the vnfortunate life of* Edgar, *sonne* / and heire to the Earle of Gloster, and his / sullen and assumed humor of / Tom of Bedlam: / *As it was played before the Kings Maiestie at Whitehall vpon* / S. Stephans *night in Christmas Hollidayes.* / By his Maiesties seruants playing vsually at the Gloabe / on the Bancke-side. / LONDON, / Printed for *Nathaniel Butter,* and are to be sold at his shop in *Pauls* / Church-yard at the signe of the Pide Bull neere / S^{t}. *Austin's* Gate. 1608." Twelve copies of the First Quarto survive. They are, however, in ten different states, because proofreading, and hence correcting, took place as the play was being printed. The instances (167 in all) in which these copies of Q1 differ one from another have been enumerated by contemporary scholarship.[1]

In 1619 appeared the Second Quarto, known as the N. Butter Quarto, and falsely dated in the same year as

---

[1] W. W. Greg, *The Variants in the First Quarto of "King Lear,"* London, 1940 (for 1939).

the first (the title page reads: "Printed for Nathaniel Butter. 1608"). The source of Q2 was apparently a copy of Q1 in which a number of sheets had been corrected.

Four years later *King Lear* was reprinted once more, this time in the first collection of Shakespeare's works, the First Folio of 1623. The source of the Folio text seems to have been, again, a corrected copy of Q1. The corrections in this copy, however, do not duplicate those in the presumptive source of Q2, but are at once more and less extensive. In some cases the Quarto which lies behind the Folio offers corrections not found in the source of Q2. In other cases, corrections incorporated in the course of Q2 are not included in the source of F1. The Folio text, moreover, omits some 300 lines found in the Quarto, and thus leads to the supposition that the copy used in preparing the Folio had been collated with the prompt book—a shorter, acting version of the play—in the possession of Shakespeare's company. The Folio text would seem, then, to stand in close relation to Shakespeare's play as it was actually performed. On the other hand, the Folio does include some 100 lines not found in the Quarto.

It is now very generally, though not unanimously, agreed that the Folio is superior to the Quarto, and ought to serve as the basis of any modern edition. The present text of *King Lear* is based, therefore, on the First Folio of 1623, except when the Folio is guilty of an obvious misprinting, or when it omits pertinent material found in the Quarto, or when its version seems to the editor so inferior to the Quarto version as to demand precedence for the latter, or when an emendation, even though perhaps unnecessary (like Edwards' "top th' legitimate"), has been canonized by use and wont.

In the preparation of this text, the spelling of Folio and Quarto has been modernized; punctuation and capitalization have been altered, when alteration seemed suitable; character designations have been expanded or clarified (F "Cor." becomes "Cordelia," F "Bastard" and "Steward" become "Edmund" and "Oswald"); contractions not affecting pronunciation have been eliminated

(F "banish'd" becomes "banished"); necessary quotation marks (as in the reading of a letter) have been supplied; as have diacritical marks whenever a syllable that is normally unemphasized must be stressed (as in "oppressèd"). These changes are not recorded.

All other departures from the Folio appearing in this text are recorded here in italic type. Unless specifically noted, these departures derive in every case from the First Quarto [Q]. If some other source is levied on, such as the Second Quarto [Q2] or Second Folio [F2] or the conjecture of an editor (for example, [Theobald]), that source is given, within brackets, immediately after the reading. There follows next, in roman type, the Folio reading which has been superseded. If an editor's emendation has been preferred to both Folio and Quarto readings, the emendation, with its provenance, is followed by the Folio and Quarto readings it replaces.

Stage directions are not given lineation. Reference to them in these notes is determined, therefore, by the line of text they follow. If a stage direction occurs at the beginning of a scene, reference is to the line of text it precedes. On occasion, the stage direction in the present text represents a conflation of Folio and Quarto. In that case, both Folio and Quarto readings are set down in the notes. Stage directions and notations of place, printed within brackets, are, unless otherwise noted, substantially from the Globe edition. The list of Dramatis Personae, first given by Rowe, is taken also from the Globe edition.

I.i. *Act I. Scene 1* Actus Primus. Scaena Prima 5 *equalities* qualities 34 s.d. *Sound . . . Attendants* Sennet. Enter King Lear, Cornwall, Albany, Gonerill, Regan, Cordelia, and attendants [F] Sound a Sennet, Enter one bearing a Coronet, then Lear, then the Dukes of Albany, and Cornwall, next Gonerill, Regan, Cordelia, with followers [Q] 70 *speak* [F omits] 98 *loved me. I* loved me 99 *Return* I return 106 *To love my father all* [F omits] 112 *mysteries* [F2] miseries [F] mistress [Q] 157 *as a pawn* as pawn 158 *nor* nere [i.e., "ne'er"] 165 *the* thy 172 *sentence* sentences 176 *diseases* disasters 190 *Gloucester* Cor[delia]

208 *on* in   216 *best object* object   227 *well* will   235 *Better thou*
Better thou hadst   250 *respects of fortune* respect and Fortunes
268 s.d. *Lear . . . Attendants* [Capell] Exit Lear and Burgundy
[Q]   283 *shame them derides* with shame derides   291 *hath not
been* hath been   299-300 *ingrafted* ingraffed   306 *let's hit* let us sit

I.ii. *Scene II* Scena Secunda   21 *top th'* [Edwards] to' th' [F]
tooth' [Q]   103-05 *Edmund . . . earth* [F omits]   142 *Fut* [F
omits]   144 *Edgar* [F omits]   145 *and pat* [Steevens] Pat [F]
and out [Q]   156-64 *as . . . come* [F omits]   165 *Why, the* The
178 *brother* [F omits]   185 *Go armed* [F omits]   191 s.d. *Exit
Edgar* Exit

I.iii. *Scene III* Scena Tertia   17-21 *Not . . . abused* [F omits]
25-26 *I would . . . speak* [F omits]   27 *Go, prepare* prepare

I.iv. *Scene IV* Scena Quarta   1 *well* will   51 *daughter* Daughters   100 *Fool* my Boy   115 *Lady the Brach* [Steevens] the
Lady Brach [F] Ladie oth'e brach [Q]   144-59 *That . . . snatching* [F omits]   158 *on't* [Q2] [F omits] an't [Q]   158 *ladies*
[Q corrected] [F omits] lodes [Q uncorrected]   167 *crown*
Crownes   182 *fools* Foole   195 *Methinks* [F omits]   222 *it
had* it's had   225 *Come, Sir* [F omits]   234 *or his* his   237-41
I . . . father [F omits]   264 *O . . . come* [F omits]   298 *the
cause* more of it   311 *Yea . . . this* [F omits]   350 *You are*
[F2] Your are [F] Y'are [Q]   350 *attasked* for [Q corrected:
"attaskt"] at task for [F] alapt [Q uncorrected]

I.v. *Scene V* Scena Quinta   1 s.d. *Enter . . . Fool* [Q2] Enter
Lear, Kent, Gentleman, and Foole   17 *Why . . . boy* What can'st
tell Boy

II.i. *Act II. Scene I* Actus Secundus. Scena Prima   21 s.d. *Enter
Edgar* [placed by Theobald] [F prints after 1. 20]   55 *But* And
72 *I should* should I   73 *ay* [F omits]   80 *I . . . him* [F omits]
80 s.d. *Tucket within* [placed by Malone] [F prints after 1. 79]
81 *why* wher   89 *strange news* strangenesse

II.ii. *Scene II* Scena Secunda   23 *clamorous* [Q corrected] clam-
ours [F] clamarous [Q uncorrected]   44 s.d. *Enter . . . drawn*
Enter Bastard, Cornewall, Regan, Gloster, Servants [F] Enter
Edmund with his rapier drawne, Gloster the Duke and Dutchesse
[Q]   77 *too* t'   80 *Renege* Revenge   81 *gale* gall   110 *flick'ring*
[Pope: "flickering"] flicking [F] flitkering [Q]   125 *dread* dead
132 *respect* respects   141 s.d. *Stocks brought out* [placed by
Dyce] [F prints after 1. 139] [Q omits]   143-47 *His . . . with*
[F omits]   145 *contemnèd'st* [Capell] [F omits] contaned [Q un-

corrected] temnest [Q corrected]   153 *For . . . legs* [F omits]
154 *Come . . . away* [F assigns to Cornwall]   154 *my good Lord*
my Lord   154 s.d. *Exeunt . . . Kent* Exit [F] [Q omits]
155 *Duke's* Duke   176 s.d. *Sleeps* [F omits]

II.iii. *Scene III* [Steevens] [F, Q omit]   4 *unusual* unusall   15
mortified bare arms mortified Armes   18 *sheepcotes* Sheeps-Cotes

II.iv.1 s.d. *Scene IV* [Steevens] [F, Q omit]   2 *messenger* Messengers   6 *thy* ahy   9 *man's* man   18-19 *No . . . have* [F omits]
30 *panting* painting   33 *whose* those   61 *the* the the   75 *have*
hause   86 s.d. *Enter . . . Gloucester* [F prints after 1. 84]
130 *mother's* Mother   167 *her pride* [F omits]   183 s.d. *Enter
Oswald* [placed by Dyce] [F and Q print after 1. 181]   185 *fickle*
fickly   188 s.d. *Enter Goneril* [placed by Johnson] [F and Q print
after 1. 186]   282 s.d. *Storm and tempest* [F prints after 1. 283]
[Q omits]   285 s.d. *Exeunt . . . Fool* [Q2] Exeunt [F] Exeunt
Lear, Leister, Kent, and Foole [Q]   294 s.d. *Enter Gloucester* [F
and Q print after 1. 293]

III.i. *Act III. Scene 1* Actus Tertius. Scena Prima   7-14 *tears
. . . all* [F omits]   30-42 *But . . . you* [F omits]

III.ii. *Scene II* Scena Secunda   3 *drowned* drown   71 *That* And
78 *True . . . boy* True boy

III.iii. *Scene III* Scaena Tertia

III.iv. *Scene IV* Scena Quarta   7 *skin: so* [Rowe] skinso [F] skin,
so [Q]   10 *thy* they   27 s.d. *Exit* [placed by Johnson] [F prints
after 1. 26] [Q omits]   38 s.d. *Enter Fool* [Duthie] Enter Edgar,
and Foole [F, which prints after 1. 36] [Q omits]   44 s.d. *Enter
Edgar* Enter Edgar, and Foole [F, which prints after 1. 36] [Q
omits]   46 *blows . . . wind* blow the windes   47 *thy cold bed*
thy bed   52 *ford* Sword   57 *Bless* Blisse   58 *Bless* blisse   63
What, has Ha's   91 *deeply* deerely   101 *sessa* [Malone] Sesey
[F] caese [Q] cease [Q2]   116 s.d. *Enter . . . torch* [F prints
after 1. 111] Enter Gloster [Q, which prints after 1. 116]   117
foul fiend Flibbertigibbet foule Flibbertigibbet   118 *till . . . cock*
at first Cocke   138 *hath* had hath

III.v. *Scene V* Scena Quinta   13 *his* this   26 *dearer* deere

III.vi. *Scene VI* Scena Sexta   5 s.d. *Exit* [placed by Capell] [F
prints after 1. 3]   17-55 *The . . . 'scape* [F omits]   22 *Now*
[Q2] [F omits] no [Q]   25 *bourn* [Capell] [F omits] broome [Q]

34 *cushions* [F omits] cushings [Q]   47 *she kicked* [Q2] [F omits]
kicked [Q]   53 *made on* [Capell] [F omits] made an [Q]   67
lym [Hanmer] Hym [F] him [Q]   68 *tike, or trundle* tight, or
Troudle   72 *Sessa!* [Malone] sese [F] [Q omits]   84 s.d. *Enter
Gloucester* [placed by Capell] [F prints after 1. 80]   97-100 *Oppressèd . . . behind* [F omits]   101-14 *When . . . lurk* [F omits]

III.vii. *Scene VII* Scena Septima   21 s.d. *Exit Oswald* [Staunton]
[F and Q omit]   23 s.d. *Exeunt . . . Edmund* [Staunton] [F
(Exit) and Q (Exit Gon. and Bast.) print after 1. 22]   28 s.d.
Enter . . . three [Q, which prints after "traitor"] Enter Gloucester,
and Servants [F, which prints as here after "control"]   59 *rash*
sticke   64 *dearn* sterne   79 s.d. *Draw and fight* [F omits]   81
s.d. *She . . . him* Killes him [F] Shee . . . behind [Q]   100-108
I'll . . . him [F omits]   100 *Second Servant* [Capell] [F omits]
Servant [Q]   101 *Third Servant* [Capell] [F omits]   2 Servant
[Q]   104 *Second Servant* [Capell] [F omits]   1 Ser. [Q]   105
roguish [Q2] [Q omits]   107 *Third Servant* [Capell] [F omits]
2 Ser. [Q]   108 s.d. *Exeunt severally* [F omits] Exit [Q]

IV.i. *Act IV Scene 1* Actus Quartus. Scena Prima   9 s.d. *led by
an Old Man* [Q, which prints after 1. 12] and an Old man [F,
which places after 1. 9, as here]   41 *Then, prithee, get thee gone*
Get thee away   60-65 *Five . . . master* [F omits]   62-63 *Flibbertigibbet* [Pope] Stiberdigebit [Q]   63 *mopping and mowing* [Theo-
bald] Mobing, & Mohing [Q]

IV.ii. *Scene II* Scena Secunda   1 s.d. *Enter Goneril and Edmund*
Enter Gonerill, Bastard, and Steward   2 s.d. [after "way"] *Enter
Oswald* [placed by Theobald] [Q prints after "master," 1.2] [F
omits]   25 s.d. *Exit Edmund* [placed by Rowe] Exit [F, which
prints after "death"] [Q omits]   28 s.d. *Exit* [F omits] Exit Stew.
[Q]   31-50 *I . . . deep* [F omits]   32 *its* ith [Q]   45 *benefited*
[Q corrected] beniflicted [Q uncorrected]   47 *these* [Jennens; Heath
conj.] the [Q uncorrected] this [Q corrected]   49 *Humanity* [Q cor-
rected] Humanly [Q uncorrected]   53-59 *that . . . so* [F omits]   56
noiseless [Q corrected] noystles [Q uncorrected]   57 *thy state
begins to threat* [Jennens] thy slayer begin threats [Q uncorrected]
thy state begins thereat [Q corrected] thy slaier begins threats
[Q2]   58 *Whilst* [Q corrected] Whil's [Q uncorrected]   62-69
Thou . . . news [F omits]   65 *dislocate* [Q3] dislecate [Qq.1,2]
68 *mew* [Q corrected] now [Q uncorrected]   68 s.d. *Enter a
Messenger* [F prints after 1. 61] Enter a Gentleman [Q, which
prints after 1. 69; and Q2, which prints after 1. 68, as here]   75
thereat enraged threat-enrag'd   79 *justicers* [Q corrected] Iustices
[F, Q]   87 s.d. *Exit* [F omits]

IV.iii. *Scene III* Scena Tertia [for Scene IV]   1 s.d. *Enter . . .
Gentleman* [F omits the entire scene]   12 *sir* [Theobald] say   17
strove [Pope] streme   21 *seemed* [Pope: "seem'd"] seeme   30
believed [Q2] beleeft   32 *moistened* [Capell] moystened her
56 *Exeunt* [Pope] Exit

IV.iv. *Scene IV* [Pope] Scena Tertia [F] [Q omits]   1 s.d. *Cordelia, Doctor, and Soldiers* Cordelia, Gentlemen, and Souldiours
[F] Cordelia, Doctor and others [Q]   3 *femiter* Fenitar   6 *century* Centery   18 *distress* desires   28 *right* Rite

IV.v. *Scene V* [Pope] Scena Quarta [F] [Q omits]   39 *meet him*
meet

IV.vi. *Scene VI* [Pope] Scena Quinta [Q omits]   17 *walk* walk'd
34 s.d. *He kneels* [F omits]   41 s.d. *He falls* [F omits]   71
whelked wealk'd   71 *enridgèd* enraged   83 *coining* crying   97
had white had the white   166 *Through* Thorough *small* great
167 *Plate sin* [Theobald] Place sinnes [Q omits]   199 *Ay . . .
dust* [F omits]   200 *Good sir* [Q2] [F and Q omit]   206 s.d.
Exit . . . follow Exit [F] Exit King running [Q]   208 *one* a
244 *I'se* [Johnson: "Ise"] ice [F] ile [Q]   247 s.d. *They fight*
[F omits]   255 s.d. *He dies* [F omits]   274 *and . . . venture*
[Q reads "Venter"] [F omits] [This line, from the First Quarto,
is almost universally omitted from editions of the play]   276
indistinguished indinguish'd   289 s.d. *Drum afar off* [F prints
after 1. 287] A drum a farre off [Q, which prints as here]

IV.vii. *Scene VII* Scaena Septima   1 s.d. *Enter . . . Gentleman*
Enter Cordelia, Kent, and Gentleman [F] Enter Cordelia, Kent,
and Doctor [Q]   24 *doubt not* doubt   24-25 *Very . . . there*
[F omits]   32 *warring* iarring   33-36 *To . . . helm* [F omits]
79-80 *and . . . lost* [F omits]   85 s.d. *Exeunt . . . Gentleman*
Exeunt   86-98 *Holds . . . fought* [F omits]

V.i. *Act V Scene I* Actus Quintus. Scena Prima   11-13 *That . . .
hers* [F omits]   16 *Fear me not* Feare not   18-19 *I . . . me*
[F omits]   23-28 *Where . . . nobly* [F omits]   33 *I . . . tent*
[F omits]   36 *pray you* pray   39 s.d. *To those going out* [F and
Q omit] *To Edgar* [F and Q omit] *Exeunt* [placed by Cambridge
edition] [Q prints after "word," 1. 39] [F omits]   46 *love* loues
50 s.d. *Exit* [placed by Dyce] [F and Q print after 1. 49]

V.ii. *Scene II* Scena Secunda

V.iii. *Scene III* Scena Tertia   13 *hear poor rogues* heere (poore
Rogues) [reference in F is to Lear and Cordelia]   26 s.d. *Exeunt*

. . . *guarded* Exit [F] [Q omits]   39-40 *I . . . do't* [F omits]   40
s.d. *Exit Captain* [F prints after 1. 38] [Q omits]   48 *and ap-*
pointed guard [Q corrected, and Q2] [F and Q omit]   55-60 *At*
. . . *place* [F omits]   56 *We* [Q corrected, and Q2] mee [Q]   58
sharpness [Q corrected, and Q2] sharpes [Q]   84 *attaint* arrest
85 *sister* Sisters   98 *he is* hes   103 *Edmund . . . ho, a herald*
[F omits]   108 s.d. *Enter a Herald* [placed by Hanmer] [F prints
after 1. 102] [Q omits]   110 *Sound, trumpet* [F omits]   110 s.d.
A trumpet sounds [F prints after 1. 109] [Q omits] trumpet [F2]
Tumpet   116 *Sound* [F omits]   116 s.d. *First trumpet* [F prints
after 1. 115] [Q omits]   118 s.d. *Enter . . . him* Enter Edgar
armed [F] Enter Edgar at the third sound, a trumpet before him
[Q]   137 *illustrious* illustirous   145 *some say* (some say)   152
s.d. *fight* Fights [F, which prints after 1. 153, "him"] [Q omits]
162 *Ask . . . know* [F gives to Edmund]   162 s.d. *Exit* [placed
here by Q: "Exit. Gonorill"] [F prints after 1. 161, "for't"]
206-23 *This . . . slave* [F omits]   215 *him* [Theobald] me [Q]
[F omits]   223 s.d. *Enter . . . knife* Enter a Gentleman [F]
Enter one with a bloudie knife [Q]   234 s.d. *Enter Kent* [placed
by Q2] [F prints after 1. 231, "Kent"] [Q prints after "allow"
in 1. 235]   240 s.d. *The . . . in* Gonerill and Regans bodies
brought out [F, which prints after 1. 232]   253 s.d. *Exit Mes-*
senger [Theobald] [F and Q omit]   259 *Howl, howl, howl, howl*
Howle, howle, howle *you are* your are   279 *them* him   291
You are [Q2] Your are [F] You'r [Q]   296 s.d. *Enter a Mes-*
senger [F, which prints after "him"] Enter Captaine [Q, placed as
here]

The Date and Source of *King Lear*

King Lear was probably written between 1603 and 1606. The evidence is as follows. Under the date of November 26, 1607, the printers Nathaniel Butter and John Busby entered the play in the Stationers' Register, thereby asserting their right to print it. That right was exercised in the following year, with the appearance of the First Quarto of 1608. The title page of that quarto (Q1) announces a performance of the play as having taken place before the King on St. Stephen's Night (December 26) in the Christmas holidays. The entry in the Stationers' Register (1607), since it refers to the Court performance as occurring on "Christmas Last," fixes the date of that performance as December 26, 1606. This date is therefore the *terminus ad quem* for the composition of the play. The earliest date, that of 1603, is more difficult to establish. Probably it is fixed by the entry in the Stationers' Register, on March 16, 1603, of Samuel Harsnett's *Declaration of Egregious Popishe Impostures.* Harsnett's work, a treatise on diabolism and an attack on the Jesuits, was written in 1602–03. It is utilized by Shakespeare in his play, chiefly for the names of the demons who lurk about Poor Tom. Assume—and it is reasonable to do so—that Shakespeare did not have access to Harsnett's *Declaration* before the date of publication, and 1603 becomes the *terminus a quo* for the writing of *King Lear.*

Astrological reference furnishes another clue. Gloucester, citing as portentous "These late eclipses in the sun and moon" (I. ii. 112), is commonly thought to be speaking of a contemporary event. There were in fact eclipses in 1601 and, more pertinently, in September (the moon) and October (the sun) of 1605. It has been suggested, moreover, that a publication of 1606, telling of "The Earth's and Moone's late and horrible obscurations," lies directly behind Gloucester's superstitious mutterings. The pamphlet in question, translated from the High Dutch and edited by the almanac writer Edward Gresham, is entitled *Strange fearful & true news which happened at Carlstadt, in the Kingdome of Croatia.* Its preface is dated February 11, 1606.

Finally, there is the re-emergence, in the period just before the first recorded performance of Shakespeare's play, of the older dramatic version of his story, *The True Chronicle History of King Leir.* Though this play was probably written about 1590, and was on the boards in 1594, it was published and perhaps acted again in 1605: on May 8, 1605, it is entered in the Stationers' Register. Presumably Shakespeare used the edition appearing in that year, in writing his own play.

The publication, then, of the old chronicle history in 1605, the notable eclipses occurring in the fall of the same year, and the appearance of Gresham's pamphlet early in 1606 seem to point to the winter of 1605–06 as the period in which Shakespeare wrote *King Lear.*

The ultimate source of the play is an ancient folk tale existing in many versions. It first appears as literature in the twelfth-century *Historia Regum Britanniae* (ii, 11-15), by Geoffrey of Monmouth. Throughout the Middle Ages and on into the Renaissance, the Lear story retained its popularity, appearing in some fifty different accounts. Shakespeare was familiar with it from the retelling in what is perhaps his most important source book, the second edition (1587) of *The Chronicles of England, Scotlande, and Irelande* by Raphael Holinshed, first compiled in 1577. From Edmund Spenser, in *The Faerie Queene* (1590), Shakespeare derived the name of Cordelia in its present form, and also the detail of her death by hanging (II. x. 27-32). Other suggestions were furnished by John Higgins, in *A Mirror for Magistrates* (1574), that immensely popular collection of stories of the falls of princes; and of course, by *The True Chronicle History of King Leir and his three daughters.* John Marston, in *The Malcontent* (1604), dramatizes a feigned suicide (4.3) that seems to parallel Gloucester's, at the Cliffs of Dover (IV. vi). The author of *The London Prodigal* (1605), a play once attributed to Shakespeare and performed by his company, anticipates the rustic dialogue affected by Edgar in his combat with Oswald (IV. vi). As previously noted, Harsnett and, possibly, Gresham were also of use to Shakespeare. So, in less tangible ways, was his great French contemporary, Montaigne, whose *Essais* were translated into English by John Florio in 1603. Numerous words and passages in Florio's translation (which Shakespeare may have read in manuscript) are echoed in *King Lear.* More impressive, however, is the impact on Shakespeare of Montaigne's skeptical thought, as expressed particularly in the *Apology for Raymond Sebonde.*

None of these sources of *Lear* includes the analogous story of Gloucester and his two sons. That story Shakespeare adapted from Sir Philip Sidney's account of the unhappy King of Paphlagonia, in his famous romantic narrative *Arcadia* (ii, 10), written early in the 1580's but not published until 1590. The tying of the subplot to the old and sufficiently horrid tale of King Lear and his daughters has, of course, the effect of engrossing the horror, until the audience is almost persuaded that ferocious cruelty is not so much an aberration as the norm. Certainly, if Lear is childed as Edgar is fathered it is no longer possible to see as merely sensational or idiosyncratic the evil that Shakespeare anatomizes in the play. Earlier writers, handling one or the other story, allow of that view. Shakespeare, in fusing the two stories, is at pains to controvert it. What is more, he darkens consistently, in manipulating his sources, whatever dark suggestion is latent in them. In the old *Leir,* in Holinshed, in Spenser, in the *Mirror for Magistrates,* the travails of the King are intermitted at last. Vice is punished and virtue rewarded: Cordelia triumphs over her wicked sisters; her father, restored to the throne, dies at the apogee, and in peace. It is true that, in some sources, Cordelia ends a suicide. But that is an irrelevant epilogue: the chief business of the tale is happily resolved.

It is left to Shakespeare to cancel that happy resolution. He is the first to educe tragedy from what is essentially a melodramatic romance. The madness of Lear is altogether his own contribution. So is the pathetic figure of the Fool. So is the murder of Cordelia, that cruelest stroke of all, which is made to fall just as the good are preparing to taste the wages of their virtue. Some sense of Shakespeare's lack of ruth, of his invention, and not least, of his tact may be gathered from a perusal of the source material on which he worked.

Selections from Raphael Holinshed
The Chronicles of England, Scotland, and Ireland

Leir the son of Baldud was admitted ruler over the Britains, in the year of the world 3105, at what time Joas reigned in Juda. This Leir was a prince of right noble demeanor, governing his land and subjects in great wealth. He made the town of Caerleir now called Leicester, which standeth upon the river of Sore. It is written that he had by his wife three daughters without other issue, whose names were Gonorilla, Regan, and Cordeilla, which daughters he greatly loved, but specially Cordeilla the youngest far above the two elder. When this Leir therefore was come to great years, & began to wax unwieldy through age, he thought to understand the affections of his daughters towards him, and prefer her whom he best loved, to the succession over the kingdom. Whereupon he first asked Gonorilla the eldest, how well she loved him: who calling her gods to record, protested that she loved him more than her own life,

which by right and reason should be most dear unto
her. With which answer the father, being well pleased,
turned to the second, and demanded of her how well
she loved him: who answered (confirming her sayings
with great oaths) that she loved him more than tongue
could express, and far above all other creatures of the
world.

Then called he his youngest daughter Cordeilla before
him, and asked of her what account she made of him,
unto whom she made this answer as followeth: "Knowing the great love and fatherly zeal that you have always borne towards me (for the which I may not answer you otherwise than I think, and as my conscience
leadeth me) I protest unto you, that I have loved you
ever, and will continually (while I live) love you as my
natural father. And if you would more understand of
the love that I bear you, ascertain yourself, that so
much as you have, so much you are worth, and so much
I love you, and no more." The father being nothing content with this answer, married his two eldest daughters,
the one unto Henninus, the duke of Cornwall, and the
other unto Maglanus, the duke of Albania, betwixt
whom he willed and ordained that his land should be
divided after his death, and the one half thereof immediately should be assigned to them in hand: but for
the third daughter Cordeilla he reserved nothing.

Nevertheless it fortuned that one of the princes of
Gallia (which now is called France), whose name was
Aganippus, hearing of the beauty, womanhood, and good
conditions of the said Cordeilla, desired to have her in
marriage, and sent over to her father, requiring that he
might have her to wife; to whom answer was made, that
he might have his daughter, but as for any dower he
could have none, for all was promised and assured to
her other sisters already. Aganippus notwithstanding this
answer of denial to receive anything by way of dower
with Cordeilla, took her to wife, only moved thereto (I
say) for respect of her person and amiable virtues. This
Aganippus was one of the twelve kings that ruled Gallia

in those days, as in British history it is recorded. But to proceed.

After that Leir was fallen into age, the two dukes that had married his two eldest daughters, thinking it long ere the government of the land did come to their hands, arose against him in armor, and reft from him the governance of the land, upon conditions to be continued for term of life: by the which he was put to his portion, that is, to live after a rate assigned to him for the maintenance of his estate, which in process of time was diminished as well by Maglanus as by Henninus. But the greatest grief that Leir took was to see the unkindness of his daughters, which seemed to think that all was too much which their father had, the same being never so little: in so much that going from the one to the other, he was brought to that misery, that scarcely they would allow him one servant to wait upon him.

In the end, such was the unkindness, or (as I may say) the unnaturalness which he found in his two daughters, notwithstanding their fair and pleasant words uttered in time past, that being constrained of necessity, he fled the land, & sailed into Gallia, there to seek some comfort of his youngest daughter Cordeilla, whom beforetime he hated. The lady Cordeilla hearing that he was arrived in poor estate, she first sent to him privily a certain sum of money to apparel himself withal, and to retain a certain number of servants that might attend upon him in honorable wise, as appertained to the estate which he had borne: and then so accompanied, she appointed him to come to the court, which he did, and was so joyfully, honorably, and lovingly received, both by his son-in-law Aganippus, and also by his daughter Cordeilla, that his heart was greatly comforted: for he was no less honored, than if he had been king of the whole country himself.

Now when he had informed his son-in-law and his daughter in what sort he had been used by his other daughters, Aganippus caused a mighty army to be put in a readiness, and likewise a great navy of ships to be rigged, to pass over into Britain with Leir his father-in-law, to see him again restored to his kingdom. It was accorded, that Cordeilla should also go with him to take possession of the land, the which he promised to leave unto her, as the rightful inheritor after his decease, notwithstanding any former grant made to her sisters or to their husbands in any manner of wise.

Hereupon, when this army and navy of ships were ready, Leir and his daughter Cordeilla with her husband took the sea, and arriving in Britain, fought with their enemies, and discomfited them in battle, in the which Maglanus and Henninus were slain; and then was Leir restored to his kingdom, which he ruled after this by the space of two years, and then died, forty years after he first began to reign.

Sir Philip Sidney from *Arcadia*

The pitiful state, and story of the Paphlagonian unkind King, and his kind son, first related by the son, then by the blind father.

It was in the kingdom of Galacia, the season being (as in the depth of winter) very cold, and as then suddenly grown to so extreme and foul a storm, that never any winter (I think) brought forth a fouler child: so that the Princes were even compelled by the hail, that the pride of the wind blew into their faces, to seek some shrouding place within a certain hollow rock offering it unto them, they made it their shield against the tempest's fury. And so staying there, till the violence thereof was passed, they heard the speech of a couple, who not perceiving them (being hid within that rude canopy) held a strange and pitiful disputation which made them step out; yet in such sort, as they might see unseen. There they perceived an aged man, and a young, scarcely come to the age of a man, both poorly arrayed, extremely weatherbeaten; the old man blind, the young man leading him:

and yet through all those miseries, in both these seemed to appear a kind of nobleness, not suitable to that affliction. But the first words they heard were these of the old man. Well Leonatus (said he) since I cannot persuade thee to lead me to that which should end my grief, & thy trouble, let me now entreat thee to leave me: fear not, my misery cannot be greater than it is, & nothing doth become me but misery; fear not the danger of my blind steps. I cannot fall worse than I am. And do not, I pray thee, do not obstinately continue to infect thee with my wretchedness. But fly, fly from this region, only worthy of me. Dear father (answered he) do not take away from me the only remnant of my happiness: while I have power to do you service, I am not wholly miserable. Ah my son (said he, and with that he groaned, as if sorrow strove to break his heart), how evil fits it me to have such a son, and how much doth thy kindness upbraid my wickedness? These doleful speeches, and some others to like purpose (well showing they had not been borne to the fortune they were in), moved the Princes to go out unto them, and ask the younger what they were? Sirs (answered he, with a good grace, and made the more agreeable by a certain noble kind of piteousness) I see well you are strangers, that know not our misery so well here known, that no man dare know, but that we must be miserable. Indeed our state is such, as though nothing is so needful unto us as pity, yet nothing is more dangerous unto us, than to make ourselves so known as may stir pity. But your presence promiseth, that cruelty shall not overrun hate. And if it did, in truth our state is sunk below the degree of fear.

This old man (whom I lead) was lately rightful Prince of this country of Paphlagonia, by the hard-hearted ungratefulness of a son of his, deprived, not only of his kingdom (whereof no foreign forces were ever able to spoil him) but of his sight, the riches which Nature grants to the poorest creatures. Whereby, & by other his unnatural dealings, he hath been driven to such grief, as even now he would have had me to have led him to the top of this rock, thence to cast himself headlong to death:

and so would have made me (who received my life of
him) to be the worker of his destruction. But noble Gentlemen (said he) if either of you have a father, and feel
what dutiful affection is engraffed in a son's heart, let me
entreat you to convey this afflicted Prince to some place
of rest & security. Amongst your worthy acts it shall be
none of the least, that a King, of such might and fame,
and so unjustly oppressed, is in any sort by you relieved.

But before they could make him answer, his father
began to speak, Ah my son (said he) how evil an his-
torian are you, that leave out the chief knot of all the dis-
course? my wickedness, my wickedness. And if thou doest
it to spare my ears, (the only sense now left me proper
for knowledge) assure thy self thou dost mistake me.
And I take witness of that sun which you see (with that
he cast up his blind eyes, as if he would hunt for light),
and wish myself in worse case than I do wish myself,
which is as evil as may be, if I speak untruly; that nothing
is so welcome to my thoughts, as the publishing of my
shame. Therefore know you Gentlemen (to whom from
my heart I wish that it may not prove ominous foretoken
of misfortune to have met with such a miser as I am)
that whatsoever my son (O God, that truth binds me to
reproach him with the name of my son) hath said, is
true. But besides those truths this also is true, that
having had in lawful marriage, of a mother fit to bear
royal children, this son (such one as partly you see,
and better shall know by my short declaration) and so
enjoyed the expectations in the world of him, till he was
grown to justify their expectations (so as I needed
envy no father for the chief comfort of mortality, to
leave another oneself after me) I was carried by a bastard son of mine (if at least I be bound to believe the
words of that base woman my concubine, his mother)
first to mislike, then to hate, lastly to destroy, to do my
best to destroy, this son (I think you think) undeserving
destruction. What ways he used to bring me to it, if I
should tell you, I should tediously trouble you with as
much poisonous hypocrisy, desperate fraud, smooth malice, hidden ambition, & smiling envy, as in any living

person could be harbored. But I list it not, no remembrance, (no, of naughtiness) delights me, but mine own; & me thinks, the accusing his trains might in some manner excuse my fault, which certainly I loathe to do. But the conclusion is, that I gave order to some servants of mine, whom I thought as apt for such charities as myself, to lead him out into a forest, & there to kill him.

But those thieves (better natured to my son than myself) spared his life, letting him go, to learn to live poorly: which he did, giving himself to be a private soldier, in a country hereby. But as he was ready to be greatly advanced for some noble pieces of service which he did, he heard news of me: who (drunk in my affection to that unlawful and unnatural son of mine) suffered myself so to be governed by him, that all favors and punishments passed by him, all offices, and places of importance, distributed to his favorites; so that ere I was aware, I had left myself nothing but the name of a King: which he shortly weary of too, with many indignities (if anything may be called an indignity, which was laid upon me) threw me out of my seat, and put out my eyes; and then (proud in his tyranny) let me go, neither imprisoning, nor killing me: but rather delighting to make me feel my misery; misery indeed, if ever there were any: full of wretchedness, fuller of disgrace, and fullest of guiltiness. And as he came to the crown by so unjust means, as unjustly he kept it, by force of stranger soldiers in citadels, the nests of tyranny, & murderers of liberty; disarming all his own countrymen, that no man durst show himself a well-willer of mine: to say the truth (I think) few of them being so (considering my cruel folly to my good son, and foolish kindness to my unkind bastard): but if there were any who fell to pity of so great a fall, and had yet any sparks of unstained duty left in them towards me, yet durst they not show it, scarcely with giving me alms at their doors; which yet was the only sustenance of my distressed life, nobody daring to show so much charity, as to lend me a hand to guide my dark steps: Till this son of mine (God knows, worthy of a more virtuous, and more fortunate father) forgetting

my abominable wrongs, not recking danger, & neglecting
the present good way he was in doing himself good, came
hither to do this kind office you see him perform towards me, to my unspeakable grief; not only because his
kindness is a glass even to my blind eyes, of my naughtiness, but that above all griefs, it grieves me he should
desperately adventure the loss of his soul-deserving life
for mine, that yet owe more to fortune for my deserts,
as if he would carry mud in a chest of crystal. For well I
know, he that now reigneth, how much soever (and with
good reason) he despiseth me, of all men despised; yet
he will not let slip any advantage to make away him,
whose just title (ennobled by courage and goodness)
may one day shake the seat of a never secure tyranny.
And for this cause I craved of him to lead me to the top
of this rock, indeed I must confess, with meaning to free
him from so serpentine a companion as I am. But he finding what I purposed only therein since he was born,
showed himself disobedient unto me. And now Gentlemen, you have the true story, which I pray you publish
to the world, that my mischievous proceedings may be
the glory of his filial piety, the only reward now left for
so great a merit. And if it may be, let me obtain that of
you, which my son denies me: for never was there more
pity in saving any, than in ending me; both because
therein my agonies shall end, and so shall you preserve
this excellent young man, who else willfully follows his
own ruin.

The matter in itself lamentable, lamentably expressed
by the old Prince (which needed not take to himself
the gestures of pity, since his face could not put off the
marks thereof) greatly moved the two Princes to compassion, which could not stay in such hearts as theirs
without seeking remedy. But by and by the occasion was
presented: for Plexirtus (so was the bastard called) came
thither with forty horse, only of purpose to murder this
brother; of whose coming he had soon advertisement,
and thought no eyes of sufficient credit in such a matter, but his own; and therefore came himself to be
actor, and spectator. And as soon as he came, not

regarding the weak (as he thought) guard of but two
men, commanded some of his followers to set their hands
to his, in the killing of Leonatus. But the young Prince
(though not otherwise armed but with a sword) how
falsely soever he was dealt with by others, would not betray himself: but bravely drawing it out, made the death
of the first that assaulted him, warn his fellows to come
more warily after him. But then Pyrocles and Musidorus
were quickly become parties (so just a defense deserving as much as old friendship) and so did behave them
among that company (more injurious, than valiant) that
many of them lost their lives for their wicked master.

Yet perhaps had the number of them at last prevailed,
if the King of Pontus (lately by them made so) had not
come unlooked for to their succor. Who (having had a
dream which had fixed his imagination vehemently upon
some great danger, presently to follow those two Princes
whom he most dearly loved) was come in all haste, following as well as he could their track with a hundred
horses in that country, which he thought (considering
who then reigned) a fit place enough to make the stage
of any tragedy.

But then the match had been so ill made for Plexirtus,
that his ill-led life, & worse-gotten honor should have
tumbled together to destruction; had there not come in
Tydeus & Telenor, with forty or fifty in their suit, to the
defense of Plexirtus. These two were brothers, of the
noblest house of that country, brought up from their
infancy with Plexirtus: men of such prowess, as not to
know fear in themselves, and yet to teach it others that
should deal with them: for they had often made their
lives triumph over most terrible dangers; never dismayed
and ever fortunate; and truly no more settled in their
valor, than disposed to goodness and justice, if either
they had lighted on a better friend, or could have
learned to make friendship a child, and not the father of
virtue. But bringing up (rather than choice) having first
knit their minds unto him, (indeed crafty enough, either to hide his faults, or never to show them, but
when they might pay home) they willingly held out the

course, rather to satisfy him, than all the world; and
rather to be good friends, than good men: so as though
they did not like the evil he did, yet they liked him that
did the evil; and though not councilors of the offense, yet
protectors of the offender. Now they having heard of this
sudden going out, with so small a company, in a country full of evil-wishing minds toward him (though they
knew not the cause) followed him; till they found him in
such case as they were to venture their lives, or else he
to lose his: which they did with such force of mind and
body, that truly I may justly say, Pyrocles & Musidorus
had never till then found any, that could make them so
well repeat their hardest lesson in the feats of arms. And
briefly so they did, that if they overcame not; yet were
they not overcome, but carried away that ungrateful master of theirs to a place of security; howsoever the Princes
labored to the contrary. But this matter being thus far
begun, it became not the constancy of the Princes so to
leave it; but in all haste making forces both in Pontus
and Phrygia, they had in few days, left him but only
that one strong place where he was. For fear having
been the only knot that had fastened his people unto
him, that once untied by a greater force, they all scattered
from him; like so many birds, whose cage had been broken.

In which season the blind King (having in the chief
city of his realm, set the crown upon his son Leonatus'
head) with many tears (both of joy and sorrow) setting
forth to the whole people, his own fault & his son's virtue,
after he had kissed him, and forced his son to accept
honor of him (as of his new-become subject) even in a
moment died, as it should seem: his heart broken with
unkindness & affliction, stretched so far beyond his limits
with this excess of comfort, as it was able no longer to
keep safe his royal spirits. But the new King (having no
less lovingly performed all duties to him dead, than alive)
pursued on the siege of his unnatural brother, as much
for the revenge of his father, as for the establishing of
his own quiet. In which siege truly I cannot but acknowledge the prowess of those two brothers, than whom the

Princes never found in all their travel two men of greater ability to perform, nor of abler skill for conduct.

But Plexirtus finding, that if nothing else, famine would at last bring him to destruction, thought better by humbleness to creep, where by pride he could not march. For certainly so had nature formed him, & the exercise of craft conformed him to all turnings of sleights, that though no man had less goodness in his soul than he, no man could better find the places whence arguments might grow of goodness to another: though no man felt less pity, no man could tell better how to stir pity: no man more impudent to deny, where proofs were not manifest; no man more ready to confess with a repenting manner of aggravating his own evil, where denial would but make the fault fouler. Now he took this way, that having gotten a passport for one (that pretended he would put Plexirtus alive into his hands) to speak with the King his brother, he himself (though much against the minds of the valiant brothers, who rather wished to die in brave defense) with a rope about his neck, barefooted, came to offer himself to the discretion of Leonatus. Where what submission he used, how cunningly in making greater the fault he made the faultiness the less, how artificially he could set out the torments of his own conscience, with the burdensome cumber he had found of his ambitious desires, how finely seeming to desire nothing but death, as ashamed to live, he begged life, in the refusing it, I am not cunning enough to be able to express: but so fell out of it, that though at first sight Leonatus saw him with no other eye, than as the murderer of his father; & anger already began to paint revenge in many colors, ere long he had not only gotten pity, but pardon, and if not an excuse of the fault past, yet an opinion of future amendment: while the poor villains (chief ministers of his wickedness, now betrayed by the author thereof) were delivered to many cruel sorts of death; he so handling it, that it rather seemed, he had rather come into the defense of an unremediable mischief already committed, than that they had done it at first by his consent.

from *The True Chronicle History of King Leir*

Scene XXIV

Enter the Gallian King and Queen, and Mumford, with a basket, disguised like country folk.

King. This tedious journey all on foot, sweet Love,
 Cannot be pleasing to your tender joints,
 Which ne'er were used to these toilsome walks.

Cordella. I never in my life took more delight
 In any journey, than I do in this:
 It did me good, when as we hapt to light
 Amongst the merry crew of country folk,
 To see what industry and pains they took,
 To win them commendations 'mongst their friends.
 Lord, how they labor to bestir themselves,
 And in their quirks to go beyond the moon,
 And so take on them with such antic fits,
 That one would think they were beside their wits!
 Come away, Roger, with your basket.

Mumford. Soft, Dame, here comes a couple of old
   youths,
 I must needs make myself fat with jesting at them.

Cordella. Nay, prithy do not, they do seem to be
 Men much o'ergone with grief and misery.
 Let's stand aside, and harken what they say.

   [*Enter Leir and Perillus very faintly.*]

Leir. Ah, my Perillus, now I see we both
 Shall end our days in this unfruitful soil.
 Oh, I do faint for want of sustenance:
 And thou, I know, in little better case.
 No gentle tree affords one taste of fruit,
 To comfort us, until we meet with men:
 No lucky path conducts our luckless steps
 Unto a place where any comfort dwells.
 Sweet rest betide unto our happy souls;
 For here I see our bodies must have end.

Perillus. Ah, my dear Lord, how doth my heart
          lament,
     To see you brought to this extremity!
     O, if you love me, as you do profess,
     Or ever thought well of me in my life,
               [*He strips up his arm.*]
     Feed on this flesh, whose veins are not so dry
     But there is virtue left to comfort you.
     O, feed on this, if this will do you good,
     I'll smile for joy, to see you suck my blood.

Leir. I am no Cannibal, that I should delight
     To slake my hungry jaws with human flesh:
     I am no devil, or ten times worse than so,
     To suck the blood of such a peerless friend.
     O, do not think that I respect my life
     So dearly, as I do thy loyal love.
     Ah, Britain, I shall never see thee more,
     That hast unkindly banishèd thy King:
     And yet thou dost not make me to complain,
     But they which were more near to me than thou.

Cordella. What do I hear? this lamentable voice,
     Me thinks, ere now I oftentimes have heard.

Leir. Ah, Gonorill, was half my kingdom's gift
     The cause that thou didst seek to have my life?
     Ah, cruel Ragan, did I give thee all,
     And all could not suffice without my blood?
     Ah, poor Cordella, did I give thee nought,
     Nor never shall be able for to give?
     O, let me warn all ages that ensueth,
     How they trust flattery, and reject the truth.
     Well, unkind girls, I here forgive you both,
     Yet the just heavens will hardly do the like;
     And only crave forgiveness at the end
     Of good Cordella, and of thee, my friend;
     Of God, whose maiesty I have offended,
     By my transgression many thousand ways:
     Of her, dear heart, whom I for no occasion
     Turned out of all, through flatterers' persuasion:
     Of thee, kind friend, who but for me, I know,

Hadst never come unto this place of woe.

Cordella. Alack, that ever I should live to see
My noble father in this misery.

King. Sweet Love, reveal not what thou art as yet,
Until we know the ground of all this ill.

Cordella. O, but some meat, some meat: do you not see,
How near they are to death for want of food?

Perillus. Lord, which didst help thy servants at their need.
Or now or never send us help with speed.
Oh comfort, comfort! yonder is a banquet,
And men and women, my Lord: be of good cheer;
For I see comfort coming very near.
O my Lord, a banquet, and men and women!

Leir. O, let kind pity mollify their hearts,
That they may help us in our great extremes.

Perillus. God save you, friends; & if this blessèd banquet
Affordeth any food or sustenance,
Even for his sake that saved us all from death,
Vouchsafe to save us from the grip of famine.

[She bringeth him to the table.]

Cordella. Here father, sit and eat, here sit and drink:
And would it were far better for your sakes.

Perillus takes Leir by the hand to the table.

Perillus. I'll give you thanks anon: my friend doth faint,
And needeth present comfort.

[Leir drinks.]

Mumford. I warrant, he ne'er stays to say grace:
O, there's no sauce to a good stomach.

Perillus. The blessed God of heaven hath thought upon us.

Leir. The thanks be his, and these kind courteous folk,
By whose humanity we are preserved.

They eat hungrily, Leir drinks.

Cordella. And may that draught be unto him, as was
    That which old Eson drank, which did renew
    His withered age, and made him young again.
    And may that meat be unto him, as was
    That which Elias ate, in strength whereof
    He walkèd forty days, and never fainted.
    Shall I conceal me longer from my father?
    Or shall I manifest myself to him?

King. Forbear a while, until his strength return,
    Lest being overjoyed with seeing thee,
    His poor weak senses should forsake their office,
    And so our cause of joy be turned to sorrow.

Perillus. What cheer, my Lord? how do you feel
    yourself?

Leir. Me thinks, I never ate such savory meat:
    It is as pleasant as the blessed manna,
    That rained from heaven amongst the Israelites:
    It hath recalled my spirits home again,
    And made me fresh, as erst I was before.
    But how shall we congratulate their kindness?

Perillus. In faith, I know not how sufficiently;
    But the best mean that I can think on, is this:
    I'll offer them my doublet in requital;
    For we have nothing else to spare.

Leir. Nay, stay, Perillus, for they shall have mine.

Perillus. Pardon, my Lord, I swear they shall have
    mine.

    Perillus proffers his doublet: they will not take it.

Leir. Ah, who would think such kindness should
    remain
    Among such strange and unacquainted men:
    And that such hate should harbor in the breast
    Of those, which have occasion to be best?

Cordella. Ah, good old father, tell to me thy grief,
    I'll sorrow with thee, if not add relief.

Leir. Ah, good young daughter, I may call thee so;
    For thou art like a daughter I did owe.

Cordella. Do you not owe her still? what, is she dead?

Leir. No, God forbid: but all my interest's gone,
 By showing myself too much unnatural:
 So have I lost the title of a father,
 And may be called a stranger to her rather.

Cordella. Your title's good still; for 'tis always known,
 A man may do as him list with his own.
 But have you but one daughter then in all?

Leir. Yes, I have more by two, than would I had.

Cordella. O, say not so, but rather see the end:
 They that are bad, may have the grace to mend:
 But how have they offended you so much?

Leir. If from the first I should relate the cause,
 'Twould make a heart of adamant to weep;
 And thou, poor soule, kindhearted as thou art,
 Dost weep already, ere I do begin.

Cordella. For God's love tell it, and when you have
  done,
 I'll tell the reason why I weep so soon.

Leir. Then know this first, I am a Briton born,
 And had three daughters by one loving wife;
 And though I say it, of beauty they were sped;
 Especially the youngest of the three,
 For her perfections hardly matched could be:
 On these I doted with a jealous love,
 And thought to try which of them loved me best,
 By asking them, which would do most for me?
 The first and second flattered me with words,
 And vowed they loved me better than their lives:
 The youngest said, she loved me as a child
 Might do: her answer I esteemed most vile,
 And presently in an outrageous mood,
 I turned her from me to go sink or swim:
 And all I had, even to the very clothes,
 I gave in dowry with the other two:
 And she that best deserved the greatest share,
 I gave her nothing, but disgrace and care.
 Now mark the sequel: When I had done thus,

I sojourned in my eldest daughter's house,
Where for a time I was entreated well,
And lived in state sufficing my content:
But every day her kindness did grow cold,
Which I with patience put up well enough,
And seemed not to see the things I saw:
But at the last she grew so far incensed
With moody fury, and with causeless hate,
That in most vile and contumelious terms,
She bade me pack, and harbor somewhere else.
Then was I fain for refuge to repair
Unto my other daughter for relief,
Who gave me pleasing and most courteous words;
But in her actions showed herself so sore,
As never any daughter did before:
She prayed me in a morning out betime,
To go to a thicket two miles from the court,
Pointing that there she would come talk with me:
There she had set a shag-haired murdering wretch,
To massacre my honest friend and me.
Then judge yourself, although my tale be brief,
If ever man had greater cause of grief.

King. Nor never like impiety was done,
Since the creation of the world begun.

Leir. And now I am constrained to seek relief
Of her, to whom I have been so unkind;
Whose censure, if it do award me death,
I must confess she pays me but my due:
But if she show a loving daughter's part,
It comes of God and her, not my desert.

Cordella. No doubt she will, I dare be sworn she will.

Leir. How know you that, not knowing what she is?

Cordella. Myself a father have a great way hence,
Used me as ill as ever you did her;
Yet, that his reverend age I once might see,
I'd creep along, to meet him on my knee.

Leir. O, no men's children are unkind but mine.

Cordella. Condemn not all, because of other's crime:

But look, dear father, look, behold and see
Thy loving daughter speaketh unto thee.

[She kneels.]

Leir. O, stand thou up, it is my part to kneel,
And ask forgiveness for my former faults.

[He kneels.]

Cordella. O, if you wish I should enjoy my breath,
Dear father rise, or I receive my death.

[He riseth.]

Leir. Then I will rise, to satisfy your mind,
But kneel again, till pardon be resigned.

[He kneels.]

Cordella. I pardon you: the word beseems not me:
But I do say so, for to ease your knee.
You gave me life, you were the cause that I
Am what I am, who else had never been.

Leir. But you gave life to me and to my friend,
Whose days had else, had an untimely end.

Cordella. You brought me up, when as I was but
young,
And far unable for to help myself.

Leir. I cast thee forth, when as thou wast but young,
And far unable for to help thyself.

Cordella. God, world and nature say I do you wrong,
That can endure to see you kneel so long.

King. Let me break off this loving controversy,
Which doth rejoice my very soul to see.
Good father, rise, she is your loving daughter,

[He riseth.]

And honors you with as respective duty.
As if you were the monarch of the world.

Cordella. But I will never rise from off my knee,
Until I have your blessing, and your pardon
Of all my faults committed any way,
From my first birth unto this present day.

Leir. The blessing, which the God of Abraham gave

Unto the tribe of Juda, light on thee,
And multiply thy days, that thou mayst see
Thy children's children prosper after thee.
Thy faults, which are just none that I do know,
God pardon on high, and I forgive below.

[She riseth.]

Cordella. Now is my heart at quiet, and doth leap
Within my breast, for joy of this good hap:
And now (dear father) welcome to our court,
And welcome (kind Perillus) unto me,
Mirror of virtue and true honesty.

Leir. O, he hath been the kindest friend to me,
That ever man had in adversity.

Perillus. My tongue doth fail, to say what heart
doth think,
I am so ravished with exceeding joy.

King. All you have spoke: now let me speak my mind,
And in few words much matter here conclude:

[He kneels.]

If ere my heart do harbor any joy,
Or true content repose within my breast,
Till I have rooted out this viperous sect,
And repossessed my father of his crown,
Let me be counted for the perjuredest man,
That ever spoke word since the world began.

[Rise.]

Mumford. Let me pray too, that never prayed before;

[Mumford kneels.]

If ere I resalute the British earth,
(As [ere't be long] I do presume I shall)
And do return from thence without my wench,
Let me gelded from my recompense.

[Rise.]

King. Come, let's to arms for to redress this wrong:
Till I am there, me thinks, the time seems long.

[Exeunt.]

Commentaries

Samuel Johnson.

From "Preface to Shakespeare" and "King Lear

PREFACE TO SHAKESPEARE

Nothing can please many, and please long, but just representations of general nature. Particular manners can be known to few, and therefore few only can judge how nearly they are copied. The irregular combinations of fanciful invention may delight awhile, by that novelty of which the common satiety of life sends us all in quest; but the pleasures of sudden wonder are soon exhausted, and the mind can only repose on the stability of truth.

Shakespeare is above all writers, at least above all modern writers, the poet of nature; the poet that holds up to his readers a faithful mirror of manners and of life. His characters are not modified by the customs of particular places, unpracticed by the rest of the world; by the peculiarities of studies or professions, which can operate but upon small numbers; or by the accidents of transient fashions or temporary opinions: they are the genuine progeny of common humanity, such as the world will always supply, and observation will always find. His persons act and speak by the influence of those general passions and principles by which all minds are agitated, and the whole system of life is continued in motion. In the writings of other poets a character is too often an individual; in those of Shakespeare it is commonly a species.

It is from this wide extension of design that so much instruction is derived. It is this which fills the plays of

From *The Plays of William Shakespeare*, London, 1765.

Shakespeare with practical axioms and domestic wisdom. It was said of Euripides, that every verse was a precept; and it may be said of Shakespeare, that from his works may be collected a system of civil and economical prudence. Yet his real power is not shown in the splendor of particular passages, but by the progress of his fable, and, the tenor of his dialogue; and he that tries to recommend him by select quotations, will succeed like the pedant in *Hierocles,* who, when he offered his house to sale, carried a brick in his pocket as a specimen. . . .

Other dramatists can only gain attention by hyperbolical or aggravated characters, by fabulous and unexampled excellence or depravity, as the writers of barbarous romances invigorated the reader by a giant and a dwarf; and he that should form his expectations of human affairs from the play, or from the tale, would be equally deceived. Shakespeare has no heroes; his scenes are occupied only by men, who act and speak as the reader thinks that he should himself have spoken or acted on the same occasion: Even where the agency is supernatural the dialogue is level with life. Other writers disguise the most natural passions and most frequent incidents; so that he who contemplates them in the book will not know them in the world: Shakespeare approximates the remote, and familiarizes the wonderful; the event which he represents will not happen, but if it were possible, its effects would be probably such as he has assigned; and it may be said, that he has not only shown human nature as it acts in real exigencies, but as it would be found in trials, to which it cannot be exposed.

This therefore is the praise of Shakespeare, that his drama is the mirror of life; that he who has mazed his imagination, in following the phantoms which other writers raise up before him, may here be cured of his delirious ecstasies, by reading human sentiments in human language; by scenes from which a hermit may estimate the transactions of the world, and a confessor predict the progress of the passions. . . .

The censure which he has incurred by mixing comic

and tragic scenes, as it extends to all his works, deserves more consideration. Let the fact be first stated, and then examined.

Shakespeare's plays are not in the rigorous and critical sense either tragedies or comedies, but compositions of a distinct kind; exhibiting the real state of sublunary nature, which partakes of good and evil, joy and sorrow, mingled with endless variety of proportion and innumerable modes of combination; and expressing the course of the world, in which the loss of one is the gain of another; in which, at the same time, the reveler is hasting to his wine, and the mourner burying his friend; in which the malignity of one is sometimes defeated by the frolic of another; and many mischiefs and many benefits are done and hindered without design.

Out of this chaos of mingled purposes and casualties the ancient poets, according to the laws which custom had prescribed, selected some the crimes of men, and some their absurdities; some the momentous vicissitudes of life, and some the lighter occurrences; some the terrors of distress, and some the gaieties of prosperity. Thus rose the two modes of imitation, known by the names of *tragedy* and *comedy,* compositions intended to promote different ends by contrary means, and considered as so little allied, that I do not recollect among the Greeks or Romans a single writer who attempted both.

Shakespeare has united the powers of exciting laughter and sorrow not only in one mind but in one composition. Almost all his plays are divided between serious and ludicrous characters, and, in the successive evolutions of the design, sometimes produce seriousness and sorrow, and sometimes levity and laughter.

That this is a practice contrary to the rules of criticism will be readily allowed; but there is always an appeal open from criticism to nature. The end of writing is to instruct; the end of poetry is to instruct by pleasing. That the mingled drama may convey all the instruction of tragedy or comedy cannot be denied, because it includes both in its alternations of exhibition, and approaches nearer than either to the appearance of life, by showing how great machinations and slender designs may promote or obviate one another, and the high and the low cooperate in the general system by unavoidable concatenation.

It is objected, that by this change of scenes the passions are interrupted in their progression, and that the principal event, being not advanced by a due gradation of preparatory incidents, wants at last the power to move, which constitutes the perfection of dramatic poetry. This reasoning is so specious, that it is received as true even by those who in daily experience feel it to be false. The interchanges of mingled scenes seldom fail to produce the intended vicissitudes of passion. Fiction cannot move so much, but that the attention may be easily transferred; and though it must be allowed that pleasing melancholy be sometimes interrupted by unwelcome levity, yet let it be considered likewise, that melancholy is often not pleasing, and that the disturbance of one man may be the relief of another; that different auditors have different habitudes; and that, upon the whole, all pleasure consists in variety. . . .

Shakespeare engaged in dramatic poetry with the world open before him; the rules of the ancients were yet known to few; the public judgment was unformed; he had no example of such fame as might force him upon imitation, nor critics of such authority as might restrain his extravagance: He therefore indulged his natural disposition, and his disposition, as Rymer has remarked, led him to comedy. In tragedy he often writes with great appearance of toil and study, what is written at last with little felicity; but in his comic scenes, he seems to produce without labor, what no labor can improve. In tragedy he is always struggling after some occasion to be comic, but in comedy he seems to repose, or to luxuriate, as in a mode of thinking congenial to his nature. In his tragic scenes there is always something wanting, but his comedy often surpasses expectation or desire. His comedy pleases by the thoughts and the language, and his tragedy for the greater part by incident and action. His tragedy seems to be skill, his comedy to be instinct.

The force of his comic scenes has suffered little diminution from the changes made by a century and a half, in manners or in words. As his personages act upon principles arising from genuine passion, very little modified by particular forms, their pleasures and vexations are communicable to all times and to all places; they are natural, and therefore durable; the adventitious peculiarities of personal habits are only superficial dyes, bright and pleasing for a little while, yet soon fading to a dim tinct, without any remains of former luster; but the discriminations of true passion are the colors of nature; they pervade the whole mass, and can only perish with the body that exhibits them. The accidental compositions of heterogeneous modes are dissolved by the chance which combined them; but the uniform simplicity of primitive qualities neither admits increase, nor suffers decay. The sand heaped by one flood is scattered by another, but the rock always continues in its place. The stream of time, which is continually washing the dissoluble fabrics of other poets, passes without injury by the adamant of Shakespeare.

If there be, what I believe there is, in every nation, a style which never becomes obsolete, a certain mode of phraseology so consonant and congenial to the analogy and principles of its respective language as to remain settled and unaltered; this style is probably to be sought in the common intercourse of life, among those who speak only to be understood, without ambition of elegance. The polite are always catching modish innovations, and the learned depart from established forms of speech, in hope of finding or making better; those who wish for distinction forsake the vulgar, when the vulgar is right; but there is a conversation above grossness and below refinement, where propriety resides, and where this poet seems to have gathered his comic dialogue. He is therefore more agreeable to the ears of the present age than any other author equally remote, and among his other excellencies deserves to be studied as one of the original masters of our language. . . .

Shakespeare with his excellencies has likewise faults, and faults sufficient to obscure and overwhelm any other merit. I shall show them in the proportion in which they appear to me, without envious malignity or superstitious veneration. No question can be more innocently discussed than a dead poet's pretensions to renown; and little regard is due to that bigotry which sets candor higher than truth.

His first defect is that to which may be imputed most of the evil in books or in men. He sacrifices virtue to convenience, and is so much more careful to please than to instruct, that he seems to write without any moral purpose. From his writings indeed a system of social duty may be selected, for he that thinks reasonably must think morally; but his precepts and axioms drop casually from him; he makes no just distribution of good or evil, nor is always careful to show in the virtuous a disapprobation of the wicked; he carries his persons indifferently through right and wrong, and at the close dismisses them without further care, and leaves their examples to operate by chance. This fault the barbarity of his age cannot extenuate; for it is always a writer's duty to make the world better, and justice is a virtue independent on time or place.

The plots are often so loosely formed, that a very slight consideration may improve them, and so carelessly pursued, that he seems not always fully to comprehend his own design. He omits opportunities of instructing or delighting which the train of his story seems to force upon him, and apparently rejects those exhibitions which would be more affecting, for the sake of those which are more easy.

It may be observed, that in many of his plays the latter part is evidently neglected. When he found himself near the end of his work, and, in view of his reward, he shortened the labor, to snatch the profit. He therefore remits his efforts where he should most vigorously exert them, and his catastrophe is improbably produced or imperfectly represented.

He had no regard to distinction of time or place, but

gives to one age or nation, without scruple, the customs, institutions, and opinions of another, at the expense not only of likelihood, but of possibility. . . .

In tragedy his performance seems constantly to be worse, as his labor is more. The effusions of passion which exigence forces out are for the most part striking and energetic; but whenever he solicits his invention, or strains his faculties, the offspring of his throes is tumor, meanness, tediousness, and obscurity.

In narration he affects a disproportionate pomp of diction and a wearisome train of circumlocution, and tells the incident imperfectly in many words, which might have been more plainly delivered in few. Narration in dramatic poetry is naturally tedious, as it is unanimated and inactive, and obstructs the progress of the action; it should therefore always be rapid, and enlivened by frequent interruption. Shakespeare found it an encumbrance, and instead of lightening it by brevity, endeavored to recommend it by dignity and splendor.

His declamations or set speeches are commonly cold and weak, for his power was the power of nature; when he endeavored, like other tragic writers, to catch opportunities of amplification, and instead of inquiring what the occasion demanded, to show how much his stores of knowledge could supply, he seldom escapes without the pity or resentment of his reader.

It is incident to him to be now and then entangled with an unwieldy sentiment, which he cannot well express, and will not reject; he struggles with it a while, and if it continues stubborn, comprises it in words such as occur, and leaves it to be disentangled and evolved by those who have more leisure to bestow upon it.

Not that always where the language is intricate the thought is subtle, or the image always great where the line is bulky; the equality of words to things is very often neglected, and trivial sentiments and vulgar ideas disappoint the attention, to which they are recommended by sonorous epithets and swelling figures.

But the admirers of this great poet have never less

reason to indulge their hopes of supreme excellence, than when he seems fully resolved to sink them in dejection, and mollify them with tender emotions by the fall of greatness, the danger of innocence, or the crosses of love. He is not long soft and pathetic without some idle conceit, or contemptible equivocation. He no sooner begins to move, than he counteracts himself; and terror and pity, as they are rising in the mind, are checked and blasted by sudden frigidity.

A quibble is to Shakespeare, what luminous vapors are to the traveler; he follows it at all adventures, it is sure to lead him out of his way, and sure to engulf him in the mire. It has some malignant power over his mind, and its fascinations are irresistible. Whatever be the dignity or profundity of his disquisition, whether he be enlarging knowledge or exalting affection, whether he be amusing attention with incidents, or enchaining it in suspense, let but a quibble spring up before him, and he leaves his work unfinished. A quibble is the golden apple for which he will always turn aside from his career, or stoop from his elevation. A quibble, poor and barren as it is, gave him such delight, that he was content to purchase it, by the sacrifice of reason, propriety and truth. A quibble was to him the fatal Cleopatra for which he lost the world, and was content to lose it.

It will be thought strange, that, in enumerating the defects of this writer, I have not yet mentioned his neglect of the unities; his violation of those laws which have been instituted and established by the joint authority of poets and critics.

For his other deviations from the art of writing I resign him to critical justice, without making any other demand in his favor, than that which must be indulged to all human excellence; that his virtues be rated with his failings: But, from the censure which this irregularity may bring upon him, I shall, with due reverence to that learning which I must oppose, adventure to try how I can defend him.

His histories, being neither tragedies nor comedies, are not subject to any of their laws; nothing more is necessary to all the praise which they expect, than that the changes of action be so prepared as to be understood, that the incidents be various and affecting, and the characters consistent, natural and distinct. No other unity is intended, and therefore none is to be sought.

In his other works he has well enough preserved the unity of action. He has not, indeed, an intrigue regularly perplexed and regularly unraveled; he does not endeavor to hide his design only to discover it, for this is seldom the order of real events, and Shakespeare is the poet of nature: But his plan has commonly what Aristotle requires, a beginning, a middle, and an end; one event is concatenated with another, and the conclusion follows by easy consequence. There are perhaps some incidents that might be spared, as in other poets there is much talk that only fills up time upon the stage; but the general system makes gradual advances, and the end of the play is the end of expectation.

To the unities of time and place he has shown no regard, and perhaps a nearer view of the principles on which they stand will diminish their value, and withdraw from them the veneration which, from the time of Corneille, they have very generally received by discovering that they have given more trouble to the poet, than pleasure to the auditor.

The necessity of observing the unities of time and place arises from the supposed necessity of making the drama credible. The critics hold it impossible, that an action of months or years can be possibly believed to pass in three hours; or that the spectator can suppose himself to sit in the theater, while ambassadors go and return between distant kings, while armies are levied and towns besieged, while an exile wanders and returns, or till he whom they saw courting his mistress, shall lament the untimely fall of his son. The mind revolts from evident falsehood, and fiction loses its force when it departs from the resemblance of reality.

From the narrow limitation of time necessarily arises the contraction of place. The spectator, who knows that he saw the first act at Alexandria, cannot suppose that he sees the next at Rome, at a distance to which not the dragons of Medea could, in so short a time, have transported him; he knows with certainty that he has not changed his place; and he knows that place cannot change itself; that what was a house cannot become a plain; that what was Thebes can never be Persepolis.

Such is the triumphant language with which a critic exults over the misery of an irregular poet, and exults commonly without resistance or reply. It is time therefore to tell him, by the authority of Shakespeare, that he assumes, as an unquestionable principle, a position, which, while his breath is forming it into words, his understanding pronounces to be false. . . .

There is no reason why a mind thus wandering in ecstasy should count the clock, or why an hour should not be a century in that calenture of the brains that can make the stage a field.

The truth is, that the spectators are always in their senses, and know, from the first act to the last, that the stage is only a stage, and that the players are only players. They came to hear a certain number of lines recited with just gesture and elegant modulation. The lines relate to some action, and an action must be in some place; but the different actions that complete a story may be in places very remote from each other. . . .

Time is, of all modes of existence, most obsequious to the imagination; a lapse of years is as easily conceived as a passage of hours. In contemplation we easily contract the time of real actions, and therefore willingly permit it to be contracted when we only see their imitation.

It will be asked, how the drama moves, if it is not credited. It is credited with all the credit due to a drama. It is credited, whenever it moves, as a just picture of a real original; as representing to the auditor what he would himself feel, if he were to do or suffer what is there feigned to be suffered or to be done. The reflection that strikes the heart is not, that the evils before us are real evils, but that they are evils to which we ourselves may be exposed. If there be any fallacy, it is not that we fancy the players, but that we fancy ourselves unhappy for a moment; but we rather lament the possibility than suppose the presence of misery, as a mother weeps over her babe, when she remembers that death may take it from her. The delight of tragedy proceeds from our consciousness of fiction; if we thought murders and treasons real, they would please no more. . . .

[Shakespeare's] plots, whether historical or fabulous, are always crowded with incidents, by which the attention of a rude people was more easily caught than by sentiment or argumentation; and such is the power of the marvelous even over those who despise it, that every man finds his mind more strongly seized by the tragedies of Shakespeare than of any other writer; others please us by particular speeches, but he always makes us anxious for the event, and has perhaps excelled all but Homer in securing the first purpose of a writer, by exciting restless and unquenchable curiosity and compelling him that reads his work to read it through.

The shows and bustle with which his plays abound have the same original. As knowledge advances, pleasure passes from the eye to the ear, but returns, as it declines, from the ear to the eye. Those to whom our author's labors were exhibited had more skill in pomps or processions than in poetical language, and perhaps wanted some visible and discriminated events, as comments on the dialogue. He knew how he should most please; and whether his practice is more agreeable to nature, or whether his example has prejudiced the nation, we still find that on our stage something must be done as well as said, and inactive declamation is very coldly heard, however musical or elegant, passionate or sublime. . . .

KING LEAR

The Tragedy of *Lear* is deservedly celebrated among the dramas of Shakespeare. There is perhaps no play which keeps the attention so strongly fixed; which so much agitates our passions and interests our curiosity. The artful involutions of distinct interests, the striking opposition of contrary characters, the sudden changes of fortune, and the quick succession of events, fill the mind with a perpetual tumult of indignation, pity, and hope. There is no scene which does not contribute to the aggravation of the distress or conduct of the action, and scarce a line which does not conduce to the progress of the scene. So powerful is the current of the poet's imagination, that the mind, which once ventures within it, is hurried irresistibly along.

On the seeming improbability of Lear's conduct, it may be observed that he is represented according to histories at that time vulgarly received as true. And perhaps if we turn our thoughts upon the barbarity and ignorance of the age to which this story is referred, it will appear not so unlikely as while we estimate Lear's manners by our own. Such preference of one daughter to another, or resignation of dominion on such conditions, would be yet credible, if told of a petty prince of Guinea or Madagascar. Shakespeare, indeed, by the mention of his Earls and Dukes, has given us the idea of times more civilized, and of life regulated by softer manners; and the truth is, that though he so nicely discriminates, and so minutely describes the characters of men, he commonly neglects and confounds the characters of ages, by mingling customs ancient and modern, English and foreign.

My learned friend Mr. Warton, who has in the *Adventurer* very minutely criticized this play, remarks, that the instances of cruelty are too savage and shocking, and that the intervention of Edmund destroys the simplicity of the story. These objections may, I think, be answered, by repeating, that the cruelty of the daughters is an historical fact, to which the poet has added little, having only drawn it into a series by dialogue and action. But I am not able to apologize with equal plausibility for the extrusion of Gloucester's eyes, which seems an act too horrid to be endured in dramatic exhibition, and such as must always compel the mind to relieve its distress by incredulity. Yet let it be remembered that our author well knew what would please the audience for which he wrote.

The injury done by Edmund to the simplicity of the action is abundantly recompensed by the addition of variety, by the art with which he is made to cooperate with the chief design, and the opportunity which he gives the poet of combining perfidy with perfidy, and connecting the wicked son with the wicked daughters, to impress this important moral, that villainy is never at a stop, that crimes lead to crimes, and at last terminate in ruin.

But though this moral be incidentally enforced, Shakespeare has suffered the virtue of Cordelia to perish in a just cause, contrary to the natural ideas of justice, to the hope of the reader, and, what is yet more strange, to the faith of chronicles. Yet this conduct is justified by the Spectator, who blames Tate for giving Cordelia success and happiness in his alteration, and declares, that, in his opinion, *the tragedy has lost half its beauty*. Dennis has remarked, whether justly or not, that, to secure the favorable reception of *Cato, the town was poisoned with much false and abominable criticism,* and that endeavors had been used to discredit and decry poetical justice. A play in which the wicked prosper, and the virtuous miscarry, may doubtless be good, because it is a just representation of the common events of human life: but since all reasonable beings naturally love justice, I cannot easily be persuaded, that the observation of justice makes a play worse; or, that if other excellencies are equal, the audience will not always rise better pleased from the final triumph of persecuted virtue.

In the present case the public has decided. Cordelia, from the time of Tate, has always retired with victory and felicity. And, if my sensations could add anything to the general suffrage, I might relate, that I was many years ago shocked by Cordelia's death, that I know not whether I ever endured to read again the last scenes of the play till I undertook to revise them as an editor.

A. C. Bradley

From *Shakespearean Tragedy*

. . . [The] chief value [of the double action in
King Lear] is not merely dramatic. It lies in the fact—
in Shakespeare without a parallel—that the subplot simply repeats the theme of the main story. Here, as there,
we see an old man "with a white beard." He, like Lear, is
affectionate, unsuspicious, foolish, and self-willed. He,
too, wrongs deeply a child who loves him not less for
the wrong. He, too, meets with monstrous ingratitude
from the child whom he favors, and is tortured and
driven to death. This repetition does not simply double
the pain with which the tragedy is witnessed: it startles
and terrifies by suggesting that the folly of Lear and the
ingratitude of his daughters are no accidents or merely
individual aberrations, but that in that dark cold world
some fateful malignant influence is abroad, turning the
hearts of the fathers against their children and of the
children against their fathers, smiting the earth with a
curse, so that the brother gives the brother to death and
the father the son, blinding the eyes, maddening the
brain, freezing the springs of pity, numbing all powers
except the nerves of anguish and the dull lust of life.

Hence too, as well as from other sources, comes that
feeling which haunts us in *King Lear,* as though we

From *Shakespearean Tragedy* by A. C. Bradley. London: Macmillan
& Co., Ltd., 1904. Reprinted by permission of Macmillan & Co., Ltd.
(London), St Martin's Press, Inc. (New York), and the Macmillan
Company of Canada, Ltd.

were witnessing something universal—a conflict not so much of particular persons as of the powers of good and evil in the world. And the treatment of many of the characters confirms this feeling. Considered simply as psychological studies few of them, surely, are of the highest interest. Fine and subtle touches could not be absent from a work of Shakespeare's maturity; but, with the possible exception of Lear himself, no one of the characters strikes us as psychologically a *wonderful* creation, like Hamlet or Iago or even Macbeth; one or two seem even to be somewhat faint and thin. And, what is more significant, it is not quite natural to us to regard them from this point of view at all. Rather we observe a most unusual circumstance. If Lear, Gloster and Albany are set apart, the rest fall into two distinct groups, which are strongly, even violently, contrasted: Cordelia, Kent, Edgar, the Fool on one side, Goneril, Regan, Edmund, Cornwall, Oswald on the other. These characters are in various degrees individualized, most of them completely so; but still in each group there is a quality common to all the members, or one spirit breathing through them all. Here we have unselfish and devoted love, there hard self-seeking. On both sides, further, the common quality takes an extreme form; the love is incapable of being chilled by injury, the selfishness of being softened by pity; and, it may be added, this tendency to extremes is found again in the characters of Lear and Gloster, and is the main source of the accusations of improbability directed against their conduct at certain points. Hence the members of each group tend to appear, at least in part, as varieties of one species; the radical differences of the two species are emphasized in broad hard strokes; and the two are set in conflict, almost as if Shakespeare, like Empedocles, were regarding Love and Hate as the two ultimate forces of the universe.

The presence in *King Lear* of so large a number of characters in whom love or self-seeking is so extreme, has another effect. They do not merely inspire in us emotions of unusual strength, but they also stir the intellect to wonder and speculation. How can there be such men and women? we ask ourselves. How comes it that humanity can take such absolutely opposite forms? And, in particular, to what omission of elements which should be present in human nature, or, if there is no omission, to what distortion of these elements is it due that such beings as some of these come to exist? This is a question which Iago (and perhaps no previous creation of Shakespeare's) forces us to ask, but in *King Lear* it is provoked again and again. And more, it seems to us that the author himself is asking this question: "Then let them anatomize Regan, see what breeds about her heart. Is there any cause in nature that makes these hard hearts?" —the strain of thought which appears here seems to be present in some degree throughout the play. We seem to trace the tendency which, a few years later, produced Ariel and Caliban, the tendency of imagination to analyze and abstract, to decompose human nature into its constituent factors, and then to construct beings in whom one or more of these factors is absent or atrophied or only incipient. This, of course, is a tendency which produces symbols, allegories, personifications of qualities and abstract ideas; and we are accustomed to think it quite foreign to Shakespeare's genius, which was in the highest degree concrete. No doubt in the main we are right here; but it is hazardous to set limits to that genius. The Sonnets, if nothing else, may show us, how easy it was to Shakespeare's mind to move in a world of "Platonic" ideas; and, while it would be going too far to suggest that he was employing conscious symbolism or allegory in *King Lear,* it does appear to disclose a mode of imagination not so very far removed from the mode with which, we must remember, Shakespeare was perfectly familiar in Morality plays and in the *Fairy Queen.*

This same tendency shows itself in *King Lear* in other forms. To it is due the idea of monstrosity—of beings, actions, states of mind, which appear not only abnormal but absolutely contrary to nature; an idea, which, of course, is common enough in Shakespeare, but appears with unusual frequency in *King Lear*, for instance in the lines:

> Ingratitude, thou marble-hearted fiend,
> More hideous when thou show'st thee in a child
> Than the sea-monster!

or in the exclamation,

> Filial ingratitude!
> Is it not as this mouth should tear this hand
> For lifting food to't?

It appears in another shape in that most vivid passage where Albany, as he looks at the face which had bewitched him, now distorted with dreadful passions, suddenly sees it in a new light and exclaims in horror:

> Thou changed and self-cover'd thing, for shame,
> Bemonster not thy feature. Were't my fitness
> To let these hands obey my blood,
> They are apt enough to dislocate and tear
> Thy flesh and bones: howe'er thou art a fiend,
> A woman's shape doth shield thee.

It appears once more in that exclamation of Kent's, as he listens to the description of Cordelia's grief:

> It is the stars,
> The stars above us, govern our conditions;
> Else one self mate and mate could not beget
> Such different issues.

(This is not the only sign that Shakespeare had been musing over heredity, and wondering how it comes about that the composition of two strains of blood or two parent souls can produce such astonishingly different products.)

This mode of thought is responsible, lastly, for a very striking characteristic of *King Lear*—one in which it has no parallel except *Timon*—the incessant references to the lower animals and man's likeness to them. These references are scattered broadcast through the whole play as though Shakespeare's mind were so busy with the subject that he could hardly write a page without some allusion to it. The dog, the horse, the cow, the sheep, the hog, the lion, the bear, the wolf, the fox, the monkey, the polecat, the civet cat, the pelican, the owl, the crow, the chough, the wren, the fly, the butterfly, the rat, the mouse, the frog, the tadpole, the wall newt, the water newt, the worm—I am sure I cannot have completed the list, and some of them are mentioned again and again. Often, of course, and especially in the talk of Edgar as the Bedlam, they have no symbolical meaning; but not seldom, even in his talk, they are expressly referred to for their typical qualities—"hog in sloth, fox in stealth, wolf in greediness, dog in madness, lion in prey," "The fitchew nor the soiled horse goes to't with a more riotous appetite." Sometimes a person in the drama is compared, openly or implicitly, with one of them. Goneril is a kite: her ingratitude has a serpent's tooth: she has struck her father most serpentlike upon the very heart: her visage is wolfish: she has tied sharp-toothed unkindness like a vulture on her father's breast: for her husband she is a gilded serpent: to Gloster her cruelty seems to have the fangs of a boar. She and Regan are dog-hearted: they are tigers, not daughters: each is an adder to the other: the flesh of each is covered with the fell of a beast. Oswald is a mongrel, and the son and heir of a mongrel: ducking to everyone in power, he is a wag-tail: white with fear, he is a goose. Gloster, for Regan, is an ingrateful fox: Albany, for his wife, has a cowish spirit and is milk-liver'd: when Edgar as the Bedlam first appeared to Lear he made him think a man a worm. As we read, the souls of all the beasts in turn seem to us to have entered the bodies of these mortals; horrible in their venom, savagery, lust, deceitfulness, sloth, cruelty, filthiness; miserable in their feebleness, nakedness, defenselessness, blindness; and man, "consider him well," is even what they are. Shakespeare, to whom the idea of the transmigration of souls was familiar and had once been material for jest,[1] seems to have been brooding on humanity, in the light of it. It is remarkable, and somewhat sad, that he seems to find none of man's better qualities in the world of the brutes (though he might well have found the prototype of the selfless love of Kent and Cordelia in the dog whom he so habitually maligns); but he seems to have been asking himself whether that which he loathes in man may not be due to some strange wrenching of this frame of things, through which the lower animal souls have found a lodgment in human forms, and there found—to the horror and confusion of the thinking mind—brains to forge, tongues to speak, and hands to act, enormities which no mere brute can conceive or execute. He shows us in *King Lear* these terrible forces bursting into monstrous life and flinging themselves upon those human beings who are weak and defenseless, partly from old age, but partly because they *are* human and lack the dreadful undivided energy of the beast. And the only comfort he might seem to hold out to us is the prospect that at least this bestial race, strong only where it is vile, cannot endure: though stars and gods are powerless, or careless, or empty dreams, yet there must be an end of this horrible world:

[1] *E.g.* in *As You Like It*, III. ii. 187, "I was never so berhymed since Pythagoras' time, that I was an Irish rat, which I can hardly remember"; *Twelfth Night*, IV. ii. 55, *"Clown.* What is the opinion of Pythagoras concerning wild fowl? *Mal.* That the soul of our grandam might haply inhabit a bird. *Clown.* What thinkest thou of his opinion? *Mal.* I think nobly of the soul, and no way approve his opinion," etc. But earlier comes a passage which reminds us of *King Lear, Merchant of Venice,* IV. i. 128:

> O be thou damn'd, inexecrable dog!
> And for thy life let justice be accused.
> Thou almost makest me waver in my faith
> To hold opinion with Pythagoras,
> That souls of animals infuse themselves
> Into the trunks of men: thy currish spirit
> Govern'd a wolf, who, hang'd for human slaughter,
> Even from the gallows did his fell soul fleet,
> And, whilst thou lay'st in thy unhallow'd dam,
> Infused itself in thee; for thy desires
> Are wolvish, bloody, starv'd and ravenous.

It will come;
Humanity must perforce prey on itself
Like monsters of the deep.

The influence of all this on imagination as we read *King Lear* is very great; and it combines with other influences to convey to us, not in the form of distinct ideas but in the manner proper to poetry, the wider or universal significance of the spectacle presented to the inward eye. But the effect of theatrical exhibition is precisely the reverse. There the poetic atmosphere is dissipated; the meaning of the very words which create it passes half-realized; in obedience to the tyranny of the eye we conceive the characters as mere particular men and women; and all that mass of vague suggestion, if it enters the mind at all, appears in the shape of an allegory which we immediately reject. A similar conflict between imagination and sense will be found if we consider the dramatic center of the whole tragedy, the Storm-scenes. The temptation of Othello and the scene of Duncan's murder may lose upon the stage, but they do not lose their essence, and they gain as well as lose. The Storm-scenes in *King Lear* gain nothing and their very essence is destroyed. It is comparatively a small thing that the theatrical storm, not to drown the dialogue, must be silent whenever a human being wishes to speak, and is wretchedly inferior to many a storm we have witnessed. Nor is it simply that, as Lamb observed, the corporal presence of Lear, "an old man tottering about the stage with a walking-stick," disturbs and depresses that sense of the greatness of his mind which fills the imagination. There is a further reason, which is not expressed, but still emerges, in these words of Lamb's: "the explosions of his passion are terrible as a volcano: they are storms turning up and disclosing to the bottom that sea, his mind, with all its vast riches." Yes, "they are *storms*." For imagination, that is to say, the explosions of Lear's passion, and the bursts of rain and thunder, are not, what for the senses they must be, two things, but manifestations of one thing. It is the powers of the tormented

soul that we hear and see in the "groans of roaring wind
and rain" and the "sheets of fire"; and they that, at intervals almost more overwhelming, sink back into darkness and silence. Nor yet is even this all; but, as those
incessant references to wolf and tiger made us see humanity "reeling back into the beast" and ravening against
itself, so in the storm we seem to see Nature herself
convulsed by the same horrible passions; the "common
mother,"

> Whose womb immeasurable and infinite breast
> Teems and feeds all,

turning on her children, to complete the ruin they have
wrought upon themselves. Surely something not less, but
much more, than these helpless words convey, is what
comes to us in these astounding scenes; and if, translated thus into the language of prose, it becomes con-
fused and inconsistent, the reason is simply that it itself
is poetry, and such poetry as cannot be transferred to the
space behind the footlights, but has its being only in
imagination. Here then is Shakespeare at his very greatest, but not the mere dramatist Shakespeare.

And now we may say this also of the catastrophe,
which we found questionable from the strictly dramatic
point of view. Its purpose is not merely dramatic. This
sudden blow out of the darkness, which seems so far
from inevitable, and which strikes down our reviving
hopes for the victims of so much cruelty, seems now
only what we might have expected in a world so wild
and monstrous. It is as if Shakespeare said to us: "Did
you think weakness and innocence have any chance
here? Were you beginning to dream that? I will show you
it is not so."

I come to a last point. As we contemplate this world,
the question presses on us, What can be the ultimate
power that moves it, that excites this gigantic war and
waste, or, perhaps, that suffers them and overrules them?
And in *King Lear* this question is not left to *us* to ask,
it is raised by the characters themselves. References to

religious or irreligious beliefs and feelings are more frequent than is usual in Shakespeare's tragedies, as frequent perhaps as in his final plays. He introduces characteristic differences in the language of the different persons about fortune or the stars or the gods, and shows how the question, What rules the world? is forced upon their minds. They answer it in their turn: Kent, for instance:

> It is the stars,
> The stars above us, govern our condition:

Edmund:

> Thou, nature, art my goddess; to thy law
> My services are bound:

and again,

> This is the excellent foppery of the world, that, when we are sick in fortune—often the surfeit of our own behavior—we make guilty of our disasters the sun, the moon and the stars; as if we were villains by necessity, fools by heavenly compulsion, . . . and all that we are evil in by a divine thrusting on:

Gloster:

> As flies to wanton boys are we to the gods;
> They kill us for their sport;

Edgar:

> Think that the clearest gods, who make them honours
> Of men's impossibilities, have preserved thee.

Here we have four distinct theories of the nature of the ruling power. And besides this, in such of the characters as have any belief in gods who love good and hate evil, the spectacle of triumphant injustice or cruelty provokes questionings like those of Job, or else the thought, often repeated, of divine retribution. To Lear at one moment the storm seems the messenger of heaven:

> Let the great gods,
> That keep this dreadful pother o'er our heads,
> Find out their enemies now. Tremble, thou wretch,
> That hast within thee undivulged crimes. . . .

At another moment those habitual miseries of the poor, of which he has taken too little account, seem to him to accuse the gods of injustice:

> Take physic, pomp;
> Expose thyself to feel what wretches feel,
> That thou mayst shake the superflux to them
> And show the heavens more just;

and Gloster has almost the same thought (IV. i. 67 ff.). Gloster again, thinking of the cruelty of Lear's daughters, breaks out,

> but I shall see
> The winged vengeance overtake such children.

The servants who have witnessed the blinding of Gloster by Cornwall and Regan, cannot believe that cruelty so atrocious will pass unpunished. One cries,

> I'll never care what wickedness I do,
> If this man come to good;

and another,

> if she live long,
> And in the end meet the old course of death,
> Women will all turn monsters.

Albany greets the news of Cornwall's death with the exclamation,

> This shows you are above,
> You justicers, that these our nether crimes
> So speedily can venge;

and the news of the deaths of the sisters with the words,

> This judgment of the heavens, that makes us tremble,
> Touches us not with pity.

Edgar, speaking to Edmund of their father, declares

> The gods are just, and of our pleasant vices
> Make instruments to plague us,

and Edmund himself assents. Almost throughout the latter half of the drama we note in most of the better characters a preoccupation with the question of the ultimate power, and a passionate need to explain by reference to it what otherwise would drive them to despair. And the influence of this preoccupation and need joins with other influences in affecting the imagination, and in causing it to receive from *King Lear* an impression which is at least as near of kin to the *Divine Comedy* as to *Othello*.

For Dante that which is recorded in the *Divine Comedy* was the justice and love of God. What did *King Lear* record for Shakespeare? Something, it would seem, very different. This is certainly the most terrible picture that Shakespeare painted of the world. In no other of his tragedies does humanity appear more pitiably infirm or more hopelessly bad. What is Iago's malignity against an envied stranger compared with the cruelty of the son of Gloster and the daughters of Lear? What are the sufferings of a strong man like Othello to those of helpless age? Much too that we have already observed—the repetition of the main theme in that of the underplot, the comparisons of man with the most wretched and the most horrible of the beasts, the impression of Nature's hostility to him, the irony of the unexpected catastrophe—these, with much else, seem even to indicate an intention to show things at their worst, and to return the sternest of replies to that question of the ultimate power and those appeals for retribution. Is it an accident, for example, that Lear's first appeal to something beyond the earth,

> O heavens,
> If you do love old men, if your sweet sway
> Allow obedience, if yourselves are old,
> Make it your cause:

is immediately answered by the iron voices of his daughters, raising by turns the conditions on which they will give him a humiliating harborage; or that his second appeal, heart-rending in its piteousness,

> You see me here, you gods, a poor old man,
> As full of grief as age; wretched in both:

is immediately answered from the heavens by the sound of the breaking storm? Albany and Edgar may moralize on the divine justice as they will, but how, in the face of all that we see, shall we believe that they speak Shakespeare's mind? Is not his mind rather expressed in the bitter contrast between their faith and the events we witness, or in the scornful rebuke of those who take upon them the mystery of things as if they were God's spies? Is it not Shakespeare's judgment on his kind that we hear in Lear's appeal,

> And thou, all-shaking thunder,
> Smite flat the thick rotundity o' the world!
> Crack nature's moulds, all germens spill at once,
> That make ingrateful man!

and Shakespeare's judgment on the worth of existence that we hear in Lear's agonized cry, "No, no, no life!"?

Beyond doubt, I think, some such feelings as these possess us, and, if we follow Shakespeare, ought to possess us, from time to time as we read *King Lear*. And some readers will go further and maintain that this is also the ultimate and total impression left by the tragedy. *King Lear* has been held to be profoundly "pessi-

mistic" in the full meaning of that word—the record of a
time when contempt and loathing for his kind had over-
mastered the poet's soul, and in despair he pronounced
man's life to be simply hateful and hideous. And if we
exclude the biographical part of this view, the rest may
claim some support even from the greatest of Shakespearean critics since the days of Coleridge, Hazlitt and
Lamb. Mr. Swinburne, after observing that *King Lear* is
"by far the most Aeschylean" of Shakespeare's works,
proceeds thus:

"But in one main point it differs radically from the
work and the spirit of Aeschylus. Its fatalism is of a darker and harder nature. To Prometheus the fetters of the
lord and enemy of mankind were bitter; upon Orestes the
hand of heaven was laid too heavily to bear; yet in
the not utterly infinite or everlasting distance we see beyond them the promise of the morning on which mystery
and justice shall be made one; when righteousness and
omnipotence at last shall kiss each other. But on the hori-
zon of Shakespeare's tragic fatalism we see no such twi-
light of atonement, such pledge of reconciliation as this.
Requital, redemption, amends, equity, explanation, pity
and mercy, are words without a meaning here.

> As flies to wanton boys are we to the gods;
> They kill us for their sport.

Here is no need of the Eumenides, children of Night
everlasting; for here is very Night herself.

"The words just cited are not casual or episodical;
they strike the keynote of the whole poem, lay the key-
stone of the whole arch of thought. There is no contest
of conflicting forces, no judgment so much as by casting
of lots: far less is there any light of heavenly harmony
or of heavenly wisdom, of Apollo or Athene from above.
We have heard much and often from theologians of the
light of revelation: and some such thing indeed we find
in Aeschylus; but the darkness of revelation is here." [2]

[2] *A Study of Shakespeare,* (1880) pp. 171, 172.

It is hard to refuse assent to these eloquent words, for they express in the language of a poet what we feel at times in reading *King Lear* but cannot express. But do they represent the total and final impression produced by the play? If they do, this impression, so far as the substance of the drama is concerned (and nothing else is in question here), must, it would seem, be one composed almost wholly of painful feelings—utter depression, or indignant rebellion, or appalled despair. And that would surely be strange. For *King Lear* is admittedly one of the world's greatest poems, and yet there is surely no other of these poems which produces on the whole this effect, and we regard it as a very serious flaw in any considerable work of art that this should be its ultimate effect. So that Mr. Swinburne's description, if taken as final, and any description of *King Lear* as "pessimistic" in the proper sense of that word, would imply a criticism which is not intended, and which would make it difficult to leave the work in the position almost universally assigned to it.

But in fact these descriptions, like most of the remarks made on *King Lear* in the present lecture, emphasize only certain aspects of the play and certain elements in the total impression; and in that impression the effect of these aspects, though far from being lost, is modified by that of others. I do not mean that the final effect resembles that of the *Divine Comedy* or the *Oresteia*: how should it, when the first of these can be called by its author a "Comedy," and when the second, ending (as doubtless the *Prometheus* trilogy also ended) with a solution, is not in the Shakespearean sense a tragedy at all? Nor do I mean that *King Lear* contains a revelation of righteous omnipotence or heavenly harmony, or even a promise of the reconciliation of mystery and justice. But then, as we saw, neither do Shakespeare's other tragedies contain these things. Any theological interpretation of the world on the author's part is excluded from them, and their effect would be disordered or destroyed equally by the ideas of righteous or of unrighteous omnipotence. Nor, in reading them, do we think of "justice" or "equity" in the sense of a strict requital or such an adjustment of merit and prosperity as our moral sense is said to demand; and there never was vainer labor than that of critics who try to make out that the persons in these dramas meet with "justice" or their "deserts." But, on the other hand, man is not represented in these tragedies as the mere plaything of a blind or capricious power, suffering woes which have no relation to his character and actions; nor is the world represented as given over to darkness. And in these respects *King Lear,* though the most terrible of these works, does not differ in essence from the rest. Its keynote is surely to be heard neither in the words wrung from Gloster in his anguish, nor in Edgar's words "the gods are just." Its final and total result is one in which pity and terror, carried perhaps to the extreme limits of art, are so blended with a sense of law and beauty that we feel at last, not depression and much less despair, but a consciousness of greatness in pain, and of solemnity in the mystery we cannot fathom. . . .

But there is another aspect of Lear's story, the influence of which modifies, in a way quite different and more peculiar to this tragedy, the impressions called pessimistic and even this impression of law. There is nothing more noble and beautiful in literature than Shakespeare's exposition of the effect of suffering in reviving the greatness and eliciting the sweetness of Lear's nature. The occasional recurrence, during his madness, of autocratic impatience or of desire for revenge serves only to heighten this effect, and the moments when his insanity becomes merely infinitely piteous do not weaken it. The old King who in pleading with his daughters feels so intensely his own humiliation and their horrible ingratitude, and who yet, at fourscore and upward, constrains himself to practice a self-control and patience so many years disused; who out of old affection for his Fool, and in repentance for his injustice to the Fool's beloved mistress, tolerates incessant and cutting reminders of his own folly and wrong; in whom the rage of the storm awakes a power and a poetic grandeur surpassing

even that of Othello's anguish; who comes in his affliction
to think of others first, and to seek, in tender solici-
tude for his poor boy, the shelter he scorns for his own
bare head; who learns to feel and to pray for the
miserable and houseless poor, to discern the falseness
of flattery and the brutality of authority, and to pierce
below the differences of rank and raiment to the common humanity beneath; whose sight is so purged by
scalding tears that it sees at last how power and place
and all things in the world are vanity except love; who
tastes in his last hours the extremes both of love's rap-
ture and of its agony, but could never, if he lived on or
lived again, care a jot for aught beside—there is no figure, surely, in the world of poetry at once so grand,
so pathetic, and so beautiful as his. Well, but Lear owes
the whole of this to those sufferings which made us
doubt whether life were not simply evil, and men like the
flies which wanton boys torture for their sport. Should
we not be at least as near the truth if we called this
poem *The Redemption of King Lear,* and declared that the
business of "the gods" with him was neither to torment
him, nor to teach him a "noble anger," but to lead him
to attain through apparently hopeless failure the very
end and aim of life? One can believe that Shakespeare
had been tempted at times to feel misanthropy and
despair, but it is quite impossible that he can have been
mastered by such feelings at the time when he produced this conception. . . .

. . . Lear's insanity, which destroys the coherence, also
reduces the poetry of his imagination. What it stimu-
lates is that power of moral perception and reflection
which had already been quickened by his sufferings. This,
however partial and however disconnectedly used, first
appears, quite soon after the insanity has declared itself,
in the idea that the naked beggar represents truth and
reality, in contrast with those conventions, flatteries, and
corruptions of the great world, by which Lear has so
long been deceived and will never be deceived again. . . .

. . . *King Lear* . . . is the tragedy in which evil is shown
in the greatest abundance; and the evil characters are

peculiarly repellent from their hard savagery, and be-cause so little good is mingled with their evil. The effect is therefore more startling than elsewhere; it is even ap-palling. But in substance it is the same as elsewhere. . . .

On the one hand we see a world which generates ter-rible evil in profusion. Further, the beings in whom this evil appears at its strongest are able, to a certain ex-tent, to thrive. They are not unhappy, and they have power to spread misery and destruction around them. All this is undeniable fact.

On the other hand this evil is *merely* destructive: it founds nothing, and seems capable of existing only on foundations laid by its opposite. It is also self-destructive. . . . These . . . are undeniable facts; and, in face of them, it seems odd to describe *King Lear* as "a play in which the wicked prosper" (Johnson).

Thus the world in which evil appears seems to be at heart unfriendly to it. And this impression is confirmed by the fact that the convulsion of this world is due to evil, mainly in the worst forms here considered, partly in the milder forms which we call the errors or defects of the better characters. Good, in the widest sense, seems thus to be the principle of life and health in the world; evil, at least in these worst forms, to be a poison. The world reacts against it violently, and, in the struggle to expel it, is driven to devastate itself.

If we ask why the world should generate that which convulses and wastes it, the tragedy gives no answer, and we are trying to go beyond tragedy in seeking one. But the world, in this tragic picture, *is* convulsed by evil, and rejects it.

. . . I might almost say that the "moral" of *King Lear* is presented in the irony of this collocation:

> *Albany.* The gods defend her!
> *Enter Lear with Cordelia dead in his arms.*

The "gods," it seems, do *not* show their approval by "de-fending" their own from adversity or death, or by giving them power and prosperity. These, on the contrary, are worthless, or worse; it is not on them, but on the renunciation of them, that the gods throw incense. They breed lust, pride, hardness of heart, the insolence of office, cruelty, scorn, hypocrisy, contention, war, murder, self-destruction. The whole story beats this indictment of prosperity into the brain. Lear's great speeches in his madness proclaim it like the curses of Timon on life and man. But here, as in *Timon,* the poor and humble are, almost without exception, sound and sweet at heart, faithful and pitiful. And here adversity, to the blessed in spirit, is blessed. It wins fragrance from the crushed flower. It melts in aged hearts sympathies which prosperity had frozen. It purges the soul's sight by blinding that of the eyes.[3] Throughout that stupendous Third Act the good are seen growing better through suffering, and the bad worse through success. The warm castle is a room in hell, the storm-swept heath a sanctuary. The judgment of this world is a lie; its goods, which we covet, corrupt us; its ills, which break our bodies, set our souls free;

> Our means secure us, and our mere defects
> Prove our commodities.

Let us renounce the world, hate it, and lose it gladly. The only real thing in it is the soul, with its courage, patience, devotion. And nothing outward can touch that.

This, if we like to use the word, is Shakespeare's "pessimism" in *King Lear*. . . .

---

3 "I stumbled when I saw," says Gloster.

Harley Granville-Barker

From *Prefaces to Shakespeare*

THE MAIN LINES OF CONSTRUCTION

King Lear, alone among the great tragedies, adds to its plot a subplot fully developed. And it suffers somewhat under the burden. After a few preliminary lines—Shakespeare had come to prefer this to the grand opening, and in this instance they are made introductory to plot and subplot too—we have a full and almost formal statement of the play's main theme and a show of the characters that are to develop it, followed by a scene which sets out the subplot as fully. The two scenes together form a sort of double dramatic prologue; and they might, by modern custom, count as a first act, for after them falls the only clearly indicated time-division in the play. The Folio, however, adds the quarrel with Goneril before an act-pause is allowed: then—whatever its authority, but according to its usual plan—sets out four more acts, the second allotted to the parallel quarrel with Regan, the third to the climax of the main theme; the fourth we may call a picture of the wreck of both Lear and Gloucester, and in it subplot and main plot are blended, and the fifth act is given to the final and rather complex catastrophe. This division, then, has thus much dramatic validity, and a producer may legitimately choose to abide by it. On the other hand, one may contend, the play's action flows unchecked throughout (but for the one check which does not coincide with the act-division of the Folio). Still it is not to be supposed that a Jacobean

Reprinted from *Prefaces to Shakespeare,* I, by Harley Granville-Barker. Reprinted by permission of Princeton University Press. Copyright 1946 by Princeton University Press.

audience did, or a modern audience would, sit through a performance without pause. Yet again, it does not follow that the Folio's act-divisions were observed as intervals in which the audience dispersed and by which the continuity of dramatic effect was altogether broken. A producer must, I think, exercise his own judgment. There may be something to be said for more "breathing-spaces," but I should myself incline to one definite interval only, to fall after Act III. . . .

The scene in which Lear divides his kingdom is a magnificent statement of a magnificent theme. It has a proper formality, and there is a certain megalithic grandeur about it, Lear dominating it, that we associate with Greek tragedy. Its probabilities are neither here nor there. A dramatist may postulate any situation he has the means to interpret, if he will abide by the logic of it after.[1] The producer should observe and even see stressed the scene's characteristics; Lear's two or three passages of such an eloquence as we rather expect at a play's climax than its opening, the strength of such single lines as

The bow is bent and drawn, make from the shaft

with its hammering monosyllables; and the hard-bitten

Nothing: I have sworn; I am firm

together with the loosening of the tension in changes to rhymed couplets, and the final drop into prose by that businesslike couple, Goneril and Regan. Then follows, with a lift into lively verse for a start, as a contrast and as the right medium for Edmund's sanguine conceit, the

[1] Later, on p. 313 of his volume, Barker says: "We must not . . . [moreover], appraise either . . . [Gloucester's initial] simplicity or Edgar's . . . with detachment—for by that light, no human being, it would seem, between infancy and dotage, could be so gullible. Shakespeare asks us to allow him the fact of the deception, even as we have allowed him Lear's partition of the kingdom. It is his starting point, the dramatist's let's pretend, which is as essential to the beginning of a play as a "let it be granted" to a proposition of Euclid. And, within bounds, the degree of pretence makes surprisingly little difference. It is what the assumption will commit him to that counts."

development of the Gloucester theme. Shakespeare does this at his ease, allows himself diversion and time. He has now both the plot of the ungrateful daughters and the subplot of the treacherous son under way.

But the phenomenon for which Shakespeareans learn to look has not yet occurred, that inexplicable "springing to life"—a springing, it almost seems, into a life of its own—of character or theme. Very soon it does occur; Lear's entrance, disburdened from the care of state, is its natural signal. On his throne, rightly enough, he showed formal and self-contained. Now he springs away; and now the whole play in its relation to him takes on a liveliness and variety; nor will the energy be checked or weakened, or, if checked, only that the next stroke may be intenser, till the climax is past, till his riven and exhausted nature is granted the oblivion of sleep. This is the master movement of the play, which enshrines the very soul of the play—and in the acting, as I have suggested, there should be no break allowed. To read and give full imaginative value to those fifteen hundred lines at a stretch is certainly exhausting; if they were written at one stretch of inspiration the marvel is that Shakespeare, with his Lear, did not collapse under the strain, yet the exactions of his performance he tempers with all his skill. Lear is surrounded by characters, which each in a different way take a share of the burden from him. Kent, the Fool, and Edgar as Poor Tom are a complement of dramatic strength; and the interweaving of the scenes concerning Oswald, Edmund, and Gloucester saves the actor's energy for the scenes of the rejection and the storm.

As the Lear theme expanded under his hand Shakespeare had begun, and perforce, to economize his treatment of the Gloucester-Edgar-Edmund story. Edgar himself is indeed dismissed from the second scene upon no more allowance of speech than

I'm sure on't, not a word.

—with which the best of actors may find it hard to make his presence felt; and at our one view of him before he had been left negative enough. Edmund is then brought rapidly into relation with the main plot, and the blending of main plot and subplot begins. Edgar also is drawn into Lear's orbit; and, for the time, to the complete sacrifice of his own interests in the play. "Poor Tom" is in effect an embodiment of Lear's frenzy, the disguise no part of Edgar's own development.

As we have seen, while Act III is at the height of its argument, Shakespeare is careful to keep alive the lower-pitched theme of Edmund's treachery, his new turn to the betrayal of his father. He affords it two scenes, of twenty-five lines each, wedged between the three dominant scenes of the storm and Lear's refuge from it. They are sufficient and no more for their own purpose; in their sordidness they stand as valuable contrast to the spiritual exaltation of the others. The supreme moment for Lear himself, the turning point, therefore, of the play's main theme, is reached in the second of the three storm-scenes, when the proud old king kneels humbly and alone in his wretchedness to pray. This is the argument's absolute height; and from now on we may feel (as far as Lear is concerned) the tension relax, through the first grim passage of his madness, slackening still through the fantastic scene of the arraignment of the joint-stools before that queer bench of justices, to the moment of his falling asleep and his conveyance away—his conveyance, we find it to be, out of the main stream of the play's action. Shakespeare then deals the dreadful blow to Gloucester. The very violence and horror of this finds its dramatic justification in the need to match in another sort—since he could not hope to match it in spiritual intensity—the catastrophe to Lear. And now we may imagine him, if we please, stopping to consider where he was. Anticlimax, after this, is all but inevitable. Let the producer take careful note how Shakespeare sets out to avoid the worst dangers of it.

Had the play been written upon the single subject of Lear and his daughters, we should now be in sight of its end. But the wealth of material Shakespeare has posited asks for use, and his own imagination, we may suppose, is still teeming. But by the very nature of the material (save Cordelia) left for development the rest of the play must be pitched in a lower key. Shakespeare marshals the action by which the wheel of Gloucester's weakness and Edmund's treachery is brought full circle with extraordinary skill and even more extraordinary economy. Yet for all this, except in a fine flash or two, the thing stays by comparison pedestrian. He is only on the wing again when Lear and Cordelia are his concern; in the scenes of their reconciliation and of the detached tragedy of Lear's death with the dead Cordelia in his arms, as in the still more detached and—as far as the mere march of the action is concerned—wholly unjustifiable scene of Lear mad and fantastically crowned with wild flowers. We must add, though, to the inspired passages the immediately preceding fantasy of Gloucester's imaginary suicide, an apt offset to the realistic horror of his blinding, and occasion for some inimitable verse. The chief fact to face, then, is that for the rest of the play, the best will be incidental and not a necessary part of the story. The producer therefore must give his own best attention to Albany, Goneril, and Regan and their close-packed contests, and to the nice means by which Edgar is shaped into a hero; and in general must see that this purposeful disciplined necessary stuff is given fullness and, as far as may be, spontaneity of life in its interpretation. If he will take care of this the marvelous moments will tend to take care of him.

Shakespeare strengthens the action at once with the fresh interest of the Edmund-Goneril-Regan intrigue, daring as it is to launch into this with the short time left him for its development and resolving. He is, indeed, driven to heroic compressions, to implications, effects by "business," action "off," almost to "love-making by reference only." Goneril's first approach to Edmund (or his to her; but we may credit the lady, I think, with the throwing of the handkerchief) is only clearly marked out for the actors by Regan's reference to it five scenes later, when she tells us that at Goneril's

> late being here
> She gave strange oeilliads and most speaking looks
> To noble Edmund.

(Regan credits her with what, if we prefer our Shake-speare modernized, we might literally translate into "giving the glad eye.") But this silent business of the earlier scene is important and must be duly marked if the arrival of the two together and Edmund's turning back to avoid meeting Albany, the "mild husband," is to have its full effect. For the first and last of their spoken love-making, excellently characteristic as it is, consists of Goneril's

> Our wishes on the way
> May prove effects. . . .
> > This trusty servant
> Shall pass between us: ere long you are like to hear,
> If you dare venture in your own behalf,
> A mistress's command. Wear this; spare speech;
> Decline your head: this kiss, if it durst speak,
> Would stretch thy spirits up into the air.
> Conceive, and fare thee well.

and Edmund's ("Spare speech," indeed!)

> Yours in the ranks of death!

—all spoken in Oswald's presence too. It is, of course, not only excellent but sufficient. The regal impudency of the woman, the falsely chivalrous flourish of the man's response—pages of dialogue might not tell us more of their relations; and, of these relations, is there much more that is dramatically worth knowing? The point for the producer is that no jot of such a constricted dramatic opportunity must be missed.

For the whole working-out of this lower issue of the play the same warning stands true; an exact and un-blurred value must be given to each significant thing. The interaction of circumstance and character is close-knit and complex, but it is clear. Keep it clear and it can be made effective to any audience that will listen, and is not distracted from listening. Let us underline this last phrase and now make the warning twofold. In working out a theme so full of incident and of contending characters Shakespeare allows for no distraction of attention at all, certainly not for the breaking of continuity which the constant shifting of realistically localized scenery must involve. The action, moreover, of these later scenes is exceptionally dependent upon to-ings and fro-ings. Given continuity of performance and no more insistence upon whereabouts than the action itself will indicate, the impression produced by the constant busy movement into our sight and out again of purposeful, passionate or distracted figures, is in itself of great dramatic value, and most congruous to the plot and counterplot of the play's ending. The order for Lear's and Cordelia's murder, the quarrel over Edmund's precedence, Albany's sudden self-assertion, Regan's sickness, Edgar's appearance, the fight, his discovery of himself, Goneril's discomfiture, the telling of Kent's secret, Regan's and Goneril's death, the alarm to save Lear and Cordelia—Shakespeare, by the Folio text, gets all this into less than two hundred lines, with a fair amount of rhetoric and incidental narrative besides. He needs no more, though bareness does nearly turn to banality sometimes. But unless we can be held in an unrelaxed grip we may not submit to the spell.

He has kept a technical master stroke for his ending:

Enter Lear with Cordelia in his arms.

There should be a long, still pause, while Lear passes slowly in with his burden, while they all stand respectful as of old to his majesty. We may have wondered a little that Shakespeare should be content to let Cordelia pass from the play as casually as she seems to in the earlier scene. But this is the last of her, not that. Dumb and dead, she that was never apt of speech—what fitter finish for her could there be? What fitter ending to the history of the two of them, which began for us with Lear on his throne, conscious of all eyes on him, while she shamed and angered him by her silence? The same company are here, or all but the same, and they await his pleasure. Even Regan and Goneril are here to pay him a ghastly homage. But he knows none of them—save for a blurred moment Kent whom he banished—none but Cordelia. And again he reproaches her silence; for

> Her voice was ever soft,
> Gentle and low, an excellent thing in woman.

Then his heart breaks. . . .

THE CHARACTERS AND THEIR INTERPLAY
LEAR

But it is upon Lear's own progress that all now centers, upon his passing from that royal defiance of the storm to the welcomed shelter of the hovel. He passes by the road of patience:

> No, I will be the pattern of all patience;
> I will say nothing,

of—be it noted—a thankfulness that he is at last simply

> a man
> More sinn'd against than sinning . . .

to the humility of

> My wits begin to turn.
> Come on, my boy. How dost, my boy? Art cold?
> I am cold myself. Where is this straw, my fellow?
> The art of our necessities is strange
> That can make vile things precious. Come, your
>   hovel . . .

and, a little later yet, mind and body still further strained towards breaking point, to the gentle dignity, when Kent would make way for him—to the more than kingly dignity of

> Prithee, go in thyself: seek thine own ease.
> This tempest will not give me leave to ponder
> On things would hurt me more. But I'll go in:
> In, boy; go first.

Now comes the crowning touch of all:

> I'll pray, and then I'll sleep.

In the night's bleak exposure he kneels down, like a child at bedtime, to pray.

> Poor naked wretches, wheresoe'er you are,
> That bide the pelting of this pitiless storm,
> How shall your houseless heads and unfed sides,
> Your loop'd and window'd raggedness, defend you
> From seasons such as these? O, I have ta'en
> Too little care of this! Take physic, pomp;
> Expose thyself to feel what wretches feel,
> That thou mayst shake the superflux to them,
> And show the heavens more just.

To this heaven of the spirit has he come, the Lear of unbridled power and pride. And how many dramatists, could they have achieved so much, would have been content to leave him here! Those who like their drama rounded and trim might approve of such a finish, which would leave us a play more compassable in performance no doubt. But the wind of a harsher doctrine is blowing through Shakespeare. Criticism, as we have seen, is apt to fix upon the episode of the storm as the height of his attempt and the point of his dramatic defeat; but it is this storm of the mind here beginning upon which he expends skill and imagination most recklessly till inspiration has had its will of him; and the drama of desperate vision ensuing it is hard indeed for actors to reduce to the positive medium of their art—without reducing it to ridicule. The three coming scenes of Lear's madness show us Shakespeare's art at its boldest. They pass beyond the needs of the plot, they belong to a larger synthesis. Yet the means they employ are simple enough; of a kind of absolute simplicity, indeed.

The boldest and simplest is the provision of Poor Tom, that living instance of all rejection. Here, under our eyes, is Lear's new vision of himself.

> What! have his daughters brought him to this pass?
> Could'st thou save nothing? Did'st thou give them all?

Side by side stand the noble old man, and the naked, scarce human wretch.

> Is man no more than this? Consider him well. Thou owest the worm no silk, the beast no hide, the sheep no wool, the cat no perfume. Ha! here's three on's are sophisticated; thou art the thing itself; unaccommodated man is no more but such a poor, bare, forked animal as thou art. Off, off, you lendings! Come; unbutton here.

Here is a volume of argument epitomized as only drama can epitomize it, flashed on us by word and action combined. And into this, one might add, has Shakespeare metamorphosed the didactics of those old Moralities which were the infancy of his art.

> What! hath your grace no better company?

gasps poor Gloucester, bewailing at once the King's wrongs and his own, as he offers shelter from the storm. But Lear, calmness itself now, will only pace up and down, arm in arm with this refuse of humanity:—nor will he seek shelter without him. So they reach the outhouse, all of his own castle that Gloucester dare offer. What a group! Kent, sturdy and thrifty of words; Gloucester, tremulous; the bedraggled and exhausted Fool; and Lear, magnificently courteous and deliberate, keeping close company with his gibbering fellow-man.

They are in shelter. Lear is silent; till the Fool—himself never overfitted, we may suppose, in body or mind for the rough and tumble of the world—rallies, as if to celebrate their safety, to a semblance of his old task. Edgar, for his own safety's sake, must play Poor Tom to the life now. Kent has his eyes on his master, watching him —at what new fantastic trick? The old king is setting two joint-stools side by side; they are Regan and Goneril, and the Fool and the beggar are to pass judgment upon them.

The lunatic mummery of the trial comes near to something we might call pure drama—as one speaks of pure mathematics or pure music—since it cannot be rendered into other terms than its own. Its effect depends upon the combination of the sound and meaning of the words and the sight of it being brought to bear as a whole directly upon our sensibility. The sound of the dialogue matters almost more than its meaning. Poor Tom and the Fool chant antiphonally; Kent's deep and kindly tones tell against the higher, agonized, weakening voice of Lear. But the chief significance is in the show. Where Lear, such a short while since, sat in his majesty, there sit the Fool and the outcast, with Kent whom he banished beside them; and he, witless, musters his failing strength to beg justice upon a joint-stool. Was better justice done, the picture ironically asks, when he presided in majesty and sanity and power?

But what, as far as Lear is concerned, is to follow? You cannot continue the development of a character in terms of lunacy—in darkness, illuminated by whatever brilliant flashes of lightning. Nor can a madman well dominate a play's action. From this moment Lear no longer is a motive force; and the needs of the story—the absolute needs of the character—would be fulfilled if, from this exhausted sleep upon the poor bed in the outhouse, he only woke to find Cordelia at his side. But Shakespeare contrives another scene of madness for him, and one which lifts the play's argument to a yet rarer height. It is delayed; and the sense of redundancy is avoided partly by keeping Lear from the stage altogether for a while, a short scene interposed sufficiently reminding us of him.

His reappearance is preluded—with what consonance! —by the fantastically imaginative episode of Gloucester's fall from the cliff. There also is Edgar, the aura of Poor Tom about him still. Suddenly Lear breaks in upon them. The larger dramatic value of the ensuing scene can hardly be overrated. For in it, in this encounter between mad Lear and blind Gloucester, the sensual man robbed of his eyes, and the despot, the light of his mind put out, Shakespeare's sublimation of the two old stories is consummated. No moral is preached to us. It is presented as it was when king and beggar fraternized in the storm and beggar and Fool were set on the bench of justice, and we are primarily to feel the significance. Yet this does not lack interpretation; less explicit than when Lear, still sane, could read the lesson of the storm, clearer than was the commentary on the mock trial. It is Edgar here that sets us an example of sympathetic listening. His asides enforce it, and the last one:

> O! matter and impertinency mixed,
> Reason in madness!

will reproach us if we have not understood. The train of fancies fired by the first sight of Gloucester, with its tragically comic

> Ha! Goneril with a white beard!

(Goneril, disguised, pursuing him still!) asks little gloss.

> They flattered me like a dog. . . . To say 'Ay' and 'No' to everything I said! . . . When the rain came to wet me once and the wind to make me chatter, when the thunder would not peace at my bidding, there I found 'em, there I smelt 'em out. Go to, they are not men o' their words; they told me I was everything; 'tis a lie, I am not ague-proof.

Gloucester's dutiful

> Is't not the king?

begins to transform him in those mad eyes. And madness sees a Gloucester there that sanity had known and ignored.

> I pardon that man's life: What was thy cause?
> Adultery?
> Thou shalt not die: die for adultery! No:
> The wren goes to't, and the small gilded fly

> Does lecher in my sight.
> Let copulation thrive; for Gloucester's bastard son
> Was kinder to his father than my daughters
> Got 'tween the lawful sheets.

Gloucester knows better; but how protest so to the mere erratic voice? Besides which there is only the kindly stranger-peasant near. A slight unconscious turn of the sightless eyes toward him, a simple gesture—unseen—in response from Edgar, patiently biding his time, will illuminate the irony and the pathos.

Does the mad mind pass logically from this to some uncanny prevision of the ripening of new evil in Regan and Goneril? Had it in its sanity secretly surmised what lay beneath the moral surface of their lives, so ready to emerge?

> Behold yon simpering dame
> Whose face between her forks presageth snow;
> That minces virtue and does shake the head
> To hear of pleasure's name;
> The fitchew, nor the soiled horse, goes to't
> With a more riotous appetite.

But a man—so lunatic logic runs—must free himself from the tyrannies of the flesh if he is to see the world clearly:

> Give me an ounce of civet, good apothecary, to sweeten my imagination.

And then a blind man may see the truth of it, so he tells the ruined Gloucester:

> Look with thine ears: see how yond justice rails upon yond simple thief. Hark in thine ear: change places, and, handy-dandy, which is the justice, which is the thief? Thou hast seen a farmer's dog bark at a beggar? . . . And the creature run from the cur? There thou might'st behold the great image of authority; a dog's obeyed in office.

It is the picture of the mock trial given words. But with a difference! There is no cry now for vengeance on the wicked. For what are we that we should smite them?

> Thou rascal beadle, hold thy bloody hand!
> Why dost thou lash that whore? Strip thine own back;
> That hotly lust'st to use her in that kind
> For which thou whip'st her. The usurer hangs the
>   cozener.
> Through tattered clothes small vices do appear;
> Robes and furr'd gowns hide all. Plate sin with gold,
> And the strong lance of justice hurtless breaks;
> Arm it in rags, a pigmy's straw doth pierce it.

Shakespeare has led Lear to compassion for sin as well as suffering, has led him mad to where he could not hope to lead him sane—to where sound common sense will hardly let us follow him:

> None does offend, none, I say, none.

To a deep compassion for mankind itself.

> I know thee well enough; thy name is Gloucester;
> Thou must be patient; we came crying hither:
> Thou know'st the first time that we smell the air
> We wawl and cry. I will preach to thee: mark. . . .
> When we are born, we cry that we are come
> To this great stage of fools.

This afterpart of Lear's madness may be redundant, then, to the strict action of the play, but to its larger issues it is most germane. It is perhaps no part of the play that Shakespeare set out to write. The play that he found himself writing would be how much the poorer without it!

The simple perfection of the scene that restores Lear to Cordelia one can leave unsullied by comment. What need of any? Let the producer only note that there is reason in the Folio's stage direction:

> *Enter Lear in a chair carried by servants.*

For when he comes to himself it is to find that he is royally attired and as if seated on his throne again. It is from this throne that he totters to kneel at Cordelia's feet. Note, too, the pain of his response to Kent's

> In your own kingdom, sir.
> Do not abuse me.

Finally, Lear must pass from the scene with all the ceremony due to royalty; not mothered—please!—by Cordelia.

Cordelia found again and again lost, what is left for Lear but to die? But for her loss, however, his own death might seem to us an arbitrary stroke; since the old Lear, we may say, is already dead. Shakespeare, moreover, has transported him beyond all worldly issues. This is, perhaps, why the action of the battle which will seemingly defeat his fortunes is minimized. What does defeat matter to him—or even victory? It is certainly the key to the meaning of the scene which follows. Cordelia, who would "out-frown false fortune's frown," is ready to face her sisters and to shame them—were there a chance of it!—with the sight of her father's wrongs. But Lear himself has no interest in anything of the sort.

> No, no, no, no! Come, let's away to prison.
> We two alone will sing like birds i' the cage:
> When thou dost ask me blessing, I'll kneel down,
> And ask of thee forgiveness: so we'll live,
> And pray, and sing, and tell old tales, and laugh
> At gilded butterflies, and hear poor rogues
> Talk of court news. . . .

He has passed beyond care for revenge or success, beyond even the questioning of rights and wrongs. Better indeed to be oppressed, if so you can be safe from contention. Prison will bring him freedom.

> Upon such sacrifices, my Cordelia,
> The gods themselves throw incense. Have I caught thee?

He that parts us shall bring a brand from heaven
And fire us hence like foxes. Wipe thine eyes;
The good years shall devour them, flesh and fell,
Ere they shall make us weep: we'll see 'em starve
   first.

Lear's death, upon one ground or another, is artisti-
cally inevitable. Try to imagine his survival; no further
argument will be needed. The death of Cordelia has been
condemned as a wanton outrage upon our feelings and
so as an aesthetic blot upon the play. But the dramatic
mind that was working to the tune of

As flies to wanton boys are we to the gods;
They kill us for their sport,

was not likely to be swayed by sentiment. The tragic
truth about life, to the Shakespeare that wrote *King Lear*,
included its capricious cruelty. And what meeter sacrifice
to this than Cordelia? Besides, as we have seen, he must
provide this new Lear with a tragic determinant, since
"the great rage . . . is kill'd in him," which precipitated
catastrophe for the old Lear. And what but Cordelia's
loss would suffice?

We have already set Lear's last scene in comparison
with his first; it will be worth while to note a little more
particularly the likeness and the difference. The same
commanding figure; he bears the body of Cordelia as
lightly as ever he carried robe, crown and scepter before.
All he has undergone has not so bated his colossal
strength but that he could kill her murderer with his bare
hands.

   I kill'd the slave that was a-hanging thee.
'Tis true, my lords, he did,

says the officer in answer to their amazed looks. Albany,
Edgar, Kent and the rest stand silent and intent around
him; Regan and Goneril are there, silent too. He stands,
with the limp body close clasped, glaring blankly at them

for a moment. When speech is torn from him, in place of the old kingly rhetoric we have only the horrible, half human

> Howl, howl, howl, howl!

Who these are, for all their dignity and martial splendor, for all the respect they show him, he neither knows nor cares. They are men of stone and murderous traitors; though, after a little, through the mist of his suffering, comes a word for Kent. All his world, of power and passion and will, and the wider world of thought over which his mind in its ecstasy had ranged, is narrowed now to Cordelia; and she is dead in his arms.

Here is the clue to the scene; this terrible concentration upon the dead, and upon the unconquerable fact of death. This thing was Cordelia; she was alive, she is dead. Here is human tragedy brought to its simplest terms, fit ending to a tragic play that has seemed to outleap human experience. From power of intellect and will, from the imaginative sweep of madness, Shakespeare brings Lear to this; to no moralizing nor high thoughts, but just to

> She's gone for ever.
> I know when one is dead and when one lives;
> She's dead as earth. Lend me a looking-glass;
> If that her breath will mist or stain the stone,
> Why, then she lives.

Lacking a glass, he catches at a floating feather. That stirs on her lips; a last mockery. Kent kneels by him to share his grief. Then to the bystanders comes the news of Edmund's death; the business of life goes forward, as it will, and draws attention from him for a moment. But what does he heed? When they turn back to him he has her broken body in his arms again.

Harry Levin

The Heights and the Depths:
A Scene from *King Lear*

Speaking of depths and heights, I hope that my title has not provoked a wider curiosity than can be sharply focused by my subtitle. I shall not be talking about the periods of Shakespeare's development, or looking for his autobiography in his dramaturgy, or assuming—with Edward Dowden and others—that he wrote his tragedies out of some private grief and later, when he felt mellower, turned back to comedies. The moods and changes that continue to interest us today are not those which we attribute to the artist in person, but those which we experience through his art. Its characteristic transitions from splendor to torment, from *O altitudo* to *de profundis,* seem to accord with a basic principle of tragic vicissitude. What I propose to discuss, in some contextual detail, is one extremely specific illustration of that principle, a text often cited but seldom re-examined, probably because our modes of stagecraft have strategically changed.

"Gain Shakespeare's effects by Shakespeare's means when you can." Such was the sound advice of Granville-Barker for the modern interpretation of Shakespeare. However, there are times when the theatrical interpreter

From *More Talking of Shakespeare*, ed. John Garrett. New York: Theatre Arts Books; London: Longmans, Green & Company, Ltd., 1959. Reprinted by permission of Longmans, Green & Company, Ltd.

cannot use Shakespearean means, even though the academic interpreter may know how a certain Shakespearean effect was accomplished. We cannot cast a boy as Cleopatra, though Shakespeare did; very few actresses are up to the part in our time, even after a long and respectable career in the theatre. Shakespeare would never have been able to spread his drama of *Antony and Cleopatra* through forty-two scenes, crossing and recrossing the Mediterranean, had he been forced to compress it within a proscenium, relying upon a succession of backdrops or a revolving stage. Working within an adaptable but permanent structure—mainly a forestage flanked by adequate exits or entrances, backed by some sort of curtained area and an upper balcony—Shakespeare achieved unlimited effects by limited means.

These were primarily verbal. To one with his gift for turning words into pictures, the absence of scenery was a stimulus to the pictorial imagination. Hence Shakespeare did his own scene-painting, verbally. "This castle hath a pleasant seat," says Duncan, praising the air; and Banquo goes on to enlarge our mental picture of Glamis Castle with his lyrical speech about the temple-haunting martlet, the pendent bed, and the heaven's breath. This delicate imagery has the quality of repose in painting, or so Sir Joshua Reynolds has commented. Repose indeed! for here the gentle Duncan will all too soon be taking his last repose; before morning that heavenly courtyard will be all the drunken porter fancies, when he envisages it as a gateway to hell; and we shall have been transported, as it were, from the heights to the depths.

Shakespeare used no programs, and does not seem to have put much faith in locality-boards.

> Alack! the night comes on, and the bleak winds
> Do sorely ruffle,

says Gloucester, thereby setting the time and place at the end of the Second Act of *King Lear*:

for many miles about
There's scarce a bush.

And with a clatter of doors being closed and shutters
banged, the clanging of gates and other sound effects
which are actually verbal, the stage is set—that vastest
and barest of stages—for the storm scenes of Act III,
which alternate between the indoors and the open air,
and gain the effect of wind and rain by means of the old
King's efforts to outscorn them. Granville-Barker's preface to *King Lear* is a practical refutation of A. C. Bradley's influential and paradoxical argument that, though it
may be Shakespeare's greatest achievement, it is too huge
for the stage. This, in turn, was a philosophical rationalization of Charles Lamb's opinion that performance was un-
bearable. Now Lamb was more of a theatergoer than
Bradley, but he could only have witnessed the play in
productions which were cruelly cut and badly adulterated.
He therefore concluded that the spectacle of an old man,
tottering about in a storm with a stick, could only be
painful or disgusting.

Other critics have recoiled more strongly from that
terrifying scene where Gloucester's eyes are put out
coram populo, not behind the scenes as in *Oedipus Rex,*
but in full view of the audience and in complete violation
of classical decorum. It is a deliberate and definitive
breach, a more flagrant gesture of indecorum than the
Elizabethan intermixture of hornpipes with funerals, or
the abasement of kings to the level of clowns in the
companionship of Lear and his Fool. Yet even that hor-
rendous act has a certain propriety as a literal climax to a
whole train of metaphors involving eyesight and suggesting moral perception, the lack of which is so fatal for
Gloucester and Lear. None so blind as those who have
eyes and see not. Their eyes may be open, but—like those
of Lady Macbeth in her sleepwalking scene—their sense is
shut. This visual metaphor is generalized into *hybris,* the
pride that goes before a tragic fall, with the self-denuncia-
tion of Antony:

But when we in our viciousness grow hard—
O misery on't!—the wise gods seel our eyes;
In our own filth drop our clear judgments; make us
Adore our errors; laugh at's while we strut
To our confusion.

When we become too intimately involved in the tragic experience, we tend to feel pain and disgust as Lamb did, rather than pity and fear. *Catharsis,* if it clears the mind through those classic emotions, does so by placing the object at an aesthetic distance from the spectator. He must, of course, apprehend it through sympathy, empathy, or some sort of identification with it. But he also achieves a sense of perspective through his detachment from it. Recent dramatic theory would stress this latter stage, which Bertolt Brecht terms "estrangement," as the most important aspect of the emotional process. But long ago Lucretius evoked the intellectual pleasure of looking out on troubled waters when one was safe ashore, of looking down on the violent conflicts of men from the heights of philosophy. Tragedy presents such knowledge, not in philosophic abstraction but in concrete exemplification. Thus, though it cries to us out of the depths, it offers us a way of temporarily detaching ourselves from the human predicament, and rising above those situations in which it has vicariously involved us.

The example for which I should like to claim your particular attention is neither the pitiful involvement of Lear in the storm nor the terrible blinding of Gloucester. It is a subsequent and incidental episode, the sixth scene of Act IV, a curiously didactic scene best known for its purple passage describing Dover Cliff. How near we really come to Dover Cliff is a moot question, as I shall try to show in my attempt to recover an unique effect which could only have been attained through Shakespearean means. Elsewhere in drama it has certain precedents and analogies, but none of them comes very close to the matter at hand. In the *Plutus* of Aristophanes, the others threaten to throw the blind god over a precipice, and the threat is averted when he reveals his name. In the repertory of Japanese Kabuki, the dance-drama *Shakkyo* concerns an old lion who pushes a young one off a cliff as a kind of test: by climbing back, the cub proves his manhood—or, rather, his lionhood.

That would seem to be the normal relationship between the two generations, father and son. Shakespeare reverses it, when Edmund accuses Edgar of maintaining that "the father should be as ward to the son." The accusation will come true ironically, when the disguised Edgar leads the blinded Gloucester. "In this play," Dame Edith Sitwell has aptly observed, "we see the upheaval of all Nature, the reversal of all histories." Tragedy always seems to hinge upon a reversal, or peripety. Here a peripety is the starting point, when the King reverses his traditional role by stepping down from the throne. As the tragedy broadens, moving out of the realm of history into the sphere of nature, it sets off a series of further reversals. The antagonism between crabbed age and flaming youth, always a latent tension in Shakespeare's plays, breaks into overt conflict in *King Lear*. It was implicit in classical comedy, to be sure, and terribly explicit in the dire prophecy of Matthew: "And brother shall deliver up brother to death, and the father his child: and children shall rise up against parents, and cause them to be put to death."

This abrogation of the most fundamental commitments, straining family ties beyond endurance and turning simple affections into complex hatreds, is still a major source of power in literature. Filial ingratitude is an obsessive theme with Proust, just as parricide is with Dostoevsky. Like the sons of old Karamazov, Edgar and Edmund incarnate the good and evil of their father's character. Science, natural philosophy, "the wisdom of nature can reason it thus and thus, yet nature finds itself scourged by the sequent effects," the superstitious Gloucester laments at the outset, anxious to blame his fate upon the stars. The worst of the many symptoms of upheaval that he enumerates is "the bond cracked between son and father." In Gloucester's own case, it is "son against father," though he suspects the wrong son as it turns out.

In the King's case, it is "father against child," and Gloucester underlines the parallel. Shakespeare never made bolder use of the double plot than when he matched the dynastic struggle of the main plot with its domestic counterpart, the Gloucester underplot. To take a *donnée* so exceptional, to hit upon so unheard-of a set of circumstances and double them, was to call the entire moral order into question, as A. W. Schlegel pointed out.

The story in outline harks back, far beyond the old play that Shakespeare adapted, through chronicle and legend, to the mounds of British prehistory and the fens of Druidical myth. But Shakespeare, shrewd folklorist that he was, found the same archetype at work in the most fashionable book of romantic fiction among his contemporaries, Sir Philip Sidney's *Arcadia*. Two heroes of that romance, in the course of their princely adventures, had encountered the blind King of Paphlagonia begging his dutiful son to lead him to headlong death from the top of a rock because, as he put it, "I cannot fall worse than I am." From the doleful speeches of father and son, it emerged that a bastard son and brother had betrayed them both through his "unnatural dealings"—a protesting phrase which Gloucester echoes at the moment when the two plots first come together in the play. The interpolated narrative ends in a battle and a reinstatement, with the blind King dying joyfully and the rightful heir forgiving his perfidious half-brother.

Sidney devotes a single chapter to this minor encounter; yet he tells us it is "worthy to be remembered for the unused examples therein, as well of true natural goodness, as of wretched ungratefulnesse." Edgar and Edmund, then, are exemplary figures, models of filial conduct, for better and worse. The worse of the two has an obvious dramatic advantage. It is always easier to portray an effectual villain than a young man of simple-minded good will. Some of Milton's critics have sympathized more with his Satan than with his Son of God. Yet the title page of the First Quarto leaves no doubt as to who, after Lear himself, is the male protagonist: who is, so to speak, the *jeune premier*. It reads in part: "With the unfortunate life of Edgar, sonne and heire to the Earle of Gloster, and his sullen and assumed humor of Tom of Bedlam." Instead of remaining just a nice young man, rather pallid and timid, Edgar is allowed to rival Shakespeare's dynamic villains by assuming a dangerous and colorful role.

Edmund has played his part from the beginning, though he already looks toward a denouement of some sort when he summons Edgar from hiding: "and pat he comes, like the catastrophe of the old comedy." Even while Edmund is soliloquizing, he is rehearsing his initial interview with his half-brother, and the notes he sings—*mi contra fa*—significantly form the forbidden interval known as *diabolus in musica*. His own "cue," as it happens, will become Edgar's: "a sigh like Tom o' Bedlam." But Edgar, at this point, is no less credulous than their father. With Gloucester he falls into Edmund's trap, is suspected of parricidal intentions, and proscribed as an outlaw. In his fugitive soliloquy, he determines

> To take the basest and most poorest shape
> That ever penury, in contempt of man,
> Brought near to beast.

He will disguise himself, paradoxically, by taking off his clothes and exposing himself to the elements. "With presented nakedness," when we next see him, he will be attempting to

> outface
> The winds and persecutions of the sky.

And Edgar seems to anticipate the storm, even as Lear seems to conjure it up with his imprecations of blast and fog.

As Edgar goes on to describe the role of Poor Tom, we can understand why it made him so popular on the Elizabethan stage. But, though it is quasi-comic, we can scarcely regard it as comic relief; rather, with its vagrant grotesquerie, it intensifies the tragic pathos. Those Bedlam beggars were harmless madmen released from their lunatic asylum, the notorious Hospital of St. Mary's of Bethlehem in London. Wandering aimlessly about the countryside, with their teeth chattering from exposure and their bare flesh lacerated by self-torture, they besought the stranger's alms with their prayers or curses. Edgar not only dresses the part; he fills it in with apt charms and exorcisms and brilliant bits of histrionic improvisation. He even seems to have worked up the names of devils from a current theological pamphlet: Turleygod, Flibbertigibbet, Frateretto, the last a likely name for a diabolical brother. Not the least of many ironies is that this innocent youth must pretend to be the victim of demonic possession, haunted by the foul fiend in many shapes—albeit these demons, on naturalistic inspection, are merely vermin.

Dramatic tradition gave Tom of Bedlam a forerunner in the person of Diccon the Bedlam, the Vice or mischief-maker in the crude old Cambridge comedy of *Gammer Gurton's Needle*. Edgar, too, will play the Vice in his later manipulations, when he intervenes on behalf of Gloucester. Meanwhile he acts as an object lesson for Lear. The extent of Lear's reversal may be grasped by contrasting the first scene of Act I with the last in Act II. In the former the bidding goes up, as Goneril and Regan bid for the kingdom with their large speeches of love. In the latter the haggling goes down, as the daughters cut down the retinue of their father. An hundred, fifty, five-and-twenty knights. "Ten, or five." "What need one?" By that time we are ready to move on with Lear from the court, the world of superfluity, to the heath, the world of necessity—from the heights toward the depths. His retort in farewell is the first of his speeches on need and its opposite, luxury, especially luxurious clothing and the difference it makes between the sophisticated courtier and the basest beggar, between man's life and beast's.

When Lear has exposed himself to the pinch of necessity, when he has felt the storm and first expressed a new insight into the houseless lives of naked wretches, it is then that the ragged Edgar appears as the personification of abject poverty and misery. "Is man no more than this?" the King demands, striving to emulate Tom by removing his own regal garments. "Unaccommodated man"—the naked wretch in the state of nature—"is no more but such a poor, bare, forked animal as thou art." Commentators have told us how richly the prose of this passage is interlarded with primitivistic speculations from Montaigne, whom Shakespeare knew so well through Florio's translation, and who had inspired so much of Hamlet's self-questioning. Lear has his own version of Hamlet's exclamation, "What a piece of work is a man!" Unaccommodate him, banish him from the commodities of the court, take away the trappings of civilization, complete his exposure to the elements. What is there left to differentiate him from all the other animals, by whose sharpened fangs we feel increasingly surrounded? Will he be naturally good, as Rousseau would argue? Or is he inherently evil, as Hobbes would have it, a wolf to his fellow man?

The Machiavellian bastard, Gloucester's natural son Edmund, dedicates himself to the goddess Nature, as he ruthlessly envisions her; while, through his cruel machinations, Edgar is placed in such a false position that their father calls his legitimate son an "unnatural villain." On the other hand, Edgar stands closer to nature; Lear hails him as a natural philosopher, who should be able to answer his questions concerning "the cause of thunder" and the other mysteries of the cosmos. This affinity, based on the fact that Edgar is Lear's godson, is confirmed by their respective plights, as Edgar keenly realizes: "He childed as I father'd!" As the pair enter the hovel together, Edgar's snatches of balladry and fairy tale transform it into a legendary dark tower, where a young squire is undergoing a ritual of knightly initiation while nameless giants objurgate: "Fie, foh, and fum." Edgar is more of a spectator than a feature of the spectacle in the ensuing scene, summing it up in the sententious understatement that "grief hath mates" or misery loves company.

This is the hallucinatory arraignment, where his own

half-hearted pretence meets Lear's actual madness, accompanied by the half-witted folly of the natural fool with his one pathetic joke: the rain rains every day for those who are excluded from the sunshine of royal favor. The only person present who can speak sanely, Kent in his servant guise of Caius, counsels patience. Edgar is so moved at times that his tears interfere with his impersonation, "mar" his "counterfeiting." Gloucester, whom Edgar has welcomed as a squinting fiend, reenters to terminate the scene by ordering that the King be conveyed on a litter to Dover. Thereafter, in his master's absence, he becomes the scapegoat. What follows is the scene of his sacrifice, upon which there is no temptation to dwell, except for pointing out that this reversal—despite its extreme brutality—is humanely mitigated by a recognition. Peripety, according to Aristotle, is most effective when it coincides with such a recognition, *anagnorisis*.

When Cornwall inquires "Where is thy lustre now?", Gloucester responds, "All dark and comfortless." Then, when the malicious Regan apprises him of Edmund's villainy, he suddenly recognizes that Edgar is innocent. Thus, at the very moment of blinding, Gloucester sees how blind he has been all along. "I stumbled when I saw," he will live to say. Now, in the absence of eyesight, he will be guided by a kind of ethical illumination. One of the servants, an old man, suggests that the "roguish madness" of "the Bedlam" would qualify him to be Gloucester's guide. Their conjunction is brought about in the first scene of Act IV. Kent has previously consoled himself with the thought that he could fall no lower than the stocks, and that any turn of Fortune's wheel would mean a rise in the world for him. Similarly, Edgar *solus* now views himself as "The lowest and most dejected thing of fortune," whose condition any change would improve. But alas, he speaks too soon. The sight of his bleeding father is worse than anything he has met so far.

"The worst is not," Edgar thereupon reflects, "so long as we can say, 'This is the worst.'" This may be regarded as Shakespeare's variation on the tragic theme of Sophocles, "Call no man happy until he is dead," or the cry from the depths when Job curses the light and gropes in the dark. Gloucester, in spite of his infirmity, half-recognizes Edgar as that thing between a madman and a beggar which makes him "think man a worm," but also made him think of his son. And it is at this significant juncture that Gloucester voices his pessimistic view of the human condition:

> As flies to wanton boys, are we to the gods;
> They kill us for their sport.

The world-view that opens up is as hopeless as Hardy's, governed by nothing more serene or secure than crass casualty and blind chance. It seems proper to Gloucester that a madman should lead a blind man, so long as he knows the way to Dover Cliff. "From that place," he declares with grim succinctness, "I shall no leading need." In his desperation, faced with what seems to be the pointless hostility of the universe, what can he do but dispatch his own "nighted life"? That is the last resort of Stoicism; and Shakespeare, in his Roman plays, consistently treats suicide as an honorable mode of death. In his tragedies with a Christian background, his attitude is shaded with disapproval, and he cites God's canon against self-slaughter.

King Lear is supposed to take place in prehistoric Britain, and to be roughly contemporaneous with the ancient Kings of Judea. Shakespeare has taken pains to have his characters invoke "the gods" in the plural and swear by conspicuously pagan divinities. But Edgar, that Good Samaritan with his faith, humility, and charity, seems to be *anima naturaliter christiana*. Curiously enough, in the original legend, where Lear regains his crown and Cordelia is dethroned again after his death, she ends by committing suicide in prison. It is her ghost which arises to retell the family history and point the moral in the standard Elizabethan collection of poetic case-histories, falls of princes or sad stories of the deaths of kings, the

Mirror for Magistrates. There the usual reversal, the change of fortune from prosperity to adversity, from the heights to the depths, is presented as a warning to those who are highly placed, lest they be precipitated.

> From greatest haps, that worldly wightes atchieue:
> To more distresse then any wretche aliue.

So Cordelia's monologue concludes. Comparably the first play performed before Queen Elizabeth, *Gorboduc,* one of whose collaborators was co-author of the *Mirror for Magistrates,* warned the queenly magistrate against the division of her realm and even foreshadowed *King Lear* in introducing a dissension between rival Dukes of Cornwall and Albany.

Downfall was the formula for tragedy that Shakespeare inherited and elaborated, not only in plot and characterization but in language and staging as well. The dying fall is its traditional posture. Its vicissitudes, such as the ups and downs of Richard II's reign, lend their thematic pattern to his tragedy, wherein his fall is a comedown literally as well as figuratively. Aloft, on the upper stage, the imagined walls of Flint Castle, Richard compares himself to Phaeton; descending to the lower stage, he condescends to pun about the "base court." Descent is even more desperate in *King John,* where Prince Arthur is killed in escaping from the Castle of Angiers. Elevation as the basis of a godlike overview is dramatized at those moments when Prospero is *"on the top,"* apparently looking down from the musicians' gallery. Antony, coming down from his vantage-point after the battle or hoisted up to Cleopatra's Monument in death, acts out the movement of his destiny. The danger of high places, the tragic vertigo, is vividly brought home in Horatio's fear lest Hamlet topple off some dreadful summit, "That beetles o'er his base into the sea." And that is all we need to know in order to establish the certainty that Shakespeare never visited Denmark, which is as conspicuous for its summits as Bohemia is for its sea-coasts.

But we must turn back to Dover Cliff. "Wherefore to

Dover?" Three times Gloucester is asked this question
by his torturers. Lear was there, of course; and Lear was
there because the French Army was there, though the
King of France had discreetly withdrawn so that his rescue party would not be mistaken for a foreign invasion. There the gleaming white cliffs, greeting the traveler
on his return from the continent, mark a perpetual bourn.
"Within these breakwaters English is spoken," writes
W. H. Auden,

> without
> Is the immense improbable atlas.

Nature in Lear, he has been chastened to learn, "is on
the very verge/ Of her confine." Just as the tempest in
his mind, in the "little world of man" or microcosm, is
a reverberation of the macrocosm, the disturbance of
outer nature; so now Gloucester, led by Edgar, has
reached the "extreme verge," the edge of the precipice.
It is like the thin line between life and death, between the
known and the unknown, that lies before Tolstoy's heroes
in *War and Peace*.

Here Edgar, the assumed madman, addresses his charge,
the blind man—and remember that we are just as blind
as Gloucester. Theatrical convention prescribes that we
accept whatever is said on the subject of immediate place
as the setting. We may grow slightly suspicious, when
Gloucester fails to notice the slant of the ground or
the sound of the sea; and we join him in remarking an
alteration of tone, since Poor Tom has shifted to blank
verse and soon embarks on his topographical passage.

> How fearful
> And dizzy 'tis to cast one's eyes so low!

His downward glance proceeds to the half-way point,
where it encounters the samphire-gatherer at his precarious business of picking the herb of Saint-Pierre from
the rocks. Thence to the beach, where the fishermen look
like mice, the birds like insects, the ships like their

boats, and the buoys are invisible. Everything suffers a diminution in scale. "I'll look no more," vows Edgar at the end of fifteen lines,

> Lest my brain turn, and the deficient sight

—a relevant phrase, "deficient sight," which universalizes the blindness of Gloucester while commenting on the trepidation of heights—

> I'll look no more,
> Lest my brain turn, and the deficient sight
> Topple down headlong.

This may strike the average reader or hearer with a distant, dizzying, vertiginous impact; Addison remarked that it could hardly be read without producing giddiness; but Dr. Johnson refused to be impressed. A precipice in the mind, he argued, should be "one great and dreadful image of irresistible destruction." Here we were too readily diverted by "the observation of particulars." Clearly, Johnson's criterion was the neo-classical grudge against concreteness that prompted him to inveigh against numbering the streaks of the tulip. In Boswell's account, he went even further when he discussed Edgar's speech with Garrick and others: "It should be all precipice—all vacuum. The crows impede your fall." It was the same Miltonic taste that emended Macbeth's "blanket of the dark" to "blank height." Yet Lessing finds Shakespeare's description superior to Milton's lines where the angels scan the "vast immeasurable abyss" of chaos. In *Paradise Lost* the declension is out of scale, Lessing asserted; the distance traversed is too vast to be fathomable in human dimensions. To jump to the beach from a cliff as high as ten masts is breath-taking danger, whereas a limitless precipitation through the void is mere astronomy. That vista may be even less thrilling today, as traffic increases in outer space.

The sense of immediacy and the sense of remoteness, the sensation of being up here one moment and down there a few seconds later, together with all the other sensations heightened by the hazards of the plunge, these feelings are concentrated into our identification with Gloucester and our prospective detachment from him. He is presumably standing at the brink as he lets go Edgar's hand, rewarding him and bidding him farewell. Whereupon Edgar, in a cryptic aside, gives us our first hint that the situation is not precisely what Gloucester believes it to be:

> Why I do trifle thus with his despair
> Is done to cure it.

From this announcement, at least, it is clear that Edgar has a stratagem for saving Gloucester; but, on a non-representational stage, it would still be difficult to foresee how the rescue might be effected. On a proscenium stage, the whole situation would be impossible; for, depending on realistic scenery, we should be fully aware whether Gloucester was or was not at the top of a hill. The best that nineteenth-century staging could do was to cut the passage heavily, letting Edgar catch Gloucester as he lurches forward into a faint, and quickly shifting to the next phase of the scene with the entrance of Lear. Meanwhile the audience would not be undergoing any throes of suspense, since the scenic arrangements would have indicated that Gloucester was perfectly safe. On occasions, the Dover Cliffs have been painted upon the backdrop; it was to be inferred that Edgar had taken Gloucester directly to the beach, where he should not have had any trouble in hearing the waves.

"*He falls,*" according to the stage direction, which editors have embellished but not improved. Most of them add "*forward*"; some add "*and swoons.*" He falls, at all events, but not far. Not so far as from the upper stage, I should guess, inasmuch as Romeo needed a rope and—lacking one—Prince Arthur lost his life. There may be a single step or a simple platform; or, again, the business may be enough—enough for Edgar to play his trick upon Gloucester and to lay bare the trick that Shakespeare has played upon ourselves, his audience. Gloucester, having gone through the motions of an ineffectual jump, lies on the ground; Edgar, assuming another character, now rushes up to revive him; and both are changed men. In complementary verses, breathless with polysyllabics, Edgar describes how Gloucester has fallen perpendicularly from a vast altitude and somehow survived: "Thy life's a miracle." Vainly, but not without irony, he exhorts him: "Look up a-height." And in contrast to all the *hybris,* the giddy exaltation of looking down from the heights, we seem to have plunged into the depths and to have touched bottom; we can fall no lower.

This is the nadir; the worst is over; we seem to be looking up; and the situation is framed by larger perspectives. "As I stood here below methought," begins Edgar, as if he were recounting a dream, a bad dream which ends with Tom of Bedlam turning into a fiend and flying away. Edgar's portrayal of his departing self is an exorcism, leaving innocence no longer possessed by guilt. Just as Gloucester utters his cry of despair—comparing the gods to boys and ourselves to flies—on his first encounter with mad Tom, so with Tom's departure Edgar voices his answering affirmation:

Think that the clearest gods, who make them honors
Of men's impossibilities, have preserv'd thee.

Providence must be at work, after all; and if we discern the workings of cosmic design in our personal destinies, then no man has a right to take his life; he must bear the slings and arrows of fortune, however outrageous they seem. To the Stoic argument for suicide Edgar would oppose the Christian attitude, in words which reverberate from the Gospel of Luke: "The things which are impossible with men are possible with God."

Since our eyes have been opened, we are bound to bear witness that Edgar himself has been fully responsible for the stratagem he now attributes to divine intervention. His intentions were kindly, where Edmund's have been malign; but he has deceived their father quite as much with his imaginary fall as Edmund earlier did with his forged letter. "Let's see," said Gloucester, snatching at that device, "come; if it be nothing, I shall not need spectacles." He saw; he stumbled; and, now that he is sightless, he is rescued by the victim of the letter. Edgar has proved to be as good a stage manager as Edmund, and in a better cause. Yet, unless his presence in the vicinity is the result of stage management on the part of the gods—unless it is providential, that is to say, rather than coincidental—we must admit that his miracle is more truly a pious fraud; and we must conclude that the gods help those who help themselves, or else those who are so fortunate as to be helped by their fellow men.

Man stands on his own feet in *King Lear*. There is no supernatural soliciting; there are no ghosts or witches or oracles; and the only demons are those which Edgar imagines while enacting his demonic role. Man takes his questionings directly to nature. Perhaps the ultimate meaning of Gloucester's fall is its symbolic gesture of expiation, re-enacting his own original sin, as well as the fall of man and his consequent progression toward self-knowledge. Other agonists have undergone it under widely differing conditions: Herman Melville narrates it, in his *White-Jacket,* as a fall from the yardarm of a ship at sea. Because he could not bear his great affliction without cursing the gods, Gloucester has attempted to shake it off "patiently." But Edgar's moral, which completes the exercise, redefines patience as the ability to bear one's sufferings, to face and endure them in calm of mind: "Bear free and patient thoughts."

Patience has been the greatest need of the King. He has resolved to be "the pattern of all patience"; whereupon he has run the gamut of passions, from rage through hysteria to delirium and finally lunacy. It is as an escaping lunatic, grotesquely decked with weeds, that he is confronted by Edgar and Gloucester at this strategic moment of the play; and it may well be the shock of this reunion that has obscured the significance of their foregoing scene. From the interchange it would appear that, if Lear stands for reason in madness, Gloucester may stand for vision in blindness. When Lear asks if he sees how the world goes, Gloucester replies: "I see it feelingly." His groping pun is heavily fraught with shame and remorse for the figure he has earlier cut: "the superfluous and lust-dieted man . . . that will not see/Because he does not feel." This parallels the insight that Lear has acquired on the heath: "to feel what wretches feel." Gloucester has immediately recognized Lear's voice; Lear rounds out the recognition scene by naming Gloucester and preaching, "Thou must be patient."

Lear is unquestionably the *persona patiens,* as Coleridge insisted; he is the agonizing figure of this passion play where all the characters suffer. Having committed his rash action, he suffers for it on and on, until he is justified in regarding himself as "a man/More sinn'd against than sinning." Edmund is the main agent, in Coleridge's estimation; certainly, he is most active in pulling the strings at the outset. "The younger rises when the old doth fall." But the defeated opportunist concedes that, with its last revolution, his wheel comes full circle. Edgar, his polar rival, is passive at first; he suffers, then he acts; and it is his suffering that prepares him for action. When Gloucester thanks and blesses him for his anonymous aid, he characterizes himself as

A most poor man, made tame to fortune's blows;
Who, by the art of known and feeling sorrows,
Am pregnant to good pity.

As such, he is the right instrument for conveying a sense of fellow-feeling, both to Lear in the hovel on the heath and to Gloucester at Dover Cliff.

It is a cruel world where the honest Kent must go incognito, and where the once-naïve Edgar has to run through a protean repertory of roles. After the disappearance of Tom of Bedlam, he is more simply a neutral benefactor, the Good Samaritan. But when he protects Gloucester from Oswald's attack and is called "bold peasant" by the courtier, he adapts himself to that appellation by replying in a rustic dialect. He disposes of

Oswald, thereby saving the life that Gloucester would
have thrown away. But he cannot disclose his identity
before he has made his appearance as a nameless cham-
pion; and even this last masquerade is preceded by
another one, that of the messenger delivering the challenge. However, the battle must precede the tournament.
Drums afar off have terminated the Cliff Scene. They
grow louder when the French forces, flying Cordelia's
colors, march to meet the British. While the engagement
is taking place off-stage, we await the outcome with
Gloucester under a tree.

Hard upon the heels of retreating soldiers, Edgar reports the defeat and capture of Lear and Cordelia, and
Gloucester reverts to his former mood of self-pity. Why
should he let himself be led any farther? "A man may
rot even here." But just as growth yields to decay, so
decay fosters growth, in the biological cycle. What is important, fulfillment, is a matter of timing. Man must rec-
oncile himself to the fact that nature will take its course.
Edgar, picking up Gloucester's negative image, trans-
poses it into the most positive statement of the play:

> Men must endure
> Their going hence, even as their coming hither;
> Ripeness is all.

Edgar's aphorism can be traced back to Montaigne's essay, "That to philosophize is to learn how to die."
Such was the end of knowledge for the tragic playwright, as well as for the skeptical philosopher. It is
rather more than a coincidence that the same sentiment
is expressed, though not imaged, at the same point in
Hamlet: "The readiness is all." The manner of one's death
and the moment of it were ultimate concerns to the
Elizabethans.

By averting the suicide and nursing his father's miseries, Edgar has saved him from despair. Could he but
live to see his son in his touch, Gloucester has feelingly
vowed, "I'd say I had eyes again." We do not witness the
recognition scene wherein this yearning is fulfilled at last.

But in the final scene, when the explanations come out, Edgar relates the circumstances of Gloucester's happy death, " 'Twixt two extremes of passion, joy and grief." These mixed emotions match the smiles and tears with which Cordelia has received the news of her father: "Sunshine and rain at once." Edmund, sincerely moved by his brother's report, resolves to do some good; but retrospective narration prolongs the delay, and his one humane impulse is thwarted; the reprieve of Cordelia comes too late. When the brothers fought and were reconciled, Edgar pronounced upon his brother and father in apocryphal terms:

> The gods are just, and of our pleasant vices
> Make instruments to plague us.

Edmund's existence is at once the consequence of, and the retribution for, Gloucester's sin.

> The dark and vicious place where thee he got
> Cost him his eyes.

Where the inequities of this world have made Gloucester and Lear more and more doubtful as to the justice of heaven, Edgar is wholeheartedly its exponent. Albany, too, can point to the death of Cornwall, fatally wounded in the very act of torturing Gloucester, as an indication that the guilty are punished here below. But so are the innocent. So is Cordelia; and this, more than anything else, I suspect, is why critics have flinched at the notion of performing the play. There is a grim sort of poetic justice in the scene where the King refuses to accept her death; and his own demise, just afterwards, is a deliverance for him. But audiences have frequently shared his and Gloucester's unwillingness to bear an unhappy ending patiently; the chronicle-history ended happily; while the adaptation by Nahum Tate, which all but replaced Shakespeare's tragedy for a hundred and fifty years, managed to marry off Cordelia to Edgar, who thanks the King with these concluding lines:

> Thy bright example shall convince the World
> (Whatever Storms of Fortune are decreed)
> That Truth and Vertue shall at last succeed.

Shakespeare's Edgar repeats to the dying Lear his optimistic counsel to Gloucester: "Look up, my lord." But he cannot contrive another miracle. The problem of evil is unresolved at the conclusion, though the prevailing catastrophe is accepted. It is, as Kent says, a presentiment of doomsday, "the promis'd end." Edgar, rather than Albany, speaks the final speech in the Folio. Well might he proclaim a farewell to dissembling and a renewal of sincerity. It is high time to "Speak what we feel, not what we ought to say." And, in his terminal couplet, our deficient sight is contrasted with the insight painfully achieved through old age:

> The oldest hath borne most: we that are young,
> Shall never see so much, nor live so long.

We leave him looking across the straits, listening to the cadence of human misery in the ebb and flow of the tides, and catching that eternal note of sadness which Sophocles heard long ago and which Matthew Arnold caught in his poem, "Dover Beach." As with Oedipus, blind and dying at Colonus, so with Gloucester at Dover. In each case, the passion of a patriarch has met with compassion on the part of a filial survivor, be it Edgar or Antigone. But it is Goethe who puts his finger on the archetype in that relationship: *"Ein alter Mann ist stets ein König Lear."* May I translate freely, in order to keep the rhyme?

> An aged man is always like King Lear.
> Effort and struggle long have passed him by;
> And love and leadership are pledged elsewhere;
> And youth must work out its own destiny.
> Come on, old fellow, come along with me.

Suggested References

The number of possible references is vast and grows alarmingly. (The *Shakespeare Quarterly* devotes a substantial part of one issue each year to a list of the previous year's work, and *Shakespeare Survey*—an annual publication—includes a substantial review of recent scholarship, as well as an occasional essay surveying a few decades of scholarship on a chosen topic.) Russell Fraser, the editor of the Signet Classic *King Lear,* offers this warning: "These comments may be ventured, regarding the titles listed here, and the critical selections above. First, no work of criticism, however excellent in itself, is to be taken as rivaling in importance, much less as supplanting, the thing it criticizes. The play's the thing! and not the commentaries thereon. Second, any work of criticism, and particularly to the degree that it is excellent, ought to be scrutinized with a cold eye whenever it pretends to the making of a definitive judgment. In the interpretation of Shakespeare, no comment is sacrosanct or final. Let the reader beware, therefore; and let him also take heart. 'Judgment, like other faculties, is improved by practice, and its advancement hindered by submission to dictatorial decisions, as the memory grows torpid by the use of a table book.' Thus Dr. Johnson."

1. SHAKESPEARE'S TIMES

Byrne, M. St. Clare. *Elizabethan Life in Town and Country*. Rev. ed. New York: Barnes & Noble, Inc., 1961. Chapters on manners, beliefs, education, etc., with illustrations.

Craig, Hardin. *The Enchanted Glass: the Elizabethan Mind in Literature.* New York and London: Oxford University Press, 1936. The Elizabethan intellectual climate.

Nicoll, Allardyce (ed.). *The Elizabethans.* London: Cambridge University Press, 1957. An anthology of Elizabethan writings, especially valuable for its illustrations from paintings, title pages, etc.

Shakespeare's England. Oxford: Clarendon Press, 1916. 2 vols. A large collection of scholarly essays on a wide variety of topics (e.g., astrology, costume, gardening, horsemanship), with special attention to Shakespeare's references to these topics.

Tillyard, E. M. W. *The Elizabethan World Picture.* London: Chatto & Windus, 1943; New York: The Macmillan Company, 1944. A brief account of some Elizabethan ideas of the universe.

Wilson, John Dover (ed.). *Life in Shakespeare's England.* 2nd ed. New York: The Macmillan Company, 1913. An anthology of Elizabethan writings on the countryside, superstition, education, the court, etc.

2. SHAKESPEARE

Bentley, Gerald E. *Shakespeare: A Biographical Handbook.* New Haven, Conn.: Yale University Press, 1961. The facts about Shakespeare, with virtually no conjecture intermingled.

Bradby, Anne (ed.). *Shakespeare Criticism, 1919-1935.* London: Oxford University Press, 1936. A small anthology of excellent essays on the plays.

Bush, Geoffrey Douglas. *Shakespeare and the Natural Condition.* Cambridge, Mass.: Harvard University Press, 1956; London: Oxford University Press, 1956. A short, sensitive account of Shakespeare's view of "Nature," touching most of the works.

Chambers, E. K. *William Shakespeare: A Study of Facts and Problems*. London: Oxford University Press, 1930. 2 vols. An invaluable, detailed reference work; not for the casual reader.

Chute, Marchette. *Shakespeare of London*. E. P. Dutton & Co., Inc., 1949. A readable biography fused with portraits of Stratford and London life.

Clemen, Wolfgang H. *The Development of Shakespeare's Imagery*. Cambridge, Mass.: Harvard University Press, 1951. (Originally published in German, 1936). A temperate account of a subject often abused.

Craig, Hardin. *An Interpretation of Shakespeare*. New York: Citadel Press, 1948. A scholar's book designed for the layman. Comments on all the works.

Dean, Leonard F. (ed.). *Shakespeare: Modern Essays in Criticism*. New York: Oxford University Press, 1957. Mostly mid-twentieth-century critical studies, covering Shakespeare's artistry.

Granville-Barker, Harley. *Prefaces to Shakespeare*. Princeton, N. J.: Princeton University Press, 1946–47. 2 vols. Essays on ten plays by a scholarly man of the theater.

Harbage, Alfred. *As They Liked It*. New York: The Macmillan Company, 1947. A sensitive, long essay on Shakespeare, morality, and the audience's expectations.

Smith, D. Nichol (ed.). *Shakespeare Criticism*. New York: Oxford University Press, 1916. A selection of criticism from 1623 to 1840, ranging from Ben Jonson to Thomas Carlyle.

Spencer, Theodore. *Shakespeare and the Nature of Man*. New York: The Macmillan Company, 1942. Shakespeare's plays in relation to Elizabethan thought.

Stoll, Elmer Edgar. *Shakespeare and Other Masters*. Cambridge, Mass.: Harvard University Press, 1940; London: Oxford University Press, 1940. Essays on tragedy, comedy, and aspects of dramaturgy with special reference to some of Shakespeare's plays.

Traversi, D. A. *An Approach to Shakespeare.* Rev. ed. New York: Doubleday & Co., Inc., 1956. An analysis of the plays, beginning with words, images, and themes, rather than with characters.

Van Doren, Mark. *Shakespeare.* New York: Henry Holt & Company, Inc., 1939. Brief, perceptive readings of all of the plays.

Whitaker, Virgil K. *Shakespeare's Use of Learning.* San Marino, Calif.: Huntington Lib., 1953. A study of the relation of Shakespeare's reading to his development as a dramatist.

3. SHAKESPEARE'S THEATER

Adams, John Cranford. *The Globe Playhouse.* Rev. ed. New York: Barnes & Noble, Inc., 1961. A detailed conjecture about the physical characteristics of the theater Shakespeare often wrote for.

Beckerman, Bernard. *Shakespeare at the Globe, 1599-1609.* New York: The Macmillan Company, 1962. On the playhouse and on Elizabethan dramaturgy, acting, and staging.

Chambers, E. K. *The Elizabethan Stage.* New York: Oxford University Press, 1923. 4 vols. Reprinted with corrections, 1945. An indispensable reference work on theaters, theatrical companies, and staging at court.

Harbage, Alfred. *Shakespeare's Audience.* New York: Columbia University Press, 1941; London: Oxford University Press, 1941. A study of the size and nature of the theatrical public.

Hodges, C. Walter. *The Globe Restored.* London: Ernest Benn, Ltd., 1953; New York: Coward-McCann, Inc., 1954. A well-illustrated and readable attempt to reconstruct the Globe Theatre.

Nagler, A. M. *Shakespeare's Stage.* Tr. by Ralph Manheim. New Haven, Conn.: Yale University Press, 1958. An excellent brief introduction to the physical aspect of the playhouse.

Smith, Irwin. *Shakespeare's Globe Playhouse*. New York: Charles Scribner's Sons, 1957. Chiefly indebted to J. C. Adams' controversial book, with additional material and scale drawings for model-builders.

Venezky, Alice S. *Pageantry on the Shakespearean Stage*. New York: Twayne Publishers, Inc., 1951. An examination of spectacle in Elizabethan drama.

4. MISCELLANEOUS REFERENCE WORKS

Abbott, E. A. *A Shakespearean Grammar*. New edition. New York: The Macmillan Company, 1877. An examination of differences between Elizabethan and modern grammar.

Bartlett, John. *A New and Complete Concordance . . . to . . . Shakespeare*. New York: The Macmillan Company, 1894. An index to most of Shakespeare's words.

Bullough, Geoffrey. *Narrative and Dramatic Sources of Shakespeare*. New York: Columbia University Press, 1957–; London: Routledge & Kegan Paul, Ltd., 1957–. 4 vols. Vols. 5 and 6 in preparation. A collection of many of the books Shakespeare drew upon.

Greg, W. W. *The Shakespeare First Folio*. New York and London: Oxford University Press, 1955. A detailed yet readable history of the first collection (1623) of Shakespeare's plays.

Kökeritz, Helge. *Shakespeare's Names*. New Haven, Conn.: Yale University Press, 1959; London: Oxford University Press, 1950. A guide to the pronunciation of some 1,800 names appearing in Shakespeare.

——. *Shakespeare's Pronunciation*. New Haven, Conn.: Yale University Press, 1953; London: Oxford University Press, 1953. Contains much information about puns and rhymes.

Linthicum, Marie C. *Costume in the Drama of Shakespeare and His Contemporaries*. New York and London: Oxford University Press, 1936. On the fabrics and dress of the age, and references to them in the plays.

Muir, Kenneth. *Shakespeare's Sources*. London: Methuen & Co., Ltd., 1957. Vol. 2 in preparation. The first volume, on the comedies and tragedies, attempts to ascertain what books were Shakespeare's sources, and what use he made of them.

Onions, C. T. *A Shakespeare Glossary*. London: Oxford University Press, 1911; 2nd ed., rev., with enlarged addenda, 1953. Definitions of words (or senses of words) now obsolete.

Partridge, Eric. *Shakespeare's Bawdy*. Rev. ed. New York: E. P. Dutton & Co., Inc., 1955; London: Routledge & Kegan Paul, Ltd., 1955. A glossary of bawdy words and phrases.

Shakespeare Quarterly. See headnote to Suggested References.

Shakespeare Survey. See headnote to Suggested References.

5. KING LEAR

Blunden, Edmund. *Shakespeare's Significances*. London: Oxford University Press, 1929.

Bradley, A. C. *Shakespearean Tragedy*. London: Macmillan & Co., Ltd., 1904. Part of the material on *King Lear* is reprinted above.

Coleridge, Samuel Taylor. *Shakespearean Criticism*, ed. Thomas Middleton Raysor. New York: E. P. Dutton & Co., Inc., 1960; London: J. M. Dent & Sons, Ltd., 1961. 2 vols.

Dowden, Edward. *Shakspere: A Critical Study of His Mind and Art*. New York: Harper & Brothers, 1918; London: H. S. King, 1875.

Fraser, Russell A. *Shakespeare's Poetics in Relation to "King Lear."* London: Routledge & Kegan Paul, Ltd., 1962.

Granville-Barker, Harley. *Prefaces to Shakespeare*. 2 vols. Princeton, N. J.: Princeton University Press, 1946–47. Part of the material on *King Lear* in Vol. I is reprinted above.

Heilman, Robert B. *This Great Stage: Image and Structure in "King Lear."* Baton Rouge, La.: Louisiana State University Press, 1948.

Knight, G. Wilson. *The Wheel of Fire.* New York and London: Oxford University Press, 1930; 5th rev. ed., New York: Meridian Books, Inc., 1957.

Lamb, Charles. "On Shakespeare's Tragedies" (1808), *The Complete Works in Prose and Verse of Charles Lamb.* London: Chatto & Windus, Ltd., 1875.

Lewis, Wyndham. *The Lion and the Fox.* London: Richards; New York: Harper & Brothers, 1927.

Lothian, John Maule. *King Lear: A Tragic Reading of Life.* London: Bell & Sons, Ltd., 1950.

Mack, Maynard. *King Lear in Our Time.* Berkeley and Los Angeles University of California Press, 1965.

Moulton, Richard G. *Shakespeare as a Dramatic Artist.* 3rd ed. Oxford: The Clarendon Press, 1893; New York: Oxford University Press, 1897. Especially Part First, Chapter X: "How Climax Meets Climax in the Centre of 'Lear.'"

Muir, Kenneth, and Sean O'Loughlin. *The voyage to Illyria.* London: Methuen & Co., Ltd., 1937.

Perrett, Wilfrid. *The Story of King Lear from Geoffrey of Monmouth to Shakespeare.* (Palaestra, XXXV) Berlin: —Mayer & Muller, 1904.

Rosen, William. *Shakespeare and the Craft of Tragedy.* Cambridge, Mass.: Harvard University Press; London: Oxford University Press, 1960.

Sewell, Arthur. *Character and Society in Shakespeare.* London and New York: Oxford University Press, 1951, 1952.

Stoll, Elmer Edgar. *Art and Artifice in Shakespeare.* London: Cambridge University Press, 1933; New York: Barnes & Noble, Inc. 1962.

Van Doren, Mark. *Shakespeare.* New York: Henry Holt & Company, Inc., 1939.

THE SIGNET CLASSIC SHAKESPEARE

Below is a listing of some of the 40 Shakespeare titles available in the most comprehensive presentation in the paperbound form.

☐ **ANTONY AND CLEOPATRA, edited by David Stevenson**
(#CQ741—95¢)

☐ **AS YOU LIKE IT, edited by Albert Gilman**
(#CT520—75¢)

☐ **HAMLET, edited by Edward Hubler** (#CQ771—95¢)

☐ **JULIUS CAESAR, edited by William & Barbara Rosen**
(#CT529—75¢)

☐ **MACBETH, edited by Sylvan Barnet** (#CT566—75¢)

☐ **MEASURE FOR MEASURE, edited by S. Nagarajan**
(#CT541—75¢)

☐ **A MIDSUMMER NIGHT'S DREAM, edited by Wolfgang Clemen** (#CT518—75¢)

☐ **MUCH ADO ABOUT NOTHING, edited by Barbara Everett**
(#CT575—75¢)

☐ **OTHELLO, edited by Alvin Kernan** (#CQ756—95¢)

☐ **RICHARD II, edited by Kenneth Muir** (#CT591—75¢)

☐ **RICHARD III, edited by Mark Eccles** (#CT587—75¢)

☐ **THE TEMPEST, edited by Robert Langbaum**
(#CT527—75¢)

☐ **TITUS ANDRONICUS, edited by Sylvan Barnet**
(#CD197—50¢)

☐ **TROILUS AND CRESSIDA, edited by Daniel Seltzer**
(#CT589—75¢)

☐ **THE WINTER'S TALE, edited by Frank Kermode**
(#CT549—75¢)

☐ **THE TWO GENTLEMEN OF VERONA, edited by Bertrand Evans** (#CD219—50¢)

THE NEW AMERICAN LIBRARY, INC.,
P.O. Box 999, Bergenfield, New Jersey 07621

Please send me the SIGNET CLASSIC BOOKS I have checked above. I am enclosing $_____(check or money order—no currency or C.O.D.'s). Please include the list price plus 25¢ a copy to cover handling and mailing costs. (Prices and numbers are subject to change without notice.)

Name_____

Address_____

City_____State_____Zip Code_____
Allow at least 3 weeks for delivery